Rev S. Boulding Gould

**Legends Of Old Testament Characters**

Volume 1, Adam To Abraham

Rev S. Boulding Gould

**Legends Of Old Testament Characters**
*Volume 1, Adam To Abraham*

ISBN/EAN: 9783741107917

Manufactured in Europe, USA, Canada, Australia, Japa

Cover: Foto ©Lupo / pixelio.de

Manufactured and distributed by brebook publishing software (www.brebook.com)

Rev S. Boulding Gould

**Legends Of Old Testament Characters**

# Legends of Old Testament Characters.

# Legends

OF

# Old Testament Characters,

FROM

THE TALMUD AND OTHER SOURCES.

BY THE
REV. S. BARING-GOULD, M.A.,

*Author of "Curious Myths of the Middle Ages," "The Origin and Development of Religious Belief," "In Exitu Israel," etc.*

VOL. I.
*ADAM TO ABRAHAM.*

London and New York:
MACMILLAN AND CO.
1871.

# PREFACE.

AN incredible number of legends exists connected with the personages whose history is given in the Old Testament. The collection now presented to the public must, by no means, be considered as exhaustive. The compiler has been obliged to limit himself as to the number, it being quite impossible to insert all. He trusts that few of peculiar interest have been omitted.

The Mussulman traditions are nearly all derived from the Talmudic writers, just as the history of Christ in the Koran is taken from the Apocryphal Gospels. The Koran follows the "Sepher Hajaschar" (Book of the Just) far more closely than the canonical Scriptures; and the "Sepher Hajaschar" is a storehouse of the Rabbinic tradition on the subject of the Patriarchs from Adam to Joshua.

The Jewish traditions are of various value. Some can be traced to their origin without fail. One class is derived from Persia, as, for instance, those of Asmodeus, the name of the demon being taken, along with his story, from Iranian sources. Another class springs from the Cabbalists, who, by permutation of the letters of a name, formed the nuclei, so to speak, from which legends spread.

Another class, again, is due to the Rabbinic commentators, who, unable to allow for poetical periphrasis, insisted on literal interpretations, and then coined fables to explain them. Thus the saying of David, "*Thou hast heard me from among the horns of the unicorns,*" which signified that David was assisted by God in trouble, was taken quite literally by the Rabbis, and a story was invented to explain it.

Another class, again, is no doubt due to the exaggeration of Oriental imagery, just as that previously mentioned is due to the deficiency of the poetic fancy in certain Rabbis. Thus, imagination and defect of imagination, each contributed to add to the store.

But when we have swept all these classes aside, there remains a residuum, small, no doubt, of genuine tradition. To this class, if I am not mistaken, belong the account of Lamech and his wives, and the story of the sacrifice of Isaac. In the latter instance, the type comes out far clearer in the Talmudic tradition than in the canonical Scriptures; and this can hardly have been the result of Jewish interpolation, knowing, as they did, that Christians pointed triumphantly to this type.

With regard to Jewish traditions, it is unfortunate that both Eisenmenger and Bartolocci, who collected many of them, were so prejudiced, so moved with violent animosity against the Rabbinic writers, that they preserved only the grotesque, absurd, and indecent legends, and wholly passed over those—and there are many of them—which are redolent of poetry, and which contain an element of truth.

A certain curious interest attaches to these legends—at least, I think so; and, should they find favour with the public, these volumes will be followed by another series on the legends connected with the New Testament characters.

The Author is not aware of any existing collection of these

legends, except that of M. Colin de Plancy, "Legendes de l'Ancien Testament," Paris, 1861; but he has found this work of little or no use to him in composing his volumes, as M. de Plancy gives no reference to authorities; and also, because nearly the whole of the contents are taken from D'Herbelot's "Bibliothèque Orientale" and Migne's "Dictionnaire des Apocryphes."

It will be necessary to add a few words on certain works largely quoted in the following pages.

1. Dr. G. Weil's "Biblische Legende der Muselmänner," Frankfurt a. M., 1845, is derived from three Arabic MS. works —"*Chamis*," by Husein Ibn Mohammed Ibn Alhasan Addiarbekri; "*Dsachirat Alulun wanatidjat Alfuhum*," by Ahmed Ibn zein Alabidin Albekri; and "*Kissat Alanbija*," by Mohammed Ibn Ahmed Alkissai.

2. The Chronicle of Abou-djafar Mohammed Tabari was translated into Persian by Abou Ali Mohammed Belami, who added sundry traditions circulating in Persia; and has been rendered into French, in part, by M. Hermann Zolenberg, for the Oriental Translation Fund, Paris, 1867.

3. The "Sepher Hajaschar," or Book of Jasher (Yaschar), is quoted from the translation by Le Chevalier P. L. B. Drach, inserted in Migne's "Dictionnaire des Apocryphes."

4. Eisenmenger, "Neuentdektes Judenthum," 2 vols. 8vo, Königsburg, 1711, contains a great many Rabbinic traditions collected from sources inaccessible to most persons.

5. Bartolocci, "Bibliotheca Magna Rabbinica," 4 vols. fol., Rome, 1675-93, is a very valuable storehouse of information, but sadly disfigured by prejudice.

# CONTENTS OF VOL. I.

PREFACE . . . . . . . . . . .

### I.

THE FALL OF THE ANGELS . . . . . . . . . .

### II.

ADAM . . . . . . . . . . . . .
   1. The Creation of Man . . . . . . . . . .
   2. The Pre-Adamites . . . . . . . . . . .

### III.

EVE . . . . . . . . . . . . .

### IV.

THE FALL OF MAN . . . . . . . . . . .

### V.

ADAM AND EVE AFTER THE FALL . . . . . . .

### VI.

CAIN AND ABEL . . . . . . . . . . . .

## VII.
THE DEATH OF ADAM . . . . . . . . . . . . . . . . PAGE 78

## VIII.
SETH . . . . . . . . . . . . . . . . . . . . . . 81

## IX.
CAINAN SON OF ENOS . . . . . . . . . . . . . . 85

## X.
ENOCH . . . . . . . . . . . . . . . . . . . . . 87
    1. The Translation of Enoch . . . . . . . . . . . . 87
    2. The Book of Enoch . . . . . . . . . . . . . . 90

## XI.
THE GIANTS . . . . . . . . . . . . . . . . . . . 95

## XII.
LAMECH . . . . . . . . . . . . . . . . . . . . 102

## XIII.
METHUSELAH . . . . . . . . . . . . . . . . . . 105

## XIV.
NOAH . . . . . . . . . . . . . . . . . . . . . 107

### XV.
Heathen Legends of the Deluge . . . . . . . . . 116

### XVI.
The Planting of the Vine . . . . . . . . . . . . 134

### XVII.
The Sons of Noah . . . . . . . . . . . . . . . . 138

### XVIII.
Relics of the Ark . . . . . . . . . . . . . . . . 141

### XIX.
Certain Descendants of Ham . . . . . . . . . . . 143

### XX.
Serug . . . . . . . . . . . . . . . . . . . . . . 148

### XXI.
The Prophet Eber . . . . . . . . . . . . . . . . 149

### XXII.
The Prophet Saleh . . . . . . . . . . . . . . . . 155

### XXIII.
The Tower of Babel . . . . . . . . . . . . . . . 165

## XXIV.

| | PAGE |
|---|---|
| ABRAHAM | 171 |
| 1. His Youth and early Struggles | 171 |
| 2. The Call of Abraham, and the Visit to Egypt | 186 |
| 3. The War with the Kings | 191 |
| 4. The Birth of Ishmael | 197 |
| 5. The Destruction of Sodom and Gomorrah | 198 |
| 6. The Birth of Isaac | 204 |
| 7. The Expulsion of Hagar and Ishmael | 208 |
| 8. The Strife between the Shepherds | 214 |
| 9. The Grove in Beer-sheba | 215 |
| 10. The Offering of Isaac | 217 |
| 11. The Death of Sarah | 228 |
| 12. The Marriage of Isaac | 232 |
| 13. The Death of Abraham | 235 |

# LEGENDARY LIVES OF THE PATRIARCHS.

## I.

### THE FALL OF THE ANGELS.

IN the beginning, before the creation of heaven and earth, God made the angels; free intelligences and free wills; out of His love He made them, that they might be eternally happy. And that their happiness might be complete, He gave them the perfection of a created nature; that is, He gave them freedom.

But happiness is only attainable by the free will agreeing in its freedom to accord with the will of God. Some of the angels by an act of free will obeyed the will of God, and in such obedience found perfect happiness; other angels by an act of free will rebelled against the will of God, and in such disobedience found misery.

Such is the catholic theory of the fall of the angels.

Historically, it is represented as a war in heaven. "*And there was war in heaven: Michael and his angels fought against the dragon; and the dragon fought and his angels, and prevailed not; neither was their place found any more in heaven. And the great dragon was cast out, that old serpent, called the Devil, and Satan, which deceiveth the whole world; he was cast out into the earth, and his angels were cast out with him.*"[1] The reason of

[1] Rev. xii. 7–9.

the revolt was that Satan desired to be as great as God. "*Thou hast said in thine heart, I will ascend into heaven, I will exalt my throne above the stars of God; I will sit also upon the mount of the congregation in the sides of the north; I will ascend above the heights of the clouds; I will be like the Most High.*"[1]

The war ended in the fall of Satan and those whom he had led into apostasy; and to this fall are referred the words of Christ, "*I saw Satan like lightning fall from heaven.*"[2]

Fabricius, in his collections of the apocryphal writings of the Old Testament, has preserved the song of triumph which the Archangel Michael sang on obtaining the victory. This is a portion of it:—

"Glory to our God! Praise to His holy Name! He is our God; glory be to Him! He is our Lord! His be the triumph! He has stretched forth His right hand; He has manifested His power, He has cast down our adversaries. They are mad who resist Him; they are accursed who depart from His commandments! He knoweth all things, and cannot err. His will is sovereignly just, and all that He wills is good, all that He advises is holy. Supreme Intelligence cannot be deceived; Perfect Being cannot will what is evil. Nothing is above that which is supreme, nothing is better than that which is perfect. None is worthy beside Him but him whom He has made worthy. He must be loved above all things and adored as the eternal King. You have abandoned your God, you have revolted against Him, you have desired to be gods; you have fallen from your high estates, you have gone down like a fallen stone. Acknowledge that God is great, that His works are perfect, and that His judgments are just. Glory be to God through ages of ages, praises of joy for all His works!" This song of the Archangel is said to have been revealed to S. Amadeus.[3]

According to the Talmudists, Satan, whose proper name is Sammael, was one of the Seraphim, with six wings.[4] He was

---

[1] Isaiah xiv. 13, 14.  [2] Luke x. 18.
[3] Fabricius (J. A.), Codex Pseudepigraphus Vet. Test. Hamb., 1722, p. 21.  [4] Jalkut Rubeni, 3, sub. tit. Sammael.

## THE FALL OF THE ANGELS.

not driven out of heaven till after he had led Adam and Eve into sin; then Sammael and his host were precipitated out of the place of bliss, with God's curse to weigh them down. In the struggle between Michael and Sammael, the falling Seraph caught the wings of Michael and tried to drag him down with him, but God saved him, whence Michael derives his name (the Rescued). This is what the Rabbi Bechai says in his commentary on the Five Books of Moses.[1]

According to a Talmudic authority, the apostate angels having fallen in a heap, God laid his little finger on them and consumed them.[2]

Sammael was the regent of the planet Mars, and this he rules still, and therefore it is that those born under the influence of that star are lovers of war and given to strife.[3]

He was chief among the angels of God, and now he is prince among devils.[4] His name is derived from Simmé, which means to blind and deceive. He stands on the *left* side of men. He goes by various names; such as the Old Serpent, the Unclean Spirit, Satan, Leviathan, and sometimes also Asael. In his fall he spat in his hatred against God, and his spittle stained the moon, and thus it is that the moon has on it spots.

After his fall, Satan took to himself four wives, Lilith and Naama the daughter of Lamech and sister of Tubal-Cain, Igereth and Machalath. Each became the mother of a great host of devils, and each rules with her host over a season of the year; and at the change of seasons there is a great gathering of devils about their mothers. Lilith is followed by four hundred and seventy-eight legions of devils, for that number is comprised in her name (לילית—478). According to some, Lilith is identical with Eve. She rules over Damascus, Naama over Tyre, Igereth over Malta and Rhodes, and Machalath over Crete.[5]

---
[1] Fol. 139, col. 1; see Eisenmenger, i. p. 831.
[2] Jalkut Rubeni, in Eisenmenger, i. p. 307.
[3] Eisenmenger, i. p. 104.
[4] Ibid., i. p. 820.  [5] Ibid., ii. 416, 420, 421.

Many traditions date the existence of angels and demons from a remote period before the creation of the world, but some connect the fall of Satan and his host with the creation of man.

Abou-Djafar-Mohammed Tabari says that when God made Adam, He bade all the angels worship him as their king and superior, as says the Koran, "All the angels adored Adam" (xv. 30), but that Satan or Eblis answered God, "I will not adore Adam, for he is made of earth and I of fire, therefore I am better than he" (vii. 11), and that God thereupon cursed Eblis and gave him the form of a devil, because of his pride, vain confidence, and disobedience.[1]

Abulfeda says, "After God had made man He thus addressed the angels: 'When I have breathed a portion of my spirit into him, bow before him and adore.' After He had inspired Adam with His spirit, all the angels of every degree adored him, except Eblis; he, through pride and envy, scorned to do this, and disobeyed God. Then God cursed him, and He cut him off from all hope in divine mercy, and He called him Scheithanan redjiman (Satan devoted to misery), and He cast him out who had been before an angel of the earth, and keeper of terrestrial things, and a guardian of Paradise."[2]

But the general opinion seems to have been that the fall of the angels preceded the creation of man. Ibn-Ezra dates it on the second day of creation, others on the first day when God "*divided the light from the darkness.*" Manasseh Ben Israel says that God has placed the devils in the clouds, that they might torment the wicked with thunder and lightnings, and showers of hail and tempests of wind, and that this took place on the second day, when the firmaments were divided.

As the fall of Satan took place through his aspiration to be God, so it is closely connected with the origin of idolatry and false worship; for now that Satan is cast out of heaven, he still seeks to exalt himself into the place of God, and therefore

---

[1] Chronique de Tabari. Paris, 1867, i. c. xxvii.
[2] Abulfeda, Hist. Ante-Islamica. Lipsiæ, 1831, p. 13.

## THE FALL OF THE ANGELS.

leads men from the worship of the true God into demonolatry. Thus the gods of the heathens were regarded by the first Christians as devils aspiring to receive that worship from men on earth which they sought and failed to obtain in heaven. Thus St. Paul tells the Corinthians that "*the Gentiles sacrifice to devils.*"[1] The temptation of Christ can only be fully understood when we bear in mind that pride and craving for worship is the prime source of Satan's actions. "*All these will I give thee*," he said to Christ, "*if Thou wilt fall down and worship me.*" It was a second attempt of Satan to set himself above the Most High.

Among the heathen, traditions of the Angelic apostasy and war have remained.

The Indian story is as follows:—

At the head of the apostate spirits is Mahisasura, or the great Asur; he and those who followed him were once good, but before the creation of the world they refused obedience to Brahma, wherefore they were cast down by the assistance of Schiva into the abyss of Onderah.[2] Mahisasura is also represented as the great serpent Vrita, against which Indra fought, and which after a desperate struggle he overcame.

The Persian tradition is that Ahriman, the chief of the rebels, is not by nature evil. He was not created evil by the Eternal One, but he became evil by revolting against His will, and the ancient books of the Parsees assert that at the last day Ahriman will return to obedience, and having been purified by fire, will regain the place among the heavenly beings which he lost. In this war the Izeds fought against the Divs, headed by Ahriman, and flung the conquered into Douzahk or hell.

The Norse story is that Loki, the spirit of evil, is one of the gods, and sat with them at their table till he declared himself their enemy, when he with his vile progeny, the wolf and the serpent, were cast out. The wolf is bound, Thorr constrains the

---
[1] 1 Cor. x. 20.
[2] Majer, Mythologische Lexicon, Th. i. p. 231.

serpent, and Loki is chained under the mountains, and a serpent distils poison on his breast; when he tosses in agony, the earth quakes.

In Egypt, Typhon was brother of Osiris, but he revolted against him.

Maximus of Tyre, and Apollonius of Rhodes, following Orpheus, speak of the war of the gods against the angels who rebelled under their chief Ophion, or the Serpent, and Pherecydes, according to Origen, sang of this event as having taken place in pre-historic times; so that the knowledge of it could only have reached man by revelation. He described the two armies face to face,—one commanded by Saturn, the supreme Creator; the other by Ophioneus, the old Dragon, and the defeat of the latter and its expulsion from the realms of bliss to Ogenos, the regions of annihilation.[1] The story of the Titans is connected with this. They were the sons of Uranus (heaven) and Ge (earth), and dwelt originally in heaven, whence they are called Uranidæ. They were twelve in number. Uranus threw out of heaven his other sons, the Hecatoncheires and the Cyclopes, and precipitated them into Tartarus. Whereupon Ge persuaded her sons, the Titans, to rise up against their father, and liberate their brethren. They did as their mother bade them, deposed Uranus, and placed on his throne their brother Cronus, who immediately re-imprisoned the Cyclopes. But Zeus with his brothers fought against the reigning Titans, cast them out of heaven, and enthroned himself on the seat of Cronus; and the Titans he enchained in the abyss under Tartarus.

This is simply the same story told over twice, and formed into a dynasty. Chronos Titan is the sáme as the Arabic Scheitan, the Erse Teitin, the Time-god, and the Biblical Satan, or Lucifer, the Son of the Morning.

Amongst the Battas of Sumatra exists a myth to this effect:

---

[1] Orig. adv. Cels. vi. 42.

Batara Guru, the supreme God, from whose daughter Putiarla Buran all mankind are descended, cast the mountain Bakkara out of heaven upon the head of the serpent, his foe, and made the home of his son Layanga-layaad-mandi on the top of this mountain. From this summit the son descended that he might bind the hands or feet of the serpent, as it shook its head and made the earth rock.

Connected with the fall of Satan is his lameness. The devil is represented in art and in legend as limping on one foot; this was occasioned by his having broken his leg in his fall.

Hephæstus, who pursued Athene and attempted to outrage divine Wisdom, was precipitated from heaven into the fire-island Lemnos, and was lamed thereby. Hermes cut the hamstring out of Typhon, therewith to string his lyre. The Norse god Loki lusted after Freya, and was lamed therefore. Wieland the smith (Völundr), who ventured to do violence to Beodohild, was lamed, and was known thereby. Phaethon, daring to drive his father's chariot of the sun, was cast out and thrown to earth.

The natives of the Caroline Islands relate that one of the inferior gods, named Merogrog, was driven by the other gods out of heaven, and he took with him a spark of fire which he gave to men.[1] This myth resembles that of Prometheus, "the contriver, full of gall and bitterness, who sinned against the gods by bestowing their honours on creatures of a day, the thief of fire," as Hermes calls him. He reappears as Tohil among the Quiches, the giver of fire, hated, yet adored.

The Northern Californians say that the supreme God once created invisible spirits, of whom one portion revolted against him, headed by a spirit named War or Touparan, and that the Great Spirit having overcome him, drove him from the plains of heaven, and confined him along with his comrades in a cavern, where he is guarded by whales.[2]

---

[1] Lettres Edifiantes, viii. p. 420.
[2] Bibliothèque Univ. de Genève, 1827; D'Anselme, i. p. 228.

The Egyptian Typhon, already alluded to, did not belong to Egypt alone, but also to Phœnicia and Asia Minor, and thence the story passed into Greece, where it took root, and has been preserved to us as the attack of the hundred-headed dragon against the heaven-god Zeus. Typhon desired to obtain supremacy over gods and men, and, in order to win for himself this sovereignty, he fought against the gods; but he was defeated, bound, and precipitated into Tartarus, or, according to another version, was buried under the flaming mountains.

According to a tradition of the Salivas, a people of New Granada, a serpent slew the nations, descended from God, who inhabited the region of the Orinoco, but a son of the God Puru fought him and overcame him, and bade him depart with his curse, and never to enter his house again, and, say these Salivas, from the flesh of the serpent sprang the Caribees, their great foes, as maggots from putrid meat.[1]

But these stories might be infinitely extended. How far they refer to a tradition common to the human race, and how far they relate to the strife between summer and winter, sun and storm-cloud, I do not pretend to decide. It is one of those vexed questions which it is impossible to determine.

[1] Hist. Naturelle de l'Orinoque, par Tos. Gumilla. Avignon, 1751, t. i. p. 172.

## II.

## ADAM.

### 1. THE CREATION OF MAN.

CERTAIN of the angels having fallen, God made men, that they might take their vacated places.

According to the most authoritative Mussulman traditions, Adam was created on Friday afternoon at the Assr-hour, or about three o'clock. The four archangels—Gabriel, Michael, Israfiel, and Asrael—were required to bring earth from the four quarters of the world, that therefrom God might fashion man. His head and breast were made of clay from Mecca and Medina, from the spot where later were the Holy Kaaba and the tomb of Mohammed. Although still lifeless, his beauty amazed the angels who had flocked to the gates of Paradise. But Eblis, envious of the beauty of Adam's as yet inanimate form, said to the angels: "How can you admire a creature made of earth? From such material nothing but fragility and feebleness can come." However, most of the angels praised God for what He had done.

The body of Adam was so great, that if he stood up his head would reach into the seventh heaven. But he was not as yet endowed with a living soul. The soul had been made a thousand years before, and had been steeped all that while in the sea of light which flowed from Allah. God now ordered the soul to enter the body. It showed some indisposition to obey; thereupon God exclaimed:

"Quicken Adam against your will, and, as a penalty for your disobedience, you shall leave the body sorely against your will." Then God blew the spirit against Adam with such force that it entered his nose, and ran up into his head, and as soon as it reached his eyes Adam opened them, and saw the throne of God with the inscription upon it: "There is no God but God, and Mohammed is His prophet." Then the soul ran into his ears, and Adam heard the song of the angels; thereupon his tongue was unloosed, for by this time the soul had reached it, and he said, "Praise be to Thee, my Creator, one and only!" And God answered him: "For this purpose are you made. You and your successors must pray to me, and you will find mercy and loving-kindness at my hands." Then the soul penetrated all the members, reaching last of all the feet of Adam, which receiving strength, he sprang up, and stood upon the earth. But when he stood upright he was obliged to close his eyes, for the light of God's throne shining directly into them blinded them. "What light is this?" he asked, as he covered his eyes with one hand, and indicated the throne with the other. "It is the light of a prophet," God answered, "who will spring from thee in later ages. By mine honour I swear, for him alone have I created the world. In heaven he bears the name of the much-lauded, and on earth he will be called Mohammed. Through him all men will be led out of error into the way of truth."

God then called all created animals before Adam, and told him their names and their natures. Then He called up all the angels, and bade them bow before Adam, the man whom He had made. Israfiel obeyed first, and God gave to him in recompense the custody of the Book of Fate; the other angels obeyed in order; only Eblis refused, in the pride of his heart, saying, "Why shall I, who am made of fire, bend before him who is made of earth?" Therefore he was cast out of the angel choirs, and was forbidden admission through the gates of

Paradise. Adam also was led out of Paradise, and he preached to the angels, who stood before him in ten thousand ranks, a sermon on the power, majesty, and goodness of God, and he showed such learning and knowledge—for he could name each beast in seventy languages—that the angels were amazed at his knowledge, which excelled their own. As a reward for having preached this sermon, God sent Adam a bunch of grapes out of Paradise by the hands of Gabriel.[1]

In the Midrash, the Rabbinical story is as follows: "When God wished to make man, He consulted with the angels, and said to them, We will make a man in our image. Then they said, What is man, that you regard him, and what is his nature? He answered, His knowledge excels yours. Then He placed all kinds of beasts before them, wild beasts and fowls of the air, and asked them their names, but they knew them not. And after Adam was made, He led them before him, and He asked Adam their names, and he replied at once, This is an ox, that is an ass, this is a horse, that is a camel, and so forth."[2]

The story told by Tabari is somewhat different.

When God would make Adam, He ordered Gabriel to bring Him a handful of every sort of clay, black, white, red, yellow, blue, and every other kind.[3] Gabriel went to the middle of the earth to the place where now is Kaaba. He wished to stoop and take the clay, but the earth said to him, "O Gabriel, what doest thou?" And Gabriel answered, "I am fetching a little clay, dust, and stone, that thereof God may make a Lord for thee." Then the earth swore by God, "Thou shalt take of me neither clay nor dust nor stone; what if of the creatures made from me some should arise who would do evil upon the earth, and shed innocent blood?" Gabriel withdrew,

[1] Weil, Biblische Legenden der Muselmänner. Frankfort, 1845, pp. 12-16.
[2] Geiger, Was hat Mohammed aus d. Judenthum aufgenommen? p. 99.
[3] So also Abulfeda, Hist. Ante-Islamica, ed. Fleischer. Lipsiæ, 1831, p. 13.

respecting the oath, and took no earth; and he said to God, "Thou knowest what the earth said to me."

Then God sent Michael and bade him fetch a little mud. But when Michael arrived, the earth swore the same oath.

And Michael respected the oath and withdrew.

Then God sent Azrael, the angel of death. He came, and the earth swore the same oath; but he did not retire, but answered and said, "I must obey the command of God in spite of thine oath."

And the angel of death stooped, and took from forty ells below the earth clay of every sort, as we have said, and therefrom God made Adam.

No one in the world had seen a form like that of Adam. Hâreth or Satan went to look at him. Adam had lain stretched in the same place for the space of about forty years. No one thought of him or knew what sort of a thing he was. Hâreth coming up to him, saw him stretched from east to west, of huge size and as dry as dry palm leaves. Then Hâreth pushed Adam, and the dry earth rattled. Hâreth was astonished. He examined the form more attentively, and he found that it was hollow. Then he went to the mouth and crept in at it, and crept out again and let the angels know the doubt that was in his breast, for he said, "This creature is nothing, its inside is empty, and a hollow thing can easily be broken. Now that God has made him, He has given him the empire of the world, but I will fight against him and drive him from the earth as I drove out the Jins. What is your advice?"

The angels answered, "O Hâreth, if we overcame the Jins it was in obedience to God's command. Now that God has created this thing, if He orders us to submit to it, we must do so." Now when Hâreth saw that the angels thought otherwise, he changed his discourse and said, "You speak the truth, I agree with you, but I wanted to prove you."

When God gave the soul to Adam, it entered his throat and passed down into his bosom and belly, and wherever it passed, the earth, the clay, the dust, and the black mud became bones, nerves, veins, flesh, skin, and the like. And when his soul entered his head, Adam sneezed, and said, "Praise be to God." And when he turned his head, he saw Paradise and all its delights; and when the soul entered his belly, he wanted to eat, so he tried to rise and get some food, but the soul had not yet reached his extremities, which were as yet mere clay, so Gabriel said: "O Adam, don't be in a hurry."[1] Then follows the story of Eblis refusing to adore Adam. According to another version of the Mussulman story, the soul showed such repugnance to enter the body, that the angel Gabriel took a flageolet, and sitting down near the head of the inanimate Adam, played such exquisite melodies that the soul descended to listen, and in a moment of ecstasy entered the feet, which began immediately to move. Thereupon the soul was given command by Allah not to leave the body again till special permission was given it by the Most High.[2]

In the Talmud we are told that the Rabbi Meir says that the dust from which Adam was made was gathered from all parts of the earth: the Rabbi Hoshea says that the body of the first man was made of dust from Babel; the head, of earth from the land of Israel, and the rest of his limbs from the soil of other countries: but the Rabbi Acha adds that his hinder quarters were fashioned out of clay from Acre.[3] When Adam was made, some of the dust remained over; of that God made locusts.[4]

A Rabbinical tale is to this effect. God was interrupted by the Sabbath in the midst of creating fauns and satyrs, after He had made man, and was obliged to postpone their completion till the Sunday, consequently these creatures are misshapen. A Talmudic account of the way in which were

---

[1] Tabari, i. c. xxvi.    [2] Collin de Plancy, p. 55.
[3] Eisenmenger, Neuentdecktes Judenthum. Königsberg, 1711., i. pp. 364-5.
[4] Bochart, Hierozoica, p. 2, l. 8, fol. 486.

spent the hours of the day in which Adam was made, is sufficiently curious.

At the first hour, God gathered the dust of the earth; in the second, He formed the embryo; in the third, the limbs were extended; in the fourth, the soul was given; at the fifth hour Adam stood upright; at the sixth, Adam named the animals. Having done this, God asked him, "And I, what is my name?"

Adam replied—"Jehovah."

At the seventh hour, Adam married Eve; at the eighth, Cain and his sister were born; at the ninth, they were forbidden to eat of the tree; at the tenth hour Adam fell; at the eleventh he was banished from Eden; and at the twelfth, he felt the sweat and pain of toil.[1]

In the Apocryphal Little Genesis, we are told that Adam did not disobey God till the expiration of the seventh year, and that he was not punished till forty-five days after. It adds, that before the Fall, Adam conversed familiarly with the animals, but that by the Fall they lost the faculty of speech.

God, say the Rabbis, made Adam so tall that his head touched the sky; and the tree of life, planted in the midst of the garden of Eden, was so broad at the base that it would take a good walker five years to march round it, and Adam's proportions accorded with those of the tree. The angels murmured, and told God that there were two sovereigns, one in heaven and one on earth. Thereupon God placed His hand on the head of Adam and reduced him to a thousand cubits.[2]

To the question, How big was Adam? the Talmud replies, He was made so tall that he stood with his head in heaven, till God pressed him down at the Fall. Rabbi Jehuda says, that as he lay stretched on the earth he covered it completely;[3] but the book Sepher Gilgulim says (fol. 20, col. 4), that when

---

[1] Tract Sanhedrim, f. 38.  [2] Jalkut Schimoni, f. 6.
[3] Tract Hagida, f. 12.

he was made, his head and throat were in Paradise, and his body in the earth. To judge how long he was, says the same book, understand that his body stretched from one end of the earth to the other, and it takes a man five hundred years to walk that distance.[1] And when Adam was created, all the beasts of earth fell down before him and desired to worship him, but he said to them, "You have come to worship me, but come and let us clothe ourselves with power and glory, and let us take Him to be king over us who has created us; for a people chooses a king, but the king does not appoint himself monarch arbitrarily." Therefore Adam chose God to be king of all the world, and the beasts, fowls, and fishes gladly consented thereto.[2] But the sun, seeing Adam, was filled with fear and became dark; and the angels quaked and were dismayed, and prayed to God to remove from them this mighty being whom He had made. Then God cast a deep sleep on Adam, and the sun and the angels looked on him lying helpless in his slumber, and they plucked up courage and feared him no more. The book Sepher Chasidim, however, says, that the angels seeing Adam so great and with his face shining above the brightness of the sun, bowed before him, and said, "Holy, holy, holy!" Whereupon God cast a sleep upon him and cut off great pieces of his flesh to reduce him to smaller proportions. And when Adam woke he saw bits of flesh strewed all round him, like shavings in a carpenter's shop, and he exclaimed "O God! how hast Thou robbed me?" but God answered, "Take these gobbets of flesh and carry them into all lands and drop them everywhere, and strew dust on them; and wherever they are laid, that land will I give to thy posterity to inherit."[3]

Many are the origins attributed to man in the various creeds of ancient and modern heathendom. Sometimes he is spoken of as having been made out of water, but more generally it is of earth that he has been made, or from which he has been

[1] Eisenmenger, i. p. 367.  [2] Ibid., i. p. 368.  [3] Ibid., i p. 369.

spontaneously born. The Peruvians believed that the world was peopled by four men and four women, brothers and sisters, who emerged from the caves near Cuzco. Among the North American Indians the earth is regarded as the universal mother. Men came into existence in her womb, and crept out of it by climbing up the roots of the trees which hung from the vault in which they were conceived and matured; or, mounting a deer, the animal brought them into daylight; or, groping in darkness, they tore their way out with their nails.[1]

The Egyptian philosophers pretended that man was made of the mud of the Nile.[2] In Aristophanes,[3] man is spoken of as πλάσματα πηλοῦ. Among some of the Chinese it is believed that man was thus formed:—"The book Fong-zen-tong says: When the earth and heaven were made, there was not as yet man or peoples. Then Niu-hoa moulded yellow earth, and of that made man. That is the true origin of men."[4]

And the ancient Chaldeans supposed man was made by the mixing of the blood of Belus with the soil.[5]

## 2. THE PRE-ADAMITES.

In 1655, Isaac de la Peyreira, a converted Jew, published a curious treatise on the Pre-Adamites. Arguing upon Romans v. 12—14, he contended that there were two creations of man; that recorded in the first chapter of Genesis and that described in the second chapter being distinct. The first race he supposed to have peopled the whole world, but that it was bad, and therefore Adam had been created with a spiritual soul, and that from Adam the Jewish race was descended, whereas the Gentile nations issued from the loins of the Pre-

---

[1] Müller, Amerikanische Urreligionen; Basle, 1855. Atherne Jones, North American Traditions, i. p. 210, &c. Heckewelder's Indian Nations, &c.
[2] Fourmont, Anciens Peuples, i. lib. ii. p. 10. [3] Aves, 666.
[4] Mémoires des Chinois, i. p. 105.
[5] Berosus, in Cory's Ancient Fragments, p. 26.

Adamites. Consequently the original sin of Adam weighed only on his descendants, and Peyreira supposed that it was his race alone which perished, with the exception of Noah and his family, in the Deluge, which Peyreira contends was partial. This book was condemned and burnt in Paris by the hands of the executioner, and the author, who had taken refuge in Brussels, was there condemned by the ecclesiastical authorities. He appealed to Rome, whither he journeyed, and he was received with favour by Alexander VII., before whom he abjured Calvinism, which he had professed.

He died at the age of 82, at Aubervilliers, near Paris, and Moreri wrote the following epigrammatic epitaph for him :—

> "La Peyrère ici gît, ce bon Israélite,
> Huguenot, catholique, enfin pré-Adamite.
> Quatre religions lui plurent à la fois ;
>  Et son indifférence était si peu commune,
> Qu'après quatre-vingts ans qu'il eut à faire un choix,
>  Le bon homme partit et n'en choisit aucune."

The Oriental book Huschenk-Nameh gives a fuller history of the Pre-Adamites. Before Adam was created, says this book, there were in the isle Muscham, one of the Maldives, men with flat heads, and for this reason they were called by the Persians, Nim-ser. They were governed by a king named Dambac.

When Adam, expelled the earthly Paradise, established himself in the Isle of Ceylon, the flat-heads submitted to him. After his death they guarded his tomb by day, and the lions relieved guard by night, to protect his body against the Divs.

## III.

## EVE.[1]

THAT man was created double, *i.e.* both male and female, is and has been a common opinion. One Rabbinical interpretation of the text, "And God created man in His own image, male-female created He them," is that Adam and Eve were formed back to back, united at the shoulders, and were hewn asunder with a hatchet; but of this more presently. The Rabbis say that when Eve had to be drawn out of the side of Adam she was not extracted by the head, lest she should be vain; nor by the eyes, lest they should be wanton; nor by the mouth, lest she should be given to gossiping; nor by the ears, lest she should be an eavesdropper; nor by the hands, lest she should be meddlesome; nor by the feet, lest she should be a gadabout; nor by the heart, lest she should be jealous; but she was drawn forth by the side: yet, notwithstanding all these precautions, she has every fault specially guarded against.[2]

They also say that, for the marriage-feast of Adam and Eve, God made a table of precious stone, and each gem was a hundred ells long and sixty ells wide, and the table was covered with costly dishes.[3]

The Mussulman tradition is, that Adam having eaten the bunch of grapes given him as a reward for having preached to the angels, fell asleep; and whilst he slept, God took from his left side a woman whom He called Hava, because she was

---

[1] It is unfortunate that I have already written on the myths relating to the formation of Eve in "Curiosities of Olden Times." I would therefore have omitted a chapter which must repeat what has been already published, but that by so doing I should leave this work imperfect. However, there is much in this chapter which was not in the article referred to.

[2] Rabboth, fol. 20 b.   [3] Eisenmenger, i. 830.

extracted from one living (Hai), and He laid her beside Adam. She resembled him exactly, except that her features were more delicate, her hair longer and divided into seven hundred locks, her form more slender, her eyes softer, and her voice sweeter than Adam's. In the meantime Adam had been dreaming that a wife had been given to him; and when he woke, great was his delight to find his dream turned into a reality. He put forth his hand to take that of Hava, but she withdrew hers, answering his words of love with, "God is my master, and I cannot give my hand to thee without His permission; and, moreover, it is not proper for a man to take a wife without making her a wedding present."

Adam thereupon sent the angel Gabriel to ask God's permission to take to him Hava as his wife. Gabriel returned with the answer that she had been created to be his helpmate, and that he was to treat her with gentleness and love. For a present he must pray twenty times for Mohammed and for the prophets, who, in due season, were to be born of him. Ridhwan, the porter of Paradise, then brought to Adam the winged horse Meimun, and to Eve a light-footed she-camel. Gabriel helped them to mount and led them into Paradise, where they were greeted by all the angels and beasts with the words: "Hail, father and mother of Mohammed!"

In the midst of Paradise was a green silk tent spread for them, supported on gold pillars, and in the tent was a throne upon which Adam and Hava were seated. Then they were bathed in one of the rivers of Paradise and brought before the presence of God, who bade them dwell in Paradise. "I have prepared you this garden for your home; in it you shall be protected from cold and heat, from hunger and thirst. Enjoy all that meets your eye, only of one fruit taste not. Beware how you break my command, and arm yourself against the subtlety of your foe, Eblis; he envies you, and stands by you seeking to destroy you, for through you was he cast out."[1]

[1] Weil, pp. 17, 18.

Tabari says that Adam was brought single into Paradise, through which he roamed eating from the fruit trees, and a deep sleep fell upon him, during which Eve was created from his left side. And when Adam opened his eyes, he saw her, and asked her who she was, and she replied, "I am thy wife; God created me out of thee and for thee, that thy heart might find repose." The angels said to Adam: "What thing is this? What is her name? Why is she made?" Adam replied, "This is Eve." Adam remained five hundred years in Paradise. It was on a Friday that Adam entered Eden.[1]

The inhabitants of Madagascar have a strange myth touching the origin of woman. They say that the first man was created of the dust of the earth, and was placed in a garden, where he was subject to none of the ills which now affect mortality; he was also free from all bodily appetites, and though surrounded by delicious fruit and limpid streams, yet felt no desire to taste of the fruit or to quaff the water. The Creator had, moreover, strictly forbidden him either to eat or to drink. The great enemy, however, came to him, and painted to him in glowing colours the sweetness of the apple, the lusciousness of the date, and the succulence of the orange.

In vain: the first man remembered the command laid upon him by his Maker. Then the fiend assumed the appearance of an effulgent spirit, and pretended to be a messenger from Heaven commanding him to eat and drink. The man at once obeyed. Shortly after, a pimple appeared on his leg; the spot enlarged to a tumour, which increased in size and caused him considerable annoyance. At the end of six months it burst, and there emerged from the limb a beautiful girl.

The father of all living was sorely perplexed what to make of his acquisition, when a messenger from heaven appeared, and told him to let her run about the garden till she was of a marriageable age, and then to take her to himself as his wife.

[1] Tabari, i. c. xxvi.

He obeyed. He called her Bahouna, and she became the mother of all races of men.

The notion of the first man having been of both sexes till the separation, was very common. He was said to have been male on the right side and female on the left, and that one half of him was removed to constitute Eve, but that the complete man consists of both sexes.

Eugubinus among Christian commentators, the Rabbis Samuel, Manasseh Ben-Israel, and Maimonides among the Jews, have given the weight of their opinion to support this interpretation. The Rabbi Jeremiah Ben-Eleazer, on the authority of the text "*Thou hast fashioned me behind and before*" (Ps. cxxxix. 4), argued that Adam had two faces, one male and the other female, and that he was of both sexes.[1]

The Rabbi Samuel Ben-Nahaman held that the first man was created double, with a woman at his back, and that God cut them apart.[2] "Adam," said other Rabbis, "had two faces and one tail, and from the beginning he was both male and female, male on one side, female on the other; but afterwards the parts were separated."[3]

The Talmudists assert that God cut off Adam's tail and thereof formed Eve.[4]

With this latter fable agrees the ludicrous myth of the Kikapoo Indians, related in my "Curiosities of Olden Times."

In Aristophanes' speech in the Symposium of Plato, a myth is given, that in the beginning there was a race of men of which every member was double, having two heads, four legs and four arms, and each of both sexes. This race, says he, was filled with pride, and it attempted to scale heaven. The Gods desired at once to reduce their might and punish their temerity, but did not wish to destroy the human race; consequently at the advice of Zeus, each androgyne was hewn

---

[1] Talmud, Tract Berachoth, f. 61; Bartolocci, Bibl. Rabbin., iv. p. 66.
[2] Bartolocci, Bibl. Rabbin., iv. p. 67.   [3] Ibid., iii. p. 395.
[4] Ibid., iii. p. 396; Eisenmenger, t. i. p. 365.

asunder, so as to leave to each half two arms and a pair of legs, one head and a single sex.

An Indian tradition is to this effect. Whilst Brahma the creator was engaged in the production of beings, he saw Kaya (body) divide itself into two parts, of which each part was of a different sex, and thence sprang the whole human race.[1]

According to another much more explicit version, Viradi, the first man, finding his solitude intolerable, fell into the deepest sorrow; and, yearning for a companion, his nature developed into two sexes united in one. Then he separated into two individuals, but found in that separation unhappiness, for he was conscious of his imperfection; then he reunited the existence of the two portions and was happy, and from that reunion the world was peopled.[2]

In Persia, Meschia and Meschiane, the first man and the first woman, were said to have formed originally but one body; but they were cut apart, and from this voluntary reunion all men are sprung.[3]

The idea so prevalent that man without woman, or woman without man, is an imperfect being, was the cause of the great repugnance with which the Jews and other nations of the East regarded celibacy. The Rabbi Eliezer, commenting on the text "He called their name Adam" (Gen. v. 2.), laid down that ne who has not a wife is not a man, for man is the recomposition of male and female into one.[4]

Bramah, says an Indian legend, being charged with the production of the human race, felt himself a prey to violent pains, till his sides opened, and from one flank emerged a boy and from the other a girl. In China, the story is told that the Goddess Amida sweated male children out of her right armpit, and female children from her left arm-pit, and these children peopled the earth.[5]

[1] Bhagavat, iii. 12, 51.  [2] Colebrooke, Miscell. Essays, p. i. 64.
[3] Bun-dehesch, p. 377.  [4] Bartolocci, Bibl. Rabbin., iv. p. 465.
[5] Mendez Pinto, Voyages, ii. p. 178.

Vishnu, according to an Indian fable, gave birth to Dharma by his right side, and to Adharma by his left side, and through Adharma death entered the world.[1] Another story is to the effect, that the right arm of Vena gave birth to Pritu, the master of the earth, and the left arm to the Virgin Archis, who became the bride of Pritu.[2]

Pygmalion, says the classic story, which is really a Phœnician myth of creation, made woman of marble or ivory, and Aphrodite, in answer to his prayers, endowed the statue with life. "Often does Pygmalion apply his hands to the work. One while he addresses it in soft terms, at another he brings it presents that are agreeable to maidens, as shells and smooth pebbles, and little birds, and flowers of a thousand hues, and lilies, and painted balls, and tears of the Heliades, that have distilled from the trees. He decks her limbs, too, with clothing, and puts a long necklace on her neck. Smooth pendants hang from her ears, and bows from her breast. All things are becoming to her."[3]

But Hesiod gives a widely different account of the creation of woman. According to him, she was sent in mockery by Zeus to be a scourge to man:—

> "The Sire who rules the earth and sways the pole
> Had spoken; laughter filled his secret soul:
> He bade the crippled god his hest obey,
> And mould with tempering water plastic clay;
> With human nerve and human voice invest
> The limbs elastic, and the breathing breast;
> Fair as the blooming goddesses above,
> A virgin likeness with the looks of love.
> He bade Minerva teach the skill that sheds
> A thousand colours in the glittering threads;
> He called the magic of love's golden queen
> To breathe around a witchery of mien,
> And eager passion's never-sated flame,
> And cares of dress that prey upon the frame;
> Bade Hermes last endue, with craft refined
> Of treacherous manners, and a shameless mind."[4]

---

[1] Bhagavat, iii. 12, 25.  
[2] Ibid., iv. 15, 27.  
[3] Ovid, Metamorph., x. 7.  
[4] Hesiod, Works and Days, 61–79.

That Eve was Adam's second wife was a common Rabbinic speculation; certain of the commentators on Genesis having adopted this view to account for the double account of the creation of woman in the sacred text,—first in Genesis i. 27, and secondly in Genesis ii. 18; and they say that Adam's first wife was named Lilith, but she was expelled from Eden, and after her expulsion Eve was created.

Abraham Ecchellensis gives the following account of Lilith, and her doings:—" There are some who do not regard spectres as simple devils, but suppose them to be of a mixed nature, part demoniacal, part human, and to have had their origin from Lilith, Adam's first wife, by Eblis, the prince of the devils. This fable has been transmitted to the Arabs from Jewish sources, by some converts of Mahomet from Cabbalism and Rabbinism, who have transferred all the Jewish fooleries to the Arabs. They gave to Adam a wife, formed of clay, along with Adam, and called her Lilith; resting on the Scripture, '*male and female created He them:*'[1] but when this woman, on account of her simultaneous creation with him, became proud and a vexation to her husband, God expelled her from Paradise, and then said, '*It is not good that the man should be alone; I will make him a help meet for him.*'[2] And this they confirm by the words of Adam when he saw the woman fashioned from his rib, '*This is now bone of my bone, and flesh of my flesh,*'[3] which is as much as to say, Now God has given me a wife and companion, suitable for me, taken from my bone and flesh, but the other wife he gave me was not of my bone and flesh, and therefore was not a suitable companion and wife for me.

" But Lilith, after she was expelled from Paradise, is said to have married the Devil, by whom she had children, who are called Jins. These were endued with six qualities, of which they share three with men, and three with devils. Like men, they generate in their own likeness, eat food, and die. Like

[1] Gen. i. 27.    [2] Gen. ii. 18.    [3] Gen. ii. 23.

devils, they are winged, and they fly where they list with great velocity; they are invisible, and they can pass through solid substances without injuring them. This race of Jins is supposed to be less noxious to men, and indeed to live in some familiarity and friendship with them, as in part sharers of their nature. The author of the history and acts of Alexander of Macedon relates, that in a certain region of India, on certain hours of the day, the young Jins assume a human form, and appear openly and play games with the native children of human parents quite familiarly."[1]

It must not be supposed that women, as they are now, are at all comparable to Eve in her pristine beauty; on this point the Talmud says: "All women in respect of Sarah are like monkeys in respect of men. But Sarah can no more be compared to Eve than can a monkey be compared with a man. In like manner it may be said, if any comparison could be drawn between Eve and Adam, she stood to him in the same relation of beauty as does a monkey to a man; but if you were to compare Adam with God, Adam would be the monkey, and God the man."[2]

Literary ladies may point to the primal mother as the first authoress; for a Gospel of Eve existed in the times of S. Epiphanius, who mentions it as being in repute among the Gnostics.[3] And the Mussulmans attribute to her a volume of Prophecies which were written at her dictation by the Angel Raphael.[4]

All ladies will be glad to learn that there is a tradition, Manichean, it is true, and anathematized by S. Clement, which nevertheless contains a large element of truth; it is to this effect, that Adam, when made, was like a beast, coarse, rude, and inanimate, but that from Eve he received his upright position, his polish, and his spirituality.[5]

[1] Abraham Ecchellensis. Hist. Arabum, p. 268.
[2] Talmud, Tract. Bava Bathra. [3] S. Epiphan. Hæres., xxvi.
[4] Tho. Bangius, Cœlum Orientis, p. 103.
[5] S. Clementi Recog., c. iv.

## IV.

## THE FALL OF MAN.

WHAT was the tree of which our first parents were forbidden to eat? In Midrash, f. 7, the Rabbi Mayer says it was a wheat-tree; the Rabbi Jehuda, that it was a grape-vine; the Rabbi Aba, that it was a Paradise-apple; the Rabbi Josse, that it was a fig-tree: therefore it was that, when driven out of Paradise, they used its leaves for a covering.

The Persian story, adopted by the Arabs, is that the forbidden fruit was wheat, and that it grew on a tree whose trunk resembled gold and its branches silver. Each branch bore five shining ears, and each ear contained five grains as big as the eggs of an ostrich, as fragrant as musk, and as sweet as honey. The people of Southern America suppose it was the banana, whose fibres form the cross, and they say that thus, in it, Adam discovered the mystery of the Redemption. The inhabitants of the island of St. Vincent think it was the tobacco plant. But, according to an Iroquois legend, the great mother of the human race lost heaven for a pot of bears' grease.[1] The story is as follows:—The first men living alone were,

> "By the viewless winds,
> Blown with resistless violence round about
> The pendant world."

Fearing the extinction of their race, and having learnt that a woman dwelt somewhere in the heavens, they deputed one of their number to seek her out. This messenger of mankind was borne to the skies on the wings of assembled birds; and

[1] Lafitau, Mœurs des Sauvages Amériquaines, i. p. 93.

then watched at the foot of a tree till the woman came forth to draw water from a neighbouring well. On her approach he addressed her, offered her bears' fat, and then seduced her. The Deity perceiving her shame, in His anger thrust her out of heaven. The tortoise received her on his back; and from the depths of the sea the fish brought clay, and thus gradually built up an island on which the universal mother brought forth her first twins.

According to the traditions of the Lamaic faith, the first men lived to the age of sixty thousand years.[1] They were invisibly nourished, and were able to raise themselves at will to the heavens. In this age of the world the transmigration of souls was universal,—all men were twice born; and in this age it was that the thousand gods settled themselves in heaven. In an unlucky hour the earth produced a honey-sweet substance: one of the men lusted after it, tasted and gave to his companions; the consequence was, that men lost the power of rising from off the earth, their size, and their wisdom, and were obliged to satisfy themselves with food produced by the soil.

The Nepaul account of the beginning of sin is as follows: "Originally," says one of the Tantras, "the earth was uninhabited. In those times the inhabitants of Abhaswara, one of the heavenly mansions, used frequently to visit the earth, and thence speedily return. It happened at length that when a few of these beings, who though half male, half female, through the innocence of their minds had never noticed their distinction of sex, came as usual to the earth, Adi Buddha suddenly created in them so violent a longing to eat, that they ate some of the earth, which had the taste of almonds; and by eating it they lost their power of flying back to their heaven, and so they remained on the earth. They were now constrained to eat the fruits of the earth for sustenance."[2]

According to the Cinghalese, the Brahmas inhabited the higher regions of the air, where they enjoyed perfect happiness.

---

[1] Pallas, Reise, i. p. 334.    [2] Hodgson, Buddhism, p. 63.

"But it came to pass that one of them beholding the earth said to himself, What thing is this? and with one of his fingers having touched the earth, he put it to the tip of his tongue, and perceived the same to be deliciously sweet; from that time all the Brahmas ate of the sweet earth for the space of sixty thousand years. In the meantime, having coveted in their hearts the enjoyment of this earth, they began to say to one another, This part is mine and that is thine; and so, fixing boundaries to their respective shares, divided the earth between them. On account of the Brahmas having been guilty of covetousness, the earth lost its sweetness, and then brought forth a kind of mushroom," which the Brahmas also coveted and divided, and of which they were also deprived; and thus they proceeded from food to food, till their nature was changed, and from spirits they became men, imbibed wicked ideas, and lost their ancient glory.[1]

According to the Chinese, man is part spirit, part animal. The spirit follows the laws of Heaven, as a disciple his master; the animal, on the other hand, is the slave of sense. At his origin, man obeyed the heavens; his first state was one of innocence and happiness; he knew neither disease nor death; he was by instinct wholly good and spiritual. But the immoderate desire to be wise, or, according to Lao-tsee, to eat, was the ruin of mankind.[2]

According to the Persian faith, the father of man had heaven for his destiny, but he must be humble of heart, pure of thought, of word and of deed, not invoking the Divs: and such in the beginning were the thoughts and acts of our first parents.

First they said, "It is Ormuzd (God) who has given the water, the earth, the trees, and the beasts of the field, and the stars, the moon, the sun, and all things pure." But Ahriman (Satan) arose, and rushed upon their thoughts and said to them,

---

[1] Upham, Sacred Books of Ceylon, iii. 156.
[2] Mémoires Chinois, i. p. 107.

"It is Ahriman who has given these things to you." Thus Ahriman deceived them, and to the end will deceive. To this lie they gave credence and became Darvands, and their souls were condemned till the great resurrection of the body. During thirty days they feasted and covered themselves with black garments. After thirty days they went to the chase; and they found a white goat, and with their lips they drew off her milk, and drank her milk and were glad. "We have tasted nothing like to this milk," said our first parents, Meschia and Meschiane; "the milk we have drunk was pleasant to the taste," but it was an evil thing to their bodies.

"Then the Div, the liar, grown more bold, presented himself a second time, and brought with him fruit of which they ate; and of a hundred excellences they before possessed, they now retained not one. And after thirty days and nights they found a white and fat sheep, and they cut off its left ear; and they fired a tree, and with their breath raised the fire to a flame; and they burned part of the branches of that tree, then of the tree khorma, and afterwards of the myrtle; and they roasted the sheep, and divided it into three portions: and of the two which they did not eat, one was carried to heaven by the bird Kehrkas.

"Afterwards they feasted on the flesh of a dog, and they clothed themselves in its skin. They gave themselves up to the chase, and with the furs of wild beasts they covered their bodies.

"And Meschia and Meschiane digged a hole in the earth and they found iron, and the iron they beat with a stone and they made for themselves an axe, and they struck at the roots of a tree, and they felled the tree and arranged its branches into a hut; and to God they gave no thanks; and the Divs took heart.

"And Meschia and Meschiane became enemies, and struck and wounded each other and separated; then from out of the place of darkness the chief of the Divs was heard to cry aloud: O man, worship the Divs! And the Div of Hate sat upon his throne. And Meschia approached and drew milk from the bull, and sprinkled it towards the north, and the Divs became strong. But during fifty winters, Meschia and Meschiane lived apart; and after that time they met, and Meschiane bare twins."[1]

The story told by the Mussulmans is as follows:—

Adam and Eve lived for five hundred years in Paradise before they ate of the tree and fell; for Eblis was outside, and could not enter the gates to deceive them.

For five hundred years Eblis sought admission, but the angel Ridhwan warned him off with his flaming sword.

One day the peacock came through the gates of Paradise. This bird with the feathers of emeralds and pearls was not only the most beautiful creature God had made, but it had also been endowed with a sweet and clear voice, wherewith it daily sang the praises of God in the highways of Eden.

This beautiful bird, thought Eblis, when he saw it, is surely vain, and will listen to the voice of flattery.

Thereupon he addressed it as a stranger, beyond the hearing of Ridhwan. "Most beautiful of all birds, do you belong to the denizens of Paradise?"

"Certainly," answered the peacock. "And who are you who look from side to side in fear and trembling?"

"I belong to the Cherubim who praise God night and day, and I have slipped out of their ranks without being observed, that I might take a glimpse of the Paradise God has prepared for the saints. Will you hide me under your feathers, and show me the garden?"

"How shall I do that which may draw down on me God's disfavour?" asked the peacock.

"Magnificent creature! take me with you. I will teach you

[1] Bundehesh in Windischmann: Zoroastrische Studien. Berlin, 1863, p. 82; and tr. A. du Perron, ii. pp. 77-80.

three words which will save you from sickness, old age, and death."

" Must then the dwellers in Paradise die?"

" All, without exception, who know not these three words."

" Is this the truth?"

" By God the Almighty it is so."

The peacock believed the oath, for it could not suppose that a creature would swear a false oath by its Creator. But, as it feared that Ridhwan would search it on its return through the gates, it hesitated to take Eblis with it, but promised to send the cunning serpent out, who would certainly devise a means of introducing Eblis into the garden.

The serpent was formerly queen of all creatures. She had a head like rubies, and eyes like emeralds. Her height was that of a camel, and the most beautiful colours adorned her skin, and her hair and face were those of a beautiful maiden. She was fragrant as musk and amber; her food was saffron; sweet hymns of praise were uttered by her melodious tongues; she slept by the waters of the heavenly river Kaulhar; she had been created a thousand years before man, and was Eve's favourite companion.

This beautiful and wise creature, thought the peacock, will desire more even than myself to possess perpetual youth and health, and will gladly admit the cherub for the sake of hearing the three words. The bird was not mistaken; as soon as it had told the story, the serpent exclaimed: "What! shall I grow old and die? Shall my beautiful face become wrinkled, my eyes close, and my body dissolve into dust? Never! rather will I brave Ridhwan's anger and introduce the cherub."

The serpent accordingly glided out of the gates of Paradise, and bade Eblis tell her what he had told the peacock.

" How shall I bring you unobserved into Paradise?" asked the serpent.

"I will make myself so small that I can sit in the nick between your front teeth," answered the fallen angel.[1]

"But how then can I answer when Ridhwan addresses me?"

"Fear not. I will whisper holy names, at which Ridhwan will keep silence."

The serpent thereupon opened her mouth, Eblis flew in and seated himself between her teeth, and by so doing poisoned them for all eternity.

When she had passed Ridhwan in security, the serpent opened her mouth and asked Eblis to take her with him to the highest heaven, where she might behold the majesty of God.

Eblis answered that he was not ready to leave yet, but that he desired to speak to Adam out of her mouth, and to this she consented, fearing Ridhwan, and greatly desiring to hear and learn the three salutary words. Having reached Eve's tent, Eblis uttered a deep sigh—it was the first that had been heard in Eden, and it was caused by envy.

"Why are you so disquieted, gentle serpent?" asked Eve.

"I am troubled for Adam's future," answered the evil spirit, affecting the voice of the serpent.

"What! have we not all that can be desired in this garden of God?"

"That is true; but the noblest fruit of the garden, the only one securing to you perfect happiness, is denied to your lips."

"Have we not abundance of fruit of every colour and flavour—only one is forbidden?"

"And if you knew why that one is forbidden, you would find little pleasure in tasting the others."

"Do you know?"

"I do, and for that reason am I so cast down. This fruit alone gives eternal youth and health, whereas all the others give weakness, disease, old age and death, which is the cessation of life with all its joys."

[1] So also Abulfeda, Hist. Ante-Islamica, p. 13.

"Why, dearest serpent, did you never tell me of this before? Whence know you these things?"

"An angel told me this as I lay under the forbidden tree."

"I must also see him," said Eve, leaving her tent and going towards the tree.

At this moment Eblis flew out of the serpent's mouth, and stood in human form beneath the tree.

"Who art thou, wondrous being, the like of whom I have not seen before?" asked Eve.

"I am a man who have become an angel."

"And how didst thou become an angel?"

"By eating of this fruit," answered the tempter,—"this fruit which is denied us through the envy of God. I dared to break His command as I grew old and feeble, and my eyes waxed dim, my ears dull, and my teeth fell out, so that I could neither speak plainly nor enjoy my food; my hands shook, my feet tottered, my head was bent upon my breast, my back was bowed, and I became so hideous that all the beasts of the garden fled from me in fear. Then I sighed for death, and hoping to find it in the fruit of this tree, I ate, and lo! instantly I was young again; though a thousand years had elapsed since I was made, they had fled with all their traces, and I enjoy perpetual health and youth and beauty."

"Do you speak the truth?" asked Eve.

"I swear by God who made me."

Eve believed this oath, and broke a branch from the wheat-tree.

Before the Fall, wheat grew to a tree with leaves like emeralds. The ears were red as rubies and the grains white as snow, sweet as honey, and fragrant as musk. Eve ate one of the grains and found it more delicious than anything she had hitherto tasted, so she gave a second grain to Adam. Adam resisted at first, according to some authorities for a whole hour, but an hour in Paradise was eighty years of our earthly reckoning. But when he saw that Eve remained well and cheerful, he yielded to her persuasions, and ate of the second grain which Eve had offered him daily, three times a day, during the hour of eighty years. Thereupon all Adam's heaven-given raiment fell from him, his crown slipped off his head, his rings dropped from his fingers, his silken garment glided like water from his shoulders, and he and Eve were naked and unadorned, and their fallen garments reproached them with the words, "Great is your misfortune; long will be your sorrows; we were created to adorn those who serve God; farewell till the resurrection!"

The throne recoiled from them and exclaimed, "Depart from me, ye disobedient ones!" The horse Meimun, which Adam sought to mount, plunged and refused to allow him to touch it, saying, "How hast thou kept God's covenant?" All the inhabitants of Paradise turned their backs on the pair, and prayed God to remove the man and the woman from the midst of them.

God himself addressed Adam with a voice of thunder, saying, "Did not I forbid thee to touch of this fruit, and caution thee against the subtlety of thy foe, Eblis?" Adam and Eve tried to fly these reproaches, but the branches of the tree Talh caught Adam, and Eve entangled herself in her long hair.

"From the wrath of God there is no escape," cried a voice from the tree Talh; "obey the commandment of God."

"Depart from Paradise," then spake God, "thou Adam, thy wife, and the animals which led you into sin. The earth shall be your abode; in the sweat of thy brow shalt thou find food; the produce of earth shall cause envy and contention; Eve (Hava) shall be afflicted with a variety of strange affections, and shall bring forth offspring in pain. The peacock shall lose its melodious voice, and the serpent its feet; dark and noisome shall be the den in which the serpent shall dwell, dust shall be its meat, and its destruction shall be a meritorious work. Eblis shall be cast into the torments of hell."

Our parents were then driven out of Paradise, and one leaf

alone was given to each, wherewith to hide their nakedness. Adam was expelled through the gate of Repentance, that he might know that through it alone could Paradise be regained; Eve was banished through the gate of Grace; the peacock and the serpent through that of Wrath, and Eblis through the gate of Damnation. Adam fell into the island Serendib (Ceylon), Eve at Jedda, the Serpent into the desert of Sahara, the Peacock into Persia, and Eblis into the river Eila.[1]

Tabari says that when the forbidden wheat had entered the belly of Adam and Eve, all the skin came off, except from the ends of the fingers. Now this skin had been pink and horny, so that they had been invulnerable in Paradise, and they were left naked and with a tender skin which could easily be lacerated; but, as often as Adam and Eve looked on their fingernails, they remembered what skin they had worn in Eden.[2]

Tabari also says that four trees pitying the shame of Adam and Eve, the Peacock, and the Serpent, in being driven naked out of Paradise, bowed their branches and gave each a leaf.

Certain Rabbis say that Adam ate only on compulsion, that he refused, but Eve "took of the tree,"—that is, broke a branch and "gave it him," with the stick.

According to the Talmudic book, Emek Hammelech (f. 23, col. 3), Eve, on eating the fruit, felt in herself the poison of Jezer hara, or Original sin, and resolved that Adam should not be without it also; she made him eat and then forced the fruit on the animals, that they might all, without exception, fall under the same condemnation, and become subject to death. But the bird Chol—that is, the Phœnix—would not be deceived, but flew away and would not eat. And now the Phœnix, says the Rabbi Joden after the Rabbi Simeon, lives a thousand years, then shrivels up till it is the size of an egg, and then from himself he emerges young and beautiful again.

We have seen what are the Asiatic myths relating to Adam and Eve; let us now turn to Africa. In Egypt it was related

[1] Weil, pp. 19-28.    [2] Tabari, i. p. 80.

that Osiris lived with Isis his sister and wife in Nysa, or Paradise, which was situated in Arabia. This Paradise was an island, surrounded by the stream Triton, but it was also a steep mountain that could only be reached on one side. It was adorned with beautiful flowers and trees laden with pleasant fruits, watered by sweet streams, and in it dwelt the deathless ones.

There Osiris found the vine, and Isis the wheat, to become the food and drink of men. There they built a golden temple, and lived in supreme happiness till the desire came on Osiris to discover the water of Immortality, in seeking which he left Nysa, and was in the end slain by Typhon.[1]

The following is a very curious negro tradition, taken down by Dr. Tutschek from a native in Tumale, near the centre of Africa.

Til (God) made men and bade them live together in peace and happiness, labour five days, and keep the sixth as a festival. They were forbidden to hurt the beasts or reptiles. They themselves were deathless, but the animals suffered death. The frog was accursed by God, because when He was making the animals it hopped over His foot. Then God ordered the men to build mountains: they did so, but they soon forgot God's commands, killed the beasts and quarrelled with one another. Wherefore Til (God) sent fire and destroyed them, but saved one of the race, named Musikdegen, alive. Then Til began to re-create beings. He stood before a wood and called, Ombo Abnatum Dgu! and there came out a gazelle and licked His feet. So He said, Stand up, Gazelle! and when it stood up, its beast-form disappeared, and it was a beautiful maiden, and He called her Mariam. He blessed her, and she bore four children, a white pair and a black pair. When they were grown up, God ordered them to marry, the white together, and the black together. In Dai, the story goes that Til cut out both Mariam's knee-caps, and of each He made a pair of chil-

[1] Diod. Sicul., i. 14 et seq.

dren. Those which were white He sent north; those which were black He gave possession of the land where they were born.

God then made the animals subject to death, but the men He made were immortal. But the new created men became disobedient, as had the first creatures; and the frog complained to Him of His injustice in having made the harmless animals subject to death, but guilty man deathless. "Thou art right," answered Til, and He cast on the men He had made, old age, sickness, and death.[1]

The Fantis relate that they are not in the same condition as that in which they were made, for their first parents had been placed in a lofty and more suitable country, but God drave them into an inferior habitation, that they might learn humility. On the Gold Coast the reason of the Fall is said to have been that the first men were offered the choice of gold or of wisdom, and they chose the former.[2]

In Ashantee the story is thus told. In the beginning, God created three white and three black men and women, and gave them the choice between good and evil. A great calabash was placed on the earth, as also a sealed paper, and God gave the black men the first choice. They took the calabash, thinking it contained everything, and in it were only a lump of gold, a bar of iron, and some other metals. The white men took the sealed paper, in which they learned everything. So God left the black men in the bush and took the white men to the sea, and He taught them how to build ships and go into another land. This fall from God caused the black men to worship the subsidiary Fetishes instead of Him.[3]

In Greenland "the first man is said to have been Kallak. He came out of the earth, but his wife issued from his thumb, and from them all generations of men have sprung. To him

[1] Ausland für Nov. 4, 1847.
[2] W. Smith, Nouveau Voyage de Guinée. Paris, 1751, ii. p. 176.
[3] Bowdler, Mission from Cape Coast to Ashantee. London, 1819, p. 344.

many attribute the origin of all things. The woman brought death into the world, in that she said, Let us die to make room for our successors."[1]

The tradition of the Dog-rib Indians near the Polar Sea, as related by Sir J. Franklin in his account of his expedition of 1825-27, is that the first man was called Tschäpiwih. He found the earth filled with abundance of all good things. He begat children and he gave to them two sorts of fruit, one white and the other black, and he bade them eat the white, but eschew the black. And having given them this command, he left them and went a long journey to fetch the sun to enlighten the world. During his absence they ate only of the white fruit, and then the father made a second journey to fetch the moon, leaving them well provided with fruit. But after a while they forgot his command, and consumed the black fruit. On his return he was angry, and cursed the ground that it should thenceforth produce only the black fruit, and that with it should come in sickness and death.

Dr. Hunter, in his "Memoirs of Captivity amongst the Indians," says that the Delawares believe that in the beginning the Red men had short tails, but they blasphemed the Great Spirit, and in punishment for their sin their tails were cut off and transformed into women, to be their perpetual worry. The same story is told by Mr. Atherne Jones, as heard by him among the Kikapoos.

The ancient Mexicans had a myth of Xolotl, making out of a man's bone the primeval mother in the heavenly Paradise; and he called the woman he had made Cihuacouhatl, which means "The woman with the serpent," or Quilatzli, which means "The woman of our flesh." She was the mother of twins, and is represented in a Mexican hieroglyph as speaking with the serpent, whilst behind her stand the twins, whose different characters are represented by different colours, one of

[1] Cranz, Historie von Grönland. Leipzig, 1770, i. p. 262.

whom is represented slaying the other.¹ Xolotl, who made her out of a bone, was cast out of heaven and became the first man. That the Mexicans had other traditions, now lost, touching this matter is probable, for they had a form of baptism for children in which they prayed that those baptized might be washed from "the original sin committed before the founding of the world." And this had to do, in all probability, with a legend akin to that of the Iroquois, who told of the primeval mother falling, and then of the earth being built up to receive her, when precipitated out of heaven.

The Caribs of South America relate that Luoguo, the first man and god, created the earth and the sea, and made the earth as fair as the beautiful garden in the heaven where dwell the gods. Luoguo dwelt among the men he had made for some while. He drew the men out of his navel and out of his thigh which he cut open. One of the first men was Racumon, who was transformed into a great serpent with a human head, and he lived twined round a great Cabatas tree and ate of its fruit, and gave to those who passed by. Then the Caribs lived to a great age, and never waxed old or died. Afterwards they found a garden planted with manioc, and on that they fed. But they became wicked, and a flood came and swept them away.²

In the South Sea Islands we find other traditions of the Fall. In Alea, one of the Caroline Islands, the tale runs thus:—

"The sister of Eliulap the first man, who was also a god, felt herself in labour, so she descended to earth and there brought forth three children. To her astonishment she found the earth barren; therefore, by her mighty word, she clothed it with herbage and peopled it with beasts and birds. And the world became very beautiful, and her sons were happy and did not feel sickness or death, but at the close of every month fell

---

[1] Humboldt, Pittoreske Ansichten d. Cordilleren; Plate xiii. and explanation, ii. pp. 41, 42.
[2] De la Borde, Reise zu den Caraiben. Nürnb. 1782, i. pp. 380-5.

into a slumber from which they awoke renewed in strength and beauty. But Erigeres, the bad spirit, envied this happiness, so he came to the world and introduced into it pain, age, and death."[1]

With the Jewish additions to the story given in Genesis, we shall conclude.

The godless Sammael had made an alliance with all the chiefs of his host against the Lord, because that the holy and ever blessed Lord had said to Adam and Eve, "*Have dominion over the fish of the sea,*" &c.; and he said, "How can I make man to sin and drive him out?" Then he went down to earth with all his host, and he sought for a companion like to himself; he chose the serpent, which was in size like a camel, and he seated himself on its back and rode up to the woman, and said to her, "*Hath God said, Ye shall not eat of every tree of the garden?*" And he thought, "I will ask more presently." Then she answered, "He has only forbidden me the fruit of the Tree of Knowledge which is in the midst of the garden. And He said, 'In the day thou touchest it thou shalt die.'" She added two words; God did not say anything to her about touching it, and she spoke of the fruit, whereas God said the Tree.

Then the godless one, Sammael, went up to the tree and touched it. But the tree cried out, "*Let not the foot of pride come against me, and let not the hand of the ungodly cast me down!* Touch me not, thou godless one!"

Then Sammael called to the woman, and said, "See, I have touched the tree and am not dead. Do you also touch it and try." But when Eve drew near to the tree she saw the Angel of Death waiting sword in hand, and she said in her heart, "Perhaps I am to die, and then God will create another wife for Adam; that shall not be, he must die too." So she gave him of the fruit. And when he took it and bit, his teeth were blunted, and thus it is that the back teeth of men are no longer sharp.[2]

[1] Allg. Hist. der Reisen, xviii. p. 395.   [2] Eisenmenger, i. pp. 827-9.

## V.

## ADAM AND EVE AFTER THE FALL.

WHEN Adam reached the earth, the Eagle said to the Whale, with whom it had hitherto lived in the closest intimacy, "Now we must part, for there is no safety for us animals since man has come amongst us. The deepest abysses of ocean must be thy refuge, and thou must protect thyself with cunning from the great foe who has entered the earth. I must soar high above the clouds, and there find a place of escape from him who is destined to be my pursuer till death."[1]

According to certain cabbalistic Rabbis, Adam, when cast out of Eden, was precipitated into Gehenna, but he escaped therefrom to earth, by repeating and pronouncing properly the mystic word Laverererareri.[2] In the Talmud it is related that when Adam heard the words of God, "*Thou shalt eat the herb of the field*" (Gen. iii. 18), he trembled in all his limbs, and exclaimed, "O Lord of all the world! I and my beast, the Ass, shall have to eat out of the same manger!" But God said to him, because he trembled, "Thou shalt eat bread in the sweat of thy brow."[3]

Learned Rabbis assert that the angel Raphael had instructed Adam in all kinds of knowledge out of a book, and this book contained mighty mysteries which the highest angels could not fathom, and knew not; and before the Fall the angels used to assemble in crowds, and listen to Adam instructing them in hidden wisdom. In that book were seventy-two parts and six

[1] Weil. p. 28.
[2] Basnage, Histoire des Juifs. La Haye, iii. p. 391.
[3] Tract. Avod., f. 1, col. 3; also Tract. Pesachim, f. 118, col. 1.

hundred and seventy writings, and all this was known; but from the middle of the book to the end were the one thousand five hundred hidden secrets of Wisdom, and these Adam began to reveal to the angels till he was arrested by the angel Haddarniel. This book Adam preserved and read in daily; but when he had sinned, it fled out of his hands and flew away, and he went into the river Gihon up to his neck, and the water washed the glory wherewith he had shone in Paradise from off his body. But God was merciful, and He restored to him the book by the hands of Raphael, and he left it to his son Seth, and Enoch and Abraham read in this book.[1]

Along with the book Adam retained the rod which God had created at the close of the Sabbath, between sun and sun; *i.e.* between nightfall and daybreak, so says the Rabbi Levi. Adam left it to Enoch, and Enoch gave it to Noah, and Noah gave it to Shem, and Shem to Abraham, and Abraham delivered it to Isaac, and Isaac gave it to Jacob; Jacob brought the staff with him to Egypt, and gave it to his son Joseph. Now when Joseph died, his house was plundered by the Egyptians, and all his effects were taken into Pharaoh's house. Jethro was a mighty magician, and when he saw the staff of Adam and read the writing thereon, he went forth into Edom and planted it in his garden. And Jethro would allow none to touch it; but when he saw Moses he said, "This is he who will deliver Israel out of Egypt." Wherefore he gave him his daughter Zipporah and the staff. But the book Midrash Vajoscha relates this rather differently, in the words of Moses himself: "After I had become great I went out, and seeing an Egyptian illtreat a Hebrew man of my brethren, I slew him and buried him in the sand. But when Pharaoh heard this he sought to slay me, and brought a sharp sword the like of which was not in the world; and therewith I was ten times smitten on my neck. But the Holy God wrought a miracle, for my neck became as hard as a marble pillar, so that the sword had

[1] Eisenmenger, i. pp. 376, 377.

no power over me. And I was forty years old when I fled out of Egypt; and I came to Jethro's house and stood by the well and found Zipporah his daughter; and when I saw her, I was pleased with her, and asked her to marry me. Then she related to me her father's custom, and it was this. 'My father proves every suitor for my hand by a tree which is in his garden; and when he comes to the tree, the tree clasps him in its branches.' Then I asked her where such a tree was, and she answered me, 'This is the staff which God created on the eve of the Sabbath, which was handed down from Adam to Joseph; but Jethro saw the staff at the plundering of Joseph's house, and he took it away with him from Pharaoh's palace and brought it here. This is the staff on which is cut the Schem hammphorasch and the ten plagues that are in store for Egypt, and these are indicated by ten letters on the staff, and they stand thus: *dam*, blood; *zephardeim*, frogs; *kinnim*, lice; *arof*, various insects; *defer*, murrain; *schechim*, blain; *barad*, hail; *arbeh*, locusts; *choschech*, darkness; and *bechor*, first born:—these will be the plagues of Egypt. This staff was for many days and years in my father's house, till he one day took it in his hand and stuck it into the earth in the garden; and then it sprouted and bloomed and brought forth almonds, and when he saw that, he proved every one who sought one of his daughters by that tree.'" These are the words of the Book Midrash Vajoscha, and thereby may be seen that the staff of Adam was of almond wood; but Yalkut Chadasch, under the title "Adam," says that the staff was of the wood of the Tree of the Knowledge of Good and Evil.[1]

When Adam and Eve were driven out of the garden, says the Talmud, they wandered disconsolate over the face of the earth. And the sun began to decline, and they looked with fear at the diminution of the light, and felt a horror like death steal over their hearts.

[1] Eisenmenger, i. pp. 377-80.

And the light of heaven grew paler, and the wretched ones clasped one another in an agony of despair.

Then all grew dark.

And the luckless ones fell on the earth, silent, and thought that God had withdrawn from them the light for ever; and they spent the night in tears.

But a beam of light began to rise over the eastern hills, after many hours of darkness, and the clouds blushed crimson, and the golden sun came back, and dried the tears of Adam and Eve; and then they greeted it with cries of gladness, and said, "*Heaviness may endure for a night, but joy cometh in the morning;* this is a law that God has laid upon nature."[1]

Among the Manichean myths prevalent among the Albigenses, was one preserved to us by the troubadour Pierre de Saint-Cloud. When Adam was driven out of Paradise, God in mercy gave him a miraculous rod, which possessed creative powers, so that he had only to strike the sea with it and it would forthwith produce the beast he might require.

Adam struck the sea, and there rose from it the sheep; then Eve took the staff and smote the water, and from it sprang the wolf, which fell on the sheep and carried it off into the wood. Then Adam took back the staff, and with it called forth the dog to hunt the wolf and recover the sheep.

According to the Mussulman tradition, Adam's beard grew after he had fallen, and it was the result of his excessive grief and penitence: how this affected his chin is not explained, the fact only is thus boldly stated. He was sorely abashed at his beard, but a voice from heaven called to him, saying, "The beard is man's ornament on earth; it distinguishes him from the feeble woman." Adam shed so many tears that all birds and beasts drank of them, and flowing into the earth they produced the fragrant plants and gum-bearing trees, for they were still endued with the strength and virtue of the food of Paradise.

[1] Talmud, Avoda Sara, fol. 8 a, and in Levy, Parabeln, p. 300.

But the tears of Eve were transformed into pearls where they dribbled into the sea, and into beautiful flowers where they sank into the soil.

Both wailed so loud that Eve's cry reached Adam on the West wind, and Adam's cry was borne to Eve on the wings of the East wind. And when Eve heard the well-known voice she clasped her hands above her head, and women to this day thus testify their sorrow; and Adam, when the voice of the weeping of Eve sounded in his ears, put his right hand beneath his beard,—thus do men to this day give evidence of their mourning. And the tears pouring out of Adam's eyes formed the two rivers Tigris and Euphrates. All nature wept with him; every bird and beast hastened to him to mingle their tears with his, but the locust was the first to arrive, for it was made of the superfluous earth which had been gathered for the creation of Adam. There are seven thousand kinds of locusts or grasshoppers, of all colours and sizes, up to the dimensions of an eagle; and they have a king to whom God addresses His commands when He would punish a rebellious nation such as that of Egypt. The black character imprinted on the locust's wing is Hebrew, and it signifies, "God is One; He overcometh the mighty; the locusts are a portion of His army which He sends against the wicked." As all nature thus wailed and lamented, from the invisible insect to the angel who upholds the world, God sent Gabriel with the words which were in after-time to save Jonah in the whale's belly, "There is no God but Thou; pardon me for Mohammed's sake, that great and last prophet, whose name is engraved on Thy throne."

When Adam had uttered these words with penitent heart, the gates of heaven opened, and Gabriel cried out, "God has accepted thy penitence, Adam! pray to Him alone, He will give thee what thou desirest, even the return to Paradise, after a certain time."

Adam prayed, "Lord, protect me from the further malice of my enemy Eblis."

"Speak the word, There is no God but God; that wounds him like a poisoned arrow."

"Lord, will not the meat and drink provided by this earth lead me into sin?"

"Drink water, and eat only clean beasts which have been slain in the name of Allah, and build mosques where you dwell, so will Eblis have no power over you."

"But if he torment me at night with evil thoughts and dreams?"

"Then rise from thy couch and pray."

"Lord, how shall I be able to distinguish between good and evil?"

"My guidance will be with thee; and two angels will dwell in thy heart, who shall warn thee against evil and encourage thee to good."

"Lord, assure me Thy grace against sin."

"That can only be obtained by good works. But this I promise thee, evil shall be punished one-fold, good shall be rewarded tenfold."

In the meanwhile the angel Michael had been sent to Eve to announce to her God's mercy. When Eve saw him, she exclaimed, "O great and almighty Archangel of God, with what weapon shall I, poor frail creature, fight against sin?"

"God," answered the Angel, "has given me for thee, the most potent weapon of modesty; that, as man is armed with faith, so mayest thou be armed with shamefacedness, therewith to conquer thy passions."

"And what will protect me against the strength of man, so much more robust and vigorous than I, in mind and in body?"

"Love and compassion," answered Michael. "I have placed these in the deepest recesses of his heart, as mighty advocates within him to plead for thee."

"And will God give me no further gift?"

"For the pangs of maternity thou shalt feel, this shall be

## ADAM AND EVE AFTER THE FALL.

thine, death in child-bearing shall be reckoned in heaven as a death of martyrdom."[1]

Eblis, seeing the mercy shown to Adam and Eve, ventured to entreat God's grace for himself, and obtained that he should not be enchained in the place of torment till the day of the general Resurrection, and that he should exercise sovereignty over the wicked and all those who should reject God's Word in this life.

"And where shall I dwell till the consummation of all things?" he asked of Allah.

"In ruined buildings, and in tombs, and in dens and cave of the mountains."

"And what shall be my nourishment?"

"All beasts slain in the name of false gods and idols."

"And how shall I slake my thirst?"

"In wine and other spirituous liquors."

"And how shall I occupy myself in hours of idleness?"

"In music, dancing, and song."

"What is the word of my sentence?"

"The curse of God till the Judgment-day."

"And how shall I fight against those men who have received Thy revelation, and are protected by the two angels?"

"Thy offspring shall be more numerous than theirs: to every man born into this world, there will be born seven evil spirits, who, however, will be powerless to injure true Believers."

God then made a covenant with Adam's successors; He rubbed Adam's back, and lo! from out of his back crawled all generations of men that were to be born, about the size of ants, and they ranged themselves on the left and on the right. At the head of those on the right stood Mohammed, then the other prophets and the faithful, distinguished from those on the left by their white and dazzling splendour. Those on the left were headed by Kabil (Cain).

---

[1] It is a popular superstition among the lower orders in England that a woman who dies in childbirth, even if she be unmarried, cannot be lost.

God then acquainted Adam with the names and fate of all his posterity; and when the recital arrived at David, to whom God had allotted only thirty years, Adam asked God, "How many years are accorded to me?"

Allah replied, "One thousand."

Then said Adam, "I make a present to David of seventy years out of my life." God consented; and knowing the shortness of Adam's memory, at all events in matters concerning himself inconveniently, He made the angels bring a formal document of resignation engrossed on parchment, and required Adam to subscribe thereto his name, and Michael and Gabriel to countersign it as witnesses.

A very similar tradition was held by the Jews, for in Midrash Jalkut (fol. 12) it is said: God showed Adam all future generations of men, with their captains, learned and literary men. Then he saw that David was provided with only three hours of life, and he said, "Lord and Creator of the world, is this unalterable?" "Such was my first intention," was the reply.

"How many years have I to live?"

"A thousand."

"And is there such a thing known in heaven as making presents?"

"Most certainly."

"Then I present seventy years of my life to David."

And what did Adam next perform? He drew up a legal document of transfer, and sealed it with his own seal, and God and Metatron did likewise.

To return to the Mussulman legend.

When all the posterity of Adam were assembled, God exclaimed to them, "Acknowledge that I am the only God, and that Mohammed is my prophet." The company on the right eagerly made this acknowledgment; those, however, on the left long hesitated,—some said only the former portion of the sentence, and others did not open their mouths.

"The disobedient," said Allah to Adam, "shall, if they

remain obstinate, be cast into hell, but the true believers shall be received into Paradise."

"So be it," replied Adam. And thus shall it be at the end of the world.

After the covenant, Allah rubbed Adam's back once more, and all his little posterity retreated into it again.

When now God withdrew His presence from Adam's sight for the remainder of our first parents' life, Adam uttered such a loud and bitter cry that the whole earth quaked.

The All-merciful was filled with compassion, and bade him follow a cloud which would conduct him to a spot where he would be directly opposite His throne, and there he was to build a temple.

"Go about this temple," said Allah, "and I am as near to you as to the angels who surround my throne." Adam, who was still the size that God had created him, easily strode from Ceylon to Mecca after the cloud, which stood over the place where he was to build. On Mount Arafa, near Mecca, to his great delight, he found Eve again, and from this circumstance the mountain takes its name (from Arafa, to recognize, to know again). They both began to build, and erected a temple having four doors—one was called Adam's door, another Abraham's door, the third Ishmael's door, and the fourth Mohammed's door. The plan of the temple was furnished by Gabriel, who also contributed a precious stone, but this stone afterwards, through the sin of men, turned black. This black stone is the most sacred Kaaba, and it was originally an angel, whose duty it had been to guard the Wheat-Tree of the knowledge of good and evil, and to warn off Adam should he approach it. But through his inattention the design of God was frustrated, and in punishment he was transformed into a stone, and he will not be released from his transformation till the Last Day.

Gabriel taught Adam also all the ceremonies of the great pilgrimage.

Adam now returned with his wife to India, and lived there till he died, but every year he made a pilgrimage to Mecca, till he lost his primitive size, and retained only the height of sixty ells.

The cause of his diminution in height was his horror and dismay at the murder of Abel, which made him shrink into himself, and he was never afterwards able to stretch himself out again to his pristine dimensions.[1]

The Book of the Penitence of Adam is a curious apocryphal work of Syriac origin; I give an outline of its contents.

God planted, on the third day, the Terrestrial Paradise; it is bounded on the east by the ocean in which, at the Last Day, the elect will wash away all those sins which have not as yet been purged away by repentance.

On leaving this garden of delights, Adam turned to take of it one last look. He saw that the Tree which had caused his fall was cursed and had withered away.

He was much surprised when night overtook him, for in Paradise he had not known darkness. As he went along his way, shedding tears, he overtook the serpent gliding over the ground, and licking the dust. That serpent he had last seen on four feet, very beautiful, with the hair of a young maiden, enamelled with brilliant colours. Now it was vile, hideous, and grovelling. The beasts which, before the Fall, had coveted its society, fled from it now with loathing.

Filled with rage at the sight of Adam and Eve, to whom it attributed its present degradation, the serpent flew at them and prostrated them. Thereupon God removed from it its sole remaining possession—the gift of speech, and it was left only its hiss of rage and shame.

Adam soon felt exhaustion, heat, fear and pain;—afflictions he had not known in Eden. As the shadows of night fell, an intense horror overwhelmed the guilty pair; they trembled in

---

[1] Weil, pp. 29-38.

every limb and cried to God. The Almighty, in compassion, consoled them by announcing to them that day would return after twelve hours of night. They were relieved by this promise, and they spent the first night in prayer.

But Satan, who never lost sight of them, fearing lest their prayers should wholly appease the divine justice, assembled his host of evil angels, surrounded himself with a brilliant light, and stood at the entrance of the cave where the banished ones prayed. He hoped that Adam would mistake him for God, and prostrate himself before him.

But Adam said to Eve: "Observe this great light and this multitude of spirits. If it were God who sent them, they would enter and tell us their message." Adam did not know then that Satan cannot approach those who pray. Then Adam addressed himself to God and said, "O my God! is there another God but Thou, who can create angels and send them to us? Lord, deign to instruct us!"

Then a heavenly angel entered the cavern and said, "Adam, fear not those whom you see; it is Satan and his host. He sought to seduce you again to your fall."

Having thus spoken, the angel fell upon Satan and tore from off him his disguise, and exposed him in his hideous nakedness to Adam and Eve. And to console them for this trial, God sent Adam gold rings, incense and myrrh, and said to him, "Preserve these things, and they will give you at night light and fragrance; and when I shall come down on earth to save you, clothed in human flesh, kings shall bring me these three tokens."

It is because of this present that the cavern into which Adam and Eve retreated has been called the Treasure-cave.

Adam and Eve, greatly cheered, blessed the Lord, and thanked Him for His goodness, and resolved to continue their repentance.

A short time after they committed a fault. Satan presented himself to them under the form of an angel of light, and

announced that he was commissioned by the Most High to
lead them to the brink of the River of the Water of Life, into
which they were to plunge and wash away their sin.

They believed, and followed him by a strange road, and he
led them to the edge of a precipice, down which he endeavoured to fling them; for, he thought, were he to destroy the
man and the woman, he would be supreme in the world God
had made. But the Almighty rescued Adam and Eve, and
drave Satan from them.

To punish themselves for their involuntary fault, Adam and
Eve separated, so as not to see one another, and resolved to
spend forty days up to their necks in the sea.

Before parting, Adam said to his wife, "Remain in the
water here, and do not quit it till I return, and spend your
time in praying the Lord to pardon us."

Now, whilst they were undergoing this penance, Satan cast
about how he might bring to naught our first parents, and he
sought them but could not find them, till on the thirty-fifth day
of their penance he perceived the two heads above the water;
then he knew at once what was their intention, and he resolved
to frustrate it. So he took upon him the form of an angel
of Heaven, and flew over the sea, singing praises to God; and
when he came to the place where Eve was, he cried, "Joy,
joy to thee! God is with thee, and He has sent me to bring
thee to Adam to announce to him that he has found favour with
the Most High."

Eve instantly scrambled out of the water, and followed Satan
to Adam, and the Evil One placed her before her husband, and
vanished. When Adam saw his wife, he was filled with dismay,
and beat his breast and wept. When she told him why she
was there, he knew that the great Enemy had been again at his
work of deception, and he fell into despair. But a voice from
Heaven bade him return with Eve to the Treasure-cave.

Hunger, thirst, cold, and prayer had completely exhausted
the pair, and Adam cried to the Lord, "O God, my Creator!

Thou hast given me reason and an enlightened heart. When Thou didst forbid me to eat of the fruit of the Tree, Eve was not yet made, and she did not hear Thy command; in Eden we hungered not, nor felt thirst or pain or fatigue. All this have we lost. And now we dare not touch the fruit of the trees or drink of water without Thy command. Our bodies are exhausted, our strength is gone; grant us wherewith to satisfy our hunger, and to quench our thirst."

God ordered the Cherubim who kept the gate of Eden, to carry to Adam two figs from the tree under which our first parents had concealed themselves after the Fall.

"Take," said the Cherubim, presenting the figs to them, "take the fruit of the tree whose leaves covered your shame."

"Oh!" cried Adam, "may God grant us some of the fruit of the Tree of Life."

But God answered, "I will give unto you this fruit and living water, to you and to your descendants, on that day that I shall descend into the abode of death and shall break the gates of iron in sunder, to bring you forth into my garden of pleasures. That which you ask of Me shall take place at the expiration of five long days and a half (*i.e.* 5,500 years), after that my blood has flowed upon thy head, O Adam, upon Golgotha."

Adam and Eve took the figs, which were very heavy, for the fruits of the earthly paradise were much larger than the fruit of this outer world in which we live. And when they were about to enter into the Cave of Treasures, they saw there a great fire; this mightily astonished them, for as yet they had not seen fire except in the flaming sword of the Cherub. Now this fire which surprised them was the work of Satan; he had collected branches and had fired them in the hope of burning down the cavern and driving Adam to despair.

The fire lasted till the morrow; Satan, without showing himself, keeping it supplied with fresh fuel. Adam and Eve did not venture to approach, but recommended themselves to

God; and the Evil One, finding that his plan had failed, let the fire die out and departed.

Adam and Eve slept the following night at the foot of a mountain near their lost Eden. Satan, beholding them, said, "God has made a compact with Adam, whom He desires to save, but I will slay him, and the earth shall be mine."

He therefore summoned his attendant angels, and they dislodged a huge rock from the mountain and hurled it upon the sleepers. But as this mass was bounding down the flank of the mountain, and was in mid-air in one of its leaps, God arrested it above the heads of the sleepers, and it sheltered them from the dews of night.

Adam and Eve awoke greatly troubled by their dreams, and they asked of God garments to cover their naked bodies, for they suffered from the scorching sun by day, and the frost by night. God replied, "Go to the shore of the sea; you will there find the skins of sheep which have been devoured by lions: of them make to yourselves raiment."

Satan heard the words of God, and he outran our first parents, that he might secure the skins and destroy them, in the hopes that Adam and Eve, finding no hides, would doubt God and think that He had failed in His word. But God fastened Satan in his naked hideousness beside the skins, immoveable, till Adam and Eve arrived, when He addressed them in these terms: "Behold him who has seduced you; see what has become of his beauty. After having made you such promises, he was about to rob you of these hides." Adam and Eve took the skins and made of them garments. A few days after, God said to them, "Go to the west till you arrive at a black land; there you will find food." They obeyed, and they saw corn full ripe, and God inspired Adam with knowledge how to make bread. But not having sickles they tore the corn up by the roots, and having made a rick of it, they slept, expecting to thrash it out and grind it on the morrow. But Satan fired this rick and reduced their harvest to ashes.

## ADAM AND EVE AFTER THE FALL.

Whilst they wept and lamented, Satan came to them as an angel, and said, "This is the work of your Enemy the Fiend, but God has sent me to bring you into a field where you will find better corn."

They followed him, nothing doubting, and he led them for eight days, and they fainted with exhaustion and were footsore. Then he left them in an unknown land; but God was their protector, He brought them back to their harvest and restored their rick of corn, and they made bread and offered to God the first sacrifice.[1]

But enough of this apocryphal work, which contains a string of absurd tricks played by Satan on our first parents, which are invariably defeated by God; of these the specimens given above are sufficient.

A curious legend exists among the Sclavonic nations by which the existence of elves is accounted for. It is said that Adam had by his wife Eve, thirty sons and thirty daughters. God asked him, one day, the number of his children. Adam was ashamed of having so many girls, so he answered, "Thirty sons and twenty-seven daughters." But from the eye of God nothing can be concealed, and He took from among Adam's daughters the three fairest, and He made them Willis, or elves; they were good and holy, and therefore did not perish in the Deluge, but entered with Noah into the ark and were saved.

The story of Adam's penitence as told by Tabari is as follows :—

The moment that Adam fell out of Paradise and touched the ground on the mountains in the centre of Ceylon, he understood in all its magnitude the greatness of his loss and his sin. He remained stupefied with his face on the earth, and did not raise it, but allowed his tears to flow upon and soak into the soil. For a hundred years he remained in this position,

---

[1] Dillman, Das Adambuch des Morgenlandes; Göttingen, 1853. This book is not to be confounded with the Testament of Adam.

and his tears formed a stream which rolled down the mountain, which still flows from Adam's Peak in the island of Ceylon, and gives their virtue to the healing plants and fragrant trees which there flourish, and are exported for medicinal purposes.

When a hundred years had elapsed, God had compassion on Adam, and sent Gabriel to him, who said, "God salutes thee, O Adam! and He bids me say to thee, Did I not create thee out of the earth by My will? Did I not give thee Paradise to be thine abode? Why these tears and sighs?"

Adam replied, "How shall I not weep, and how shall I abstain from sighing? Have I not lost the protection of God, and have I not disobeyed His will?"

Gabriel said, "Do not afflict thyself. Recite the words I shall teach thee, and God will grant thee repentance which He will accept," as it is written in the Koran, 'Adam learnt of His Lord words; and the Lord returned to Him, for He is merciful, and He returns.' Adam recited these words, and in the joy he felt at the prospect of finding mercy, he wept, and his joyous tears watered the earth, and from them sprang up the narcissus and the ox-eye.

Then said Adam to Gabriel, "What shall I now do?"

And Gabriel gave to Adam wheat-grains from out of Paradise, the fruit of the Forbidden Tree, and he bade him sow it, and he said, "This shall be thy food in future."

Afterwards, Gabriel taught Adam to draw iron out of the rock and to make instruments of husbandry. And all that Adam sowed sprang up in the self-same hour that it was sown, for the blessing of God was upon it. And Adam reaped and thrashed and winnowed. Then Gabriel bade him take two stones from the mountain, and he taught him with them to grind the corn; and when he had made flour, he said to the angel, "Shall I eat now?" But Gabriel answered, "Not so;" and he showed him how to build an oven of iron. It was from this oven that the water of the deluge at Koufa flowed. He taught him also to make dough and to bake.

But Adam was hungry, and he said, "Let me eat now," and the angel stayed him, and answered, "Tarry till the bread be cold and stale," but he would not, but ate. Therefore he suffered from pain in his belly. Next, Gabriel by the command of Allah brought out of Eden the ox and fruit; of these latter there were ten kinds whose exterior was edible, but whose insides were useless to eat, such as the apricot, the peach, and the date. And there were three that could not be eaten anyhow. Then he brought ten more whose insides and outsides might be eaten, such as the grape, the fig, and the apple. Said Gabriel to Adam, "Sow these," and he sowed them. These are the trees that the angel brought out of Paradise.

Now Adam was all alone on the peak in the midst of Ceylon, and his head was in the first heaven. The sun burnt him, so that all his hair fell off; and God, in compassion, bade Gabriel pass his wing over Adam's head, and Adam thereupon shrank to the height of sixty cubits. And then he could no longer hear the voices of the angels in heaven, and he was sore distressed.

Then God said to him, "I have made this world thy prison, but I send to thee out of heaven a house of rubies, in order that thou mayest enter in and walk round it, and therein find repose for thy heart."

Thereupon out of heaven descended "the visited house," and it was placed where now stands the temple of Mecca. The black stone which is there was originally white and shining. It was placed in the ruby house. Whosoever looked in that direction from ten parasangs off, could see the light of that house shining like a fire up to the heaven, and in the midst of that red light shone the white stone like a star.

. Afterwards, Gabriel conducted Adam to that house that he might go in procession round it. All the places where his foot was planted became verdant oases, with rivers of water and many flowers and trees, but all the tract between was barren.

Gabriel taught Adam how to make the pilgrimage; and if anyone now goes there without knowing the ceremonies, he needs a guide.

Then Adam met with Eve again, and they rejoiced together; and she went back with him to Ceylon. Now at that time there was in the world no other pair than Adam and Eve, and no other house than the mansion of rubies.

Now Eblis had made his prayer to Allah that he might be allowed to live till Israfiel should sound the last trumpet. And he asked this, because those who are alive when that trumpet sounds, shall not die any more, for Death will be brought in, in the shape of a sheep, and will be slaughtered; and when Death is slaughtered, no one will be able to die.

And God said, "I give thee the time till all creatures must die."

Then Eblis said, "Just as Thou didst turn me out of the right way, so shall I pervert those whom Thou hast made." Satan went to man and said to him, "God has driven me out of Paradise, never to return there, and He has taken from me the sovereignty of this world to give it to thee. Why should we not be friends and associate together, and I can advise thee on thy concerns?"

And Adam thought to himself, "I must be the companion of this one, but I will make use of him." So he suffered him to be his comrade.

The first act of treachery he did was this.

Every child Adam had by Eve died when born. Eve became pregnant for the fourth time, and Eblis said to Adam, "I believe this child will be good-looking and will live."

"I am of the same opinion," answered Adam.

"If my prophecy turns out right," said the Evil One, "give the child to me."

"I will give it," said Adam.

## ADAM AND EVE AFTER THE FALL.

Now the child, when born, was very fair to look upon, and Adam, though he repented of his rash promise, did not venture to break his word; so he gave the child to Eblis, that is to say, he named it Abd-el-Hareth, or Servant of Hareth, instead of Abd-Allah, Servant of God. And after living two years it died.[1]

Thus Satan became an associate in the affairs of man.

But others tell the conclusion of the story somewhat differently. They say that the child Abd-el-Hareth became the progenitor of the whole race of Satyrs, nightmares, and hobgoblins.

Maimonides says that the Sabians attribute to Adam the introduction of the worship of the moon, on which account they call him the prophet or apostle of the moon.[2]

A large number of books are attributed to Adam. The passage in Genesis, *This is the Book of the generations of Adam*,[3] led many to suppose that Moses quoted from a book written by our first parent. That such an apocryphal book did exist in after-times, appears from the fact of Pope Gelasius in his decrees rejecting it as spurious. He speaks of it as "the book which is called the Book of the generations of Adam or Geneseos." And the Rabbis say that this book was written by Adam, after he had seen all his posterity brought out before him, as already related. And this book, they say, Adam gave to Enoch.[4]

Beside this, there existed an Apocalypse of Adam, which is mentioned by S. Epiphanius, who quotes a passage from it, in which Adam describes the Tree of Life, which produced twelve kinds of fruit every year.[5] And George Syncellus, in his Chronicle, extracts a portion of an apocryphal Life of Adam.

Amongst the Revelations of S. Amadeus are found two

---

[1] Tabari, i., capp. xxviii. xxix.
[2] In More Nevochim, quoted by Fabricius, i. p. 5.
[3] Gen. v. i.    [4] Fabricius, i. p. 11.
[5] Adv. Hæresi, c. 5.

psalms, which, in vision, he heard had been composed by Adam. One was on the production of Eve, the other is a hymn of repentance, a joint composition of the two outcasts. It runs as follows:—

*Adam.*—" Adonai, my Lord God, have mercy upon me for Thy great goodness, and according to the multitude of Thy mercies do away my transgressions. I am bowed down with trouble, Thy waves and storms have gone over me. Deliver me, O God, and save me from the flood of many waters. Hear my words, O Heavens, and all ye that dwell in them. May the Angels bear up all my thoughts and words to Thee, and may the celestial virtues declare them. May the Lord bend His compassionate ear to my lowly petition. May He hear my prayer, and let the cry of my heart reach Him. Thou, O God, art the true and most brilliant light; all other lights are mingled with darkness. Thou art the sun that knowest no down-setting, that dwellest in inaccessible light. Thou art the end to which all flesh come. Thou art the only satisfaction of all the blessed."

*Eve.*—" Adonai, Lord God, have mercy upon me for Thy great goodness, and for the multitude of Thy mercies do away my transgressions. Thou before all things didst create the immoveable heaven as a holy and exalted home, and Thou didst adorn it with angel spirits, to whom Thou didst in goodness declare thy purposes. They were the bright morning stars who sang to Thee through ages of ages. Thou didst form the moveable heaven and Thou didst set in it the watery clouds. Those waters are under the immoveable heaven, and are above all that live and move. Thou didst create the light; the beauteous sun, the moon with the five planets didst Thou place in the midst, and didst fix the signs and constellations. Thou didst produce four elements, and didst kindle all with Thy wisdom."

*Adam.*—" Adonai, Lord God, have mercy upon me for Thy great goodness, and for the multitude of Thy mercies do away my transgressions. Thou hast cast out the proud and rebel dragon with Thy mighty arm. Thou hast put down the mighty from their seat and hast exalted the humble and meek. Thou hast filled the hungry with good things, and the rich Thou hast sent empty away. Thou didst fashion me in Thine own image of the dust of earth, and destine me, mortal, to be immortal; and me, frail, to endure. Thou didst lead me into the place of life and joy, and didst surround me with all good things; Thou didst put all things under my feet, and didst reveal to me Thy great name, Adonai. Thou didst give me Eve, to be a help meet for me, whom Thou didst draw from my side."

*Adam.*—" Adonai, Lord and God, have mercy upon me for Thy great goodness, and for the multitude of Thy mercies do away my transgressions; for Thou hast made me the head of all men. Thou hast inspired me and my consort with Thy wisdom, and hast given us a free will and placed our lot in our own hands. But Thou hast given us precepts and laws, and hast placed life and death before us that we might keep Thy commandments, and in keeping them find life; but if we keep them not, we shall die. Lucifer, the envious one, saw and envied. He fought against us and prevailed. Conquered by angels, he conquered man, and subjugated all his race. I have sinned. I am he who have committed iniquity. If I had refused in my free will, neither Eve nor the Enemy could have obtained my destruction. But being in honour I had no understanding and I lost my dignity. I am like to the cattle, the horse, and the mule, which have no understanding."

*Eve.*—" Adonai, Lord and God, have mercy upon me for Thy great goodness, and for the multitude of Thy mercies do away mine offences. Great is our God, and great is His mercy; His goodness is unmeasured. He will supply the remedy to our sin, that if we will to rise, we may be able to arise; He has appointed His Son, the glorifier of all, and our Redeemer; and He has appointed the Holy Mother to be our mediatrix, in whose image He has built me, Eve, the mother of all flesh. He has fashioned the Mother after the likeness of her daughter. He has made the father after the image and likeness of His Son; and He will blot out our transgressions for His merits, if we yield our wills thereto, and receive His sacraments. He will receive a free-will offering, and He will not despise a contrite heart. To those going towards Him, He will fly with welcome, He will pardon their offences and will crown them with glory."

*Adam.*—" Adonai, Lord and God, have mercy upon me for Thy great goodness, and for the multitude of Thy mercies do away mine offences. O God, great is the abundance of Thy sweetness. Blessed are all they that hope in Thee. After the darkness Thou bringest in the light; and pain is converted into joy. Thou repayest a thousand for a hundred, and for a thousand thou givest ten thousand. For the least things, Thou rewardest with the greatest things; and for temporal joys, Thou givest those that are eternal. Blessed are they that keep Thy statutes, and bend their necks to Thy yoke. They shall dwell in Thy tabernacle and rest upon Thy holy hill. They shall be denizens of Thy courts with Thee, whose roofs shine above gold and precious stones. Blessed are they who believe in the triune God, and will to know His ways. We all sing, Glory to the Father, and to the Son, and to the Holy Ghost, and we magnify our God. As in the beginning the angels sang, so shall we now and ever, and in ages of ages. Amen." [1]

Manasseh Ben-Israel has preserved a prophecy of Adam, that the world is to last seven thousand years. He says this secret was handed down from Adam to Enoch, and from Enoch to Noah, and from Noah to Shem.[2]

At Hebron is a cave, "which," says an old traveller, "Christians and Turks point out as having been the place where Adam and Eve bewailed their sins for a hundred years.

---

[1] Eusebius Nierembergius, De Origine S. Scripturæ. Lugd., 1641, p. 46.
[2] Fabricius, i. p. 33.

This spot is towards the west, in a valley, about a hundred paces from the Damascene field; it is a dark grotto, not very long or broad, very low, in a hard rock, and not apparently artificial, but natural. This valley is called *La valle de' Lagrime*, the Vale of Tears, as they shed such copious tears over their transgressions."[1]

Abu Mohammed Mustapha Ben-Alschit Hasen, in his Universal History, says that Adam's garment of fig-leaves, in which he went out of Eden, was left by him, when he fell, on Adam's Peak in Ceylon. There it dried to dust, and the dust was scattered by the wind over the island, and from this sprang the odoriferous plants which grow there.[2]

Adam is said to have not gone altogether empty-handed out of Paradise. Hottinger, in his Oriental History, quoting Jewish authorities, says: "Adam having gone into the land of Babel, took with him many wonderful things, amongst others a tree with flowers, leaves and branches of gold, also a stone tree, also the leaves of a tree so strong that they were inconsumable in fire, and so large as to be able to shelter under them ten thousand men of the stature of Adam; and he carried about with him two of these leaves, of which one would shelter two men, or clothe them."[3] Of these trees we read in the Gemara that the Rabbi Canaan asked of the Rabbi Simon, son of Assa, who had gone to see them, whether this was true. He was told in reply that it was so, and that at the time of the Captivity the Jews had seated themselves under these trees, and in their shadow had found consolation.

But Palestine seems also to have possessed some of the trees of Adam's planting, for Jacob Vitriacus in his Jewish History says: "There are in that land wonderful trees, which for their pre-excellence are called Apples of Paradise, bearing oblong fruit, very sweet and unctuous, having a most delicious

---

[1] Ferdinand de Troilo, Orientale Itinerario. Dresd., 1676, p. 323.
[2] Selden, De Synedriis, ii. p. 452.
[3] Hottinger, Historia Orientalis, lib. i. c. 8.

savour, bearing in one cluster more than a hundred compressed berries. The leaves of this tree are a cubit long and half a cubit wide. There are three other trees producing beautiful apples or citrons, in which the bite of a man's teeth is naturally manifest, wherefore they are called Adam's Apples."[1] Hottinger says that at Tripoli grows a tree called Almaus, or Adam's apple, with a green head, and leaves like outspread fingers, no branches, but only leaves, and with a fruit like a bean-pod, of delicious flavour, and an odour of roses. Buntingius, in his Itinerary, describes an Adam's apple which he tasted at Alexandria, and he said the taste was like pears, and the clusters of prodigious size, with twenty in each cluster, like magnificent bunches of grapes. But the most remarkable fact about them was that, if one of the fruit were cut with a knife, the figure of a crucifix was found to be contained in it.[2] And this tree was supposed to have been the forbidden tree, and the fruit to have thus brought hope as it also brought death to the eater. Nider, "In Formicario," also relates that this fruit, thus marked with the form of the Crucified, grows in Granada.[3]

"At Beyrut, of which S. Nicodemus was the first bishop," writes the Friar, Ignatius von Rheinfelden, " I saw a wonderful fruit which is called by the Arabs, Mauza, and by the Christians Adam's fig. This fruit grows upon a trunk in clusters of fifty or more, and hangs down towards the ground on account of its weight. The fruit is in shape something like a cucumber, and is a span long, yellow, and tasting something like figs. The Christians of those parts say it is the fruit of which Adam and Eve ate in Paradise, and they argue thus : first, there are no apples in those parts ; secondly, S. Jerome translated the word in the Bible, Mauza ; thirdly, if the fruit be cut, within it is seen the figure of a crucifix, and they conclude thereby that

---

[1] Jacobus Vitriacus, Hist. Hierosol., c. lxxxv.
[2] As King Charles's oak may be seen in the fern-root.
[3] Fabricius, i. p. 84.

the first parents were showed by this figure how their sin would be atoned; fourthly, the leaves being three ells long and half an ell wide, were admirably adapted to make skirts of, when Adam and Eve were conscious of their nakedness. And Holy Scripture says nothing of apples, but says merely—fruit. But whether this was the fruit or not, I leave to others to decide."[1]

Adam is said by the Easterns to have received from Raphael a magic ring, which became his symbol, and which he handed down to his descendants selected to know and read mysteries. This was no other than the 'crux ansata,' or handled cross, so common on Egyptian monuments as the hieroglyph of Life out of death. The circle symbolized the apple, and thus the Carthusian emblem, which bears the motto "Stat crux dum volvitur orbis," is in reality the mystic symbol of Adam. "Which," says the Arabic philosopher, Ibn-ephi, "Mizraim received from Ham, and Ham from Noah, and Noah from Enoch, and Enoch from Seth, and Seth from Adam, and Adam from the angel Raphael. Ham wrought with it great marvels, and Hermes received it from him and placed it amongst the hieroglyphics. But this character signifies the progress and motion of the Spirit of the world, and it was a magic seal, kept secret among their mysteries, and a ring constraining demons."[2]

[1] Neue Ierosolymitanische Pilgerfahrt. Würtzburg, 1667, p. 47.
[2] Stephanus Le Moyne, Notæ ad Varia Sacra, p. 863.

## VI.

## CAIN AND ABEL.

AFTER that the child given to Satan died, says Tabari, Adam had another son, and he called him Seth, and Seth was prophet in the room of his father, after the death of Adam.

Adam had many more children; every time that Eve bore, she bare twins, whereof one was male, the other female, and the twins were given to one another as husband and wife.

Now Adam sought to give to Abel the twin sister of Cain, when she was old enough to be married, but Cain (Kabil, in Arabic) was dissatisfied.[1] Adam said to the brothers, Cain and Abel, "Go, my sons, and sacrifice to the Lord; and he whose sacrifice is accepted, shall have the young girl. Take each of you offerings in your hand and go, sacrifice to the Lord, and He shall decide."

Abel was a shepherd, and he took the fattest of the sheep, and bore it to the place of sacrifice; but Cain, who was a tiller of the soil, took a sheaf of corn, the poorest he could find, and placed it on the altar. Then fire descended from heaven and consumed the offering of Abel, so that not even the cinders remained; but the sheaf of Cain was left untouched.

Adam gave the maiden to Abel, and Cain was sore vexed.

One day, Abel was asleep on a mountain. Cain took a stone and crushed his head. Then he threw the corpse on

---

[1] Abulfeda, p. 15. In the Apocryphal book, The Combat of Adam (Dillman, Das Christliche Adambuch des Morgenlandes; Göttingen, 1853), the same reason for hostility is given. In that account, Satan appears to Cain, and prompts him to every act of wickedness.

his back, and carried it about, not knowing what to do with it; but he saw two crows fighting, and one killed the other; then the crow that survived dug a hole in the earth with his beak, and buried the dead bird. Cain said, "I have not the sense of this bird. I too will lay my brother in the ground." And he did so.

When Adam learned the death of his son, he set out in search of Cain, but could not find him; then he recited the following lines:—

"Every city is alike, each mortal man is vile,
The face of earth has desert grown, the sky has ceased to smile,
Every flower has lost its hue, and every gem is dim.
Alas! my son, my son is dead; the brown earth swallows him!
We one have had in midst of us whom death has not yet found,
No peace for him, no rest for him, treading the blood-drenched ground."[1]

This is how the story is told in the Midrash:[2] Cain and Abel could not agree, for, what one had, the other wanted; then Abel devised a scheme that they should make a division of property, and thus remove the possibility of contention. The proposition pleased Cain. So Cain took the earth, and all that is stationary, and Abel took all that is moveable.

But the envy which lay in the heart of Cain gave him no rest. One day he said to his brother, "Remove thy foot, thou standest on my property; the plain is mine."

Then Abel ran upon the hills, but Cain cried, "Away, the hills are mine!" Then he climbed the mountains, but still Cain followed him, calling, "Away! the stony mountains are mine."

In the Book of Jasher the cause of quarrel is differently stated. One day the flock of Abel ran over the ground Cain had been ploughing; Cain rushed furiously upon him and bade him leave the spot. "Not," said Abel, "till you have paid me for the skins of my sheep and wool of their fleeces used for your clothing." Then Cain took the coulter from his plough, and with it slew his brother.[3]

[1] Tabari, i. c. xxx.   [2] Jalkut, fol. 11a.   [3] Yaschar, p. 1089

The Targum of Jerusalem says, the subject of contention was that Cain denied a Judgment to come and Eternal Life; and Abel argued for both.[1] The Rabbi Menachem, however, asserts that the point on which they strove was whether a word was written *zisit* or *zizis* in the Parascha.[2]

"And when they were in the field together, the brothers quarrelled, saying, 'Let us divide the world.' One said, 'The earth you stand on is my soil.' The other said, 'You are standing on my earth.' One said, 'The Holy Temple shall stand on my lot;' the other said, 'It shall stand on my lot.' So they quarrelled. Now there were born with Abel two daughters, his sisters. Then said Cain, 'I will take the one I choose, I am the eldest;' Abel said, 'They were born with me, and I will have them both to wife.' And when they fought, Abel flung Cain down and was above him; and he lay on Cain. Then Cain said to Abel, 'Are we not both sons of one father; why wilt thou kill me?' And Abel had compassion, and let Cain get up. And so Cain fell on him and killed him. From this we learn not to render good to the evil, for, because Abel showed mercy to Cain, Cain took advantage of it to slay Abel."[3]

S. Methodius the Younger refers to this tradition. He says: "Be it known that Adam and Eve when they left Paradise were virgins. But the third year after the expulsion from Eden, they had Cain, their first-born, and his sister Calmana; and after this, next year, they had Abel and his sister Deborah. But in the three hundredth year of Adam's life, Cain slew his brother, and Adam and Eve wailed over him a hundred years."[4]

Eutychius, Patriarch of Alexandria, says, "When Adam and Eve rebelled against God, He expelled them from Para-

---

[1] Targums, ed. Etheridge, London, 1862, i. p. 172.
[2] Eisenmenger, i. p. 320.
[3] Liber Zenorena, quoted by Fabricius, i. p. 108.
[4] S. Methodius, jun., Revelationes, c. 3.

dise at the ninth hour on Friday to a certain mountain in India, and He bade them produce children to increase and multiply upon the earth. Adam and Eve therefore became parents, first of a boy named Cain, and of a girl named Azrun, who were twins; then of another boy named Abel, and of a twin sister named Owain, or in Greek Laphura.

"Now, when the children were grown up, Adam said to Eve, 'Let Cain marry Owain, who was born with Abel, and let Abel have Azrun, who was born with Cain.' But Cain said to his mother, 'I will marry my own twin sister, and Abel shall marry his.' For Azrun was prettier than Owain. But when Adam heard this, he said, "It is contrary to the precept that thou shouldst marry thy twin sister.'

"Now Cain was a tiller of the ground, but Abel was a pastor of sheep. Adam said to them, 'Take of the fruits of the earth, and of the young of the sheep, and ascend the top of this holy mountain, and offer there the best and choicest to God." Abel offered of the best and fattest of the first-born of the flock. Now as they were ascending the summit of the mountain, Satan put it into the head of Cain to kill his brother, so as to get Azrun. For that reason his oblation was not accepted by God. Therefore he was the more inflamed with rage against Abel, and as they were going down the mount, he rushed upon him and beat him about the head with a stone and killed him. Adam and Eve bewailed Abel a hundred years with the greatest grief. . . . And God cast out Cain whilst he was still unmarried into the land of Nod. But Cain carried off with him his sister Azrun."[1]

The Rabbi Zadok said, "This was the reason why Cain slew Abel. His twin sister and wife was not at all good-looking. Then he said, 'I will kill my brother Abel, and carry off his wife.'"[2]

Gregory Abulfaraj gives this account of the strife: "Accord-

---

[1] Eutychius, Patriarcha Alex., Annales.   [2] Pirke R. Eliezer, c. xxi.

ing to the opinion of Mar Theodosius, thirty years after he was expelled from Paradise, Adam knew his wife Eve, and she bore twins, Cain and his sister Climia; and after thirty more years she bore Abel and his twin sister Lebuda. Then, seventy years after when Adam wanted to marry one of the brothers with the twin sister of the other, Cain refused, asking to have his own twin sister."[1]

The Pseudo-Athanasius says, "Up to this time no man had died so that Cain should know how to kill. The devil instructed him in this in a dream."[2]

Leonhard Marius on Genesis iv. says, "As to what instrument Cain used, Scripture is silent. Chrysostom calls it a sword; Prudentius, a spade; Irenæus, an axe; Isidore says simply, steel; but artists generally paint a club, and Abulensis thinks he was killed with stones." Reuchlin thinks, as iron was not discovered till the times' of Tubal-cain, the weapon must have been made of wood, and he points out how much more this completes the type of Christ.[3]

Cain and Abel had been born and had lived with Adam in the land of Adamah; but after Cain slew his brother, he was cast out into the land Erez, and wherever he went, swords sounded and flashed as though thirsting to smite him. And he fled that land and came to Acra, where he had children, and his descendants who live there to this day have two heads.[4]

Before Cain slew his brother, says the Targum of Jerusalem, the earth brought forth fruits as the fruits of Eden; but from the day that blood was spilt upon it, thistles and thorns sprang up; for the face of earth grew sad, its joy was gone, the stain was on its brow.

Abel's offering had been of the fattest of his sheep, the Targum adds, but Cain offered flax.[5]

Abel's offering, say certain Rabbis, was not perfect; for he

---

[1] Historia Dynastiarum, ed. Pocock; Oxon. 1663, p. 4.
[2] Ad Antiochum, quæst. 56.   [3] Fabricius, i. p. 112.
[4] Eisenmenger, i. p. 462.   [5] Targum, i. p. 173.

offered the chief part to God, but the remainder he dedicated to the Devil; and Cain offered the chief part to Satan, and only the remainder to God.[1]

The Rabbi Johanan said, Cain exclaimed when accused by God of the murder, "My iniquity is greater than I can bear," and this is supposed to mean, "My iniquity is too great to be atoned for, except by my brother rising from the earth and slaying me." What did the Holy One then? He took one letter of the twenty-two which are in the Law, and He wrote it on the arm of Cain, as it is written, "He put a mark upon him.'[2]

After Abel was slain, the dog which had kept his sheep guarded his body, says the Midrash. Adam and Eve sat beside it and wept, and knew not what to do. Then said a raven whose friend was dead, "I will teach Adam a lesson," and he dug a hole in the soil and laid his friend there and covered him up. And when Adam saw this, he said to Eve, "We will do the same with Abel." God rewarded the raven for this by promising that none should ever injure his young, that he should always have meat in abundance, and that his prayer for rain should be immediately answered.[3]

But the Rabbi Johanan taught that Cain buried his brother to hide what he had done from the eye of God, not knowing that God can see even the most secret things.[4]

According to some Rabbis, all good souls are derived from Abel and all bad souls from Cain. Cain's soul was derived from Satan, his body alone was from Eve; for the Evil Spirit Sammael, according to some, Satan, according to others, deceived Eve, and thus Cain was the son of the Evil One.[5] All the children of Cain also became demons of darkness and nightmares, and therefore it is, say the Cabbalists, that there is no mention in Genesis of the death of any of Cain's offspring.[6]

When Cain had slain his brother, we are told in Scripture

[1] Jalkut Chadasch, fol. 6, col. i.
[2] Pirke R. Eliezer, c. xxi.
[3] Ibid.
[4] Ibid.
[5] Eisenmenger, ii. p. 8.
[6] Ibid., ii. p. 428.

that he fled. Certain Rabbis give the reason :—He feared lest
Satan should kill him: now Satan has no power over any one
whose face he does not see, thus he had none over Lot's wife
till she turned her face towards Sodom, and he could see it;
and Cain fled, to keep his face from being seen by the Evil One,
and thus give him an opportunity of taking his life.[1]

With regard to the mark put upon Cain, there is great diverg-
ing of opinion. Some say that his tongue turned white; others,
that he was given a peculiar dress; others, that his face became
black; but the most prevalent opinion is that he became covered
with hair, and a horn grew in the midst of his forehead.

The Little Genesis says, Cain was born when Adam was
aged seventy, and Abel when he was seventy-seven.

The book of the penitence of Adam gives us some curious
details. When Cain had killed his brother, he was filled with
terror, for he saw the earth quivering. He cast the body into a
hole and covered it with dust, but the earth threw the body
out. Then he dug another hole and heaped earth on his
brother's corpse, but again the earth rejected it.

When God appeared before him, Cain trembled in all his
limbs, and God said to him, "Thou tremblest and art in fear;
this shall be thy sign." And from that moment he quaked
with a perpetual ague.

The Rabbis give another mark as having been placed on
Cain. They say that a horn grew out of the midst of his forehead. He was killed by a son of Lamech, who, being short-
sighted, mistook him for a wild beast; but in the Little
Genesis it is said that he was killed by the fall of his house,
in the year 930, the same day that Adam died. According to
the same authority, Adam and Eve bewailed Abel twenty-eight
years.

The Talmud relates the following beautiful incident.

God had cursed Cain, and he was doomed to a bitter punish-

---

[1] Eisenmenger, ii. p. 455.

ment; but moved, at last, by Cain's contrition, He placed on his brow the symbol of pardon.

Adam met Cain, and looked with wonder on the seal or token, and asked,—

"How hast thou turned away the wrath of the Almighty?"

"By confession of sin and repentance," answered the fratricide.

"Woe is me!" cried Adam, smiting his brow; "is the virtue of repentance so great, and I knew it not! And by repentance I might have altered my lot!"[1]

Tabari says that Cain was the first worshipper of fire. Eblis (Satan) appeared to him and told him that the reason of the acceptance of Abel's sacrifice was, that he had invoked the fire that fell on it and consumed it; Cain had not done this, and therefore fire had not come down on his oblation. Cain believed this, and adored fire, and taught his children to do the same.[2]

Cain, says Josephus, having wandered over the earth with his wife, settled in the land of Nod. But his punishment, so far from proving of advantage to him, proved only a stimulus to his violence and passion; and he increased his wealth by rapine, and he encouraged his children and friends to live by robbery and in luxury. He also corrupted the primitive simplicity in which men lived, by the introduction amongst them of weights and measures, by placing boundaries, and walling cities.[3]

John Malala says the same: "Cain was a tiller of the ground till he committed the crime of slaying his brother; after that, he lived by violence, his hand being against every man, and he invented and taught men the use of weights, measures, and boundaries."[4]

The passage in Genesis "*Whosoever slayeth Cain, vengeance shall be taken on him seven-fold*,"[5] has been variously interpreted.

---

[1] Tract. Avoda Sara.
[2] Tabari, i. c. xix.
[3] Antiq. Judæ., lib. i. c. 2.
[4] Excerpta Chronologica, p. 2.
[5] Gen. iv. 15.

Cosmas Indopleustes renders it thus, "Whosoever slayeth Cain will discharge seven vengeances;" that is, he will deliver him from those calamities to which he is subject when living.[1]

But Malala renders it otherwise; he says it is to be thus understood: "Every murderer shall die for his sin, but thou who didst commit the first homicide, and art therefore the originator of this crime, shalt be punished seven-fold; that is, thou shalt undergo seven punishments." For Cain had committed seven crimes. First, he was guilty of envy; then, of treachery; thirdly, of murder; fourthly, of killing his brother; fifthly, this was the first murder ever committed; sixthly, he grieved his parents; and seventhly, Cain lied to God. Thus the sin of Cain was seven-fold; therefore seven-fold was his punishment. First, the earth was accursed on his account; secondly, he was sentenced to labour; thirdly, the earth was forbidden from yielding to him her strength; fourthly, he was to become timid and conscience-stricken; fifthly, he was to be a vagabond on the earth; sixthly, he was to be cast out from God's presence; seventhly, a mark was to be placed upon him.

The Mussulmans say that the penitence of Cain, whom they call Kabil, was not sincere. He was filled with remorse, but it was mingled with envy and hatred, because he was regarded with disfavour by the rest of the sons of Adam.

Near Damascus is shown a place at the foot of a mountain where Cain slew Abel.[2]

The legends of the death of Cain will be found under the title of Lamech.

"Half a mile from the gates of Hebron," says the Capuchin Friar, Ignatius von Rheinfelden, in his Pilgrimage to Jerusalem, "begins the valley of Mamre, in which Abraham saw the three angels; the *Campus Damascenus* lies toward the west; there, Adam was created; and the spot is pointed out where Cain killed his brother Abel. The earth there is red, and may be

---

[1] Cosmas Indopleustes, Cosmographia, lib. v.
[2] D'Herbelot, Bibliothèque Orientale, *sub voce* Cabil, i. p. 438.

moulded like wax."[1] Salmeron says the same, "Adam was made of the earth or dust of the *Campus Damascenus.*" And St. Jerome on Ezekiel, chap. xvii., says: "Damascus is the place where Abel was slain by his brother Cain; for which cause the spot is called Damascus, that is, Blood-drinking." This Damascus near Hebron is not to be confused with the city Damascus.

[1] Neue Ierosolymitanische Pilger-fahrt. Von P. F. Ignat. von Rheinfelden. Würtzburg, 1667. P. ii. p. 8.

## VII.

## THE DEATH OF ADAM.

ACCORDING to a Mussulman tradition, Adam was consoled for the loss of Abel by the discovery of how to make wheat-bread. The story is as follows :—

The angel Gabriel was sent out of Paradise to give him the rest of the wheat-grains Eve had plucked from the forbidden tree, together with two oxen, and various instruments of husbandry. Hitherto he had fed on roots and berries, and had known nothing of sowing grain; acting under Gabriel's directions, he ploughed the land, but the plough stuck, and Adam impatiently smote one of the oxen, and it spoke to him and said, "Wherefore hast thou smitten me?"

Adam replied, "Because thou dost not draw the plough."

"Adam!" said the ox, "when thou wast rebellious, did God smite thee thus?"

"O God!" cried Adam to the Almighty, "is every beast to reproach me, and recall to me my sin?"

Then God heard his cry, and withdrew from beasts the power of speech, lest they should cast their sin in the teeth of men.

But as the plough was still arrested, Adam dug into the soil, and found that the iron had been caught by the body of his son Abel.

When the wheat was sprung up, Gabriel gave Adam fire from hell, which however he had previously washed seventy times in the sea, or it would have consumed the earth and all things thereon. In the beginning, wheat-grains were the size of ostrich eggs, but under Edris (Enoch) they were no bigger than goose eggs; under Elias they were the size of hen's eggs; under Christ, when the Jews sought to slay him, they were no larger than grapes; it was in the time of Uzeir (Esdras) that they diminished to their present proportions.

After Adam and Eve had been instructed in all that appertained to agriculture, Gabriel brought them a lamb and showed Adam how to slay it in the name of God, how to shear off the wool, and skin the sheep. Eve was instructed in the art of spinning and weaving by the angel, and she made of the wool, first a veil for herself, and then a shirt for her husband.

The first pair brought up their grandsons and great grandsons, to the number of 40,000 according to some, and 70,000 according to others, and taught them all that they had learned of the angel.

After the death of Abel, and after Cain had been slain by the avenging angel, Eve bore a third son, named Seth, who became the father of the race of the prophets.

Finally, when Adam had reached his nine hundred and thirtieth year, the Angel of Death appeared under the form of a goat, and ran between his legs.

Adam recoiled with horror, and exclaimed, "God has given me one thousand years; wherefore comest thou now?"

"What!" exclaimed the Angel of Death, "hast thou not given seventy years of thy life to the prophet David?"

Adam stoutly denied that he had done so. Then the Angel of Death drew the document of transfer from out of his beard, and presented it to Adam, who could no longer refuse to go.

His son Seth washed and buried him, after that the angel Gabriel, or, according to some accounts, Allah himself, had blessed him: Eve died a year later.

Learned men are not agreed as to the place of their burial; some traditions name India, others the Mount Kubeis, and others again, Jerusalem—God alone knows![1]

[1] Weil, pp. 40-3.

Tabari says that Adam made Seth his testamentary executor. "When Adam was dead, Gabriel instructed Seth how to bury him, and brought him the winding sheet out of heaven. And Gabriel said to Seth, 'Thou art sole executor of thy father, therefore it is thy office to perform the religious functions.' Then Seth recited over Adam thirty *Tebirs*. Four of these *Tebirs* were the legal prayers, the others were supererogatory, and were designed to exalt the virtues of Adam. Some say that Adam was buried near Mecca on Mount Abui-Kubais."[1]

According to the apocryphal "Life of Adam and Eve," Adam before his death called to his bedside all his sons and daughters, and they numbered fifteen thousand males, and females unnumbered. Adam is said to have been the author of several psalms; amongst others, Psalm civ., *Benedic anima mea*, and Psalm cxxxix., *Domine probasti;* as may be gathered from the 14th, 15th, and 16th verses: "*My bones are not hid from thee: though I was made secretly, and fashioned beneath in the earth. Thine eyes did see my substance, yet being imperfect; and in Thy book were all my members written; which day by day were fashioned, when as yet there was none of them.*"

The Arabs say that when Adam dictated his last will and testament, the angel Gabriel descended from heaven to receive it, accompanied by sixty-two millions of angels, each provided with clean white sheets of parchment and pens, and that the will was sealed by Gabriel.[2]

Tradition is not agreed as to the place of Adam's burial. Khaithemah says that Adam was buried near Mecca on Mount Abu-Kubais. But the ancient Persians assert that he was buried in Ceylon, where his sepulchre was guarded by lions at the time of the war of the giants.[3]

But the most generally received tradition is this:—

The body of Adam was taken by Noah into the ark, and when the ark rested on Ararat, Noah and his sons removed the

---

[1] Tabari, i. c. xxxiii. [2] Colin de Plancy, p. 78. [3] Herbelot, i. p. 95.

## THE DEATH OF ADAM.

body from it, and they followed an angel who led them to the place where the first father was to lie. Shem or Melchizedek—for they are one, as we shall see presently—being consecrated by God to the priesthood, performed the religious rites; and buried Adam at the centre of the earth, which is Jerusalem; but, say some, he was buried by Shem along with Eve, in the cave of Machpelah, in Hebron. But others relate that Noah on leaving the ark distributed the bones of Adam among his sons, and that he gave the head to Shem, who buried it in Jerusalem. Some, taking this mystically, suppose that by this is meant the sin and punishment of Adam, which was transmitted to all the sons of Noah, but that to Shem was given the head, the Messiah who was to regenerate the world.[1] S. Basil of Seleucia says: "According to Jewish traditions, the skull of Adam was found there (*i.e.* on Golgotha), and this, they say, Solomon knew by his great wisdom. And because it was the place of Adam's skull, therefore the hill was called Golgotha, or Calvary."[2]

With this a great concourse of Fathers agree; whose testimony has been laboriously collected by Gretser in his famous and curious book "De Cruce." And this tradition has become a favourite subject for artists, who, in their paintings or sculptures, represent the skull of Adam at the foot of the Cross of Christ.

The apocryphal "Testament of Adam" still exists.

The tomb of Eve is shown at Jedda. "On entering the great gate of the cemetery, one observes on the left a little wall three feet high, forming a square of ten to twelve feet. There lies the head of our first mother. In the middle of the cemetery is a sort of cupola, where reposes the navel of her body; and at the other extremity, near the door of egress, is another little wall also three feet high, forming a lozenge-shaped enclosure: there are her feet. In this place is a large piece of cloth,

---

[1] Moses bar Cepha. Commentarius de Paradiso, P. i. c. 14. Fabricius, i. p. 75.     [2] S. Basil Seleuc., Orat. xxxviii.

whereon the faithful deposit their offerings, which serve for the maintenance of a constant burning of perfumes over the midst of her body. The distance between her head and feet is four hundred feet. How we have shrunk since the creation !¹ "

The bones of Adam and Eve, says Tabari, were taken by Noah into the ark with him, and were reburied by him.

This article may be fitly concluded with the epitaph of Adam, composed by Gabriel Alvarez, and published by him in his " Historia Ecclesiæ Antediluvianæ," Madrid, 1713.

"Here lies, reduced to a pinch of dust, he who, from a pinch of dust, was formed to govern the earth,
ADAM,
the son of None, the father of All, the stepfather of All and of himself.
Having never wailed as a child, he spent his life in weeping, the result of penitence.
Powerful, Wise, Immortal, Just,
he sold for the price of disobedience, power, wisdom, justice, immortality.
Having abused the privilege of Free-will, which weapon he had received for the preservation of Knowledge and Grace, by one stroke he struck with death himself and all the human race.
The Omnipotent Judge
who in His Justice took from him righteousness, by His Mercy restored it to him whole again :
by whose goodness it has fallen out, that we may call that crime happy, which obtained such and so great A Redeemer.
Thenceforth Free-will, which he in happiness used to bring forth Misery, is used in Misery to bring forth Happiness.
For if we, partakers of his pernicious inheritance, partake also of his penitential example, and lend our ears to salutary counsels,
Then we (who by our Free-will could lose ourselves) can be saved by the grace of the Redeemer, and the co-operation of our Free-will.
The First Adam Lived to Die ;
The Second Adam Died to Live.
Go, and imitate the penitence of the First Adam ;
Go, and celebrate the goodness of the Second Adam."

---

¹ Lettre de H. A. D., Consul de France en Abyssinie, 1841.

## VIII.

## SETH.

WHEN Seth had ascended the throne of his father, says Tabari, he was the greatest of the sons of Adam. Every year he made the pilgrimage to the Kaaba, and he ruled the world with equity, and everything flourished during his reign. At the age of fifty he had a son; he called his name Enoch and named him his executor. He died at the age of nine hundred.[1]

Seth and the other sons of Adam waged perpetual war against the Divs, or giants, the sons of Kabil, or Cain.

Rocail was another son of Adam, born next after Seth.

He possessed, says the Tahmurath Nâmeh, the most wonderful knowledge in all mysteries. He had a genius so quick and piercing, that he seemed to be rather an angel than a man.

Surkrag, a great giant, son of Cain, commanded in the mountains of Kaf, which encompass the centre of the earth. This giant asked Seth to send him Rocail, his brother, to assist him in governing his subjects. Seth consented, and Rocail became the vizier or prime minister of Surkrag, in the mountains of Kaf.

After having governed many centuries, and knowing, by divine revelation, that the time of his death drew nigh, he thus addressed Surkrag: "I am about to depart hence and enter on another existence; but before I leave, I wish to

[1] Tabari, i. c. xxxiv.

## VIII.

### SETH.

Seth had ascended the throne of his father, says
he was the greatest of the sons of Adam. Every year
e the pilgrimage to the Kaaba, and he ruled the world
nity, and everything flourished during his reign. At
of fifty he had a son; he called his name Enoch
med him his executor. He died at the age of nine
.l.¹

and the other sons of Adam waged perpetual war
the Divs, or giants, the sons of Kabil, or Cain.
il was another son of Adam, born next after Seth.
ossessed, says the Tahmurath Námeh, the most w...
wledge in all mysteries. He had a genius so ...
, that he seemed to be rather an angel than a man.
rag, a great giant, son of Cain, comm... n the
ins of Kaf, which encompass the centre of the earth.
nt asked Seth to send him Rocail, his brother...
governing his subjects. Seth consent... and ...
the vizier or prime minister of S...
Kaf.

having governed many centuries and ...
revelation, that the time of his ...
ldressed Surkrag: "I am about to ...
n another exi...

bequeath to you some famous work, which shall perpetuate my name into remote ages."

Thereupon Rocail erected an enormous sepulchre, adorned with statues of various metals, made by talismanic art, which moved, and spake, and acted like living men.[1]

According to the Rabbinic traditions, Seth was one of the thirteen who came circumcised into the world. The rest were Adam, Enoch, Noah, Shem, Terah, Jacob, Joseph, Moses, Samuel, David, Isaiah, and Jeremiah.[2] The book Schene Luchôth says that the soul of righteous Abel passed into the body of Seth, and afterwards this same soul passed into Moses; thus the law, which was known to Adam and in which Abel had been instructed, was not new to Moses.[3]

The Little Genesis says, that Seth was instructed by the angels in what was to take place in the world; how its iniquity was to grow, and a flood was to overwhelm it; and how the Messiah would come and restore all things. Seth was remarkable for the majesty and beauty of his appearance, as he had inherited much of the loveliness of unfallen man. He married his sister Azur, or, according to others, Noræa or Horæa.

Suidas, under the heading 'Σήδ,' says: "Seth was the son of Adam: of this it is said, the sons of God went in unto the daughters of men; that is to say, the sons of Seth went in unto the daughters of Cain. For in that age Seth was called God, because he had discovered Hebrew letters, and the names of the stars; but especially on account of his great piety, so that he was the first to bear the name of God."

Theodoret thus refers the verse,—"*And to Seth, to him also there was born a son; and he called his name Enos: then began men to call upon the name of the Lord,*" or as our marginal reading is, "*then began men to call themselves by the name of the Lord;*"

---

[1] D'Herbelot, i. p. 125, s. v. Rocail.
[2] Midrash Tillim, fol. 10, col. 2.
[3] Eisenmenger, i. p. 645.

"Aquila interpreted it thus, 'then Seth began to be called by the name of the Lord.' These words intimate his piety, which deserved that he should receive the sacred name; and he was called God by his acquaintance, and his children were termed the sons of God, just as we are called Christians after Christ."[1]

The origin of this tradition seems to be the fact that Seth was the name of an ancient Egyptian deity, at first regarded as the giver of light and civilization, but afterwards identified with Typhon by the Egyptians, who considered Seth to be the chief god of the Hyksos or shepherd kings; and in their hatred of these oppressors, the name of Seth was everywhere obliterated on their monuments, and he was regarded as one with the great adversary, Typhon; and was represented as an ass, or with an ass's head.[2]

Abulfaraj, in his history, says that Seth discovered letters, and that, desirous to recover the Blessed Life, he and his sons went to Mount Hermon, where they served God in piety and continence, and associated not with the people of the land, nor took to themselves wives; wherefore they were called the sons of God.[3]

Flavius Josephus relates that after the things that were to take place had been revealed to Seth,—how the earth was to be destroyed, first with water and then with fire,—lest those things which he had discovered should perish from the memory of his posterity, he set up two pillars, one of brick, the other of stone, and he wrote thereon all the science he had acquired, hoping that, in the event of the brick pillar perishing by the rain, the stone one would endure.[4]

Freculphus adds that Jubal assisted the sons of Seth in engraving on the columns all that was known of the conduct and order of the heavens, and all the arts then known.[5]

[1] Theodoret, Quæst. in Gen. xlvii.
[2] Plutarch, Isis and Osiris, ed. Parthey; pp. 72, 88, and notes pp. 183, 238.
[3] Abulfaraj, Hist. Dynast., ed. Pocock, p. 5.
[4] Joseph. Antiq. Judaic., lib. i. c. 2.
[5] Freculphus, Chron. lib. i. c. 12.

The stone pillar was to be seen, in the time of Josephus, in Syria.

Anastasius of Sinai says that, when God created Adam after His image and likeness, He breathed into him grace, and illumination, and a ray of the Holy Spirit. But when he sinned, this glory left him, and his face became clouded. Then he became the father of Cain and Abel. But afterwards it is said in Scripture, "*He begat a son in his own likeness, after his image; and called his name Seth;*" which is not said of Cain and Abel; and this means that Seth was begotten in the likeness of unfallen man and after the image of Adam in Paradise; and he called his name Seth, that is, by interpretation, Resurrection, because in him he saw the resurrection of his departed beauty, and wisdom, and glory, and radiance of the Holy Spirit. And all those then living, when they saw how the face of Seth shone with divine light, and heard him speak with divine wisdom, said, He is God; therefore his sons were commonly called the sons of God.[1]

As Seth was an ancient Egyptian Sun-god, the origin of the myth of his shining face can be ascertained without difficulty.

To Seth were attributed several apocryphal writings.

[1] Anastasius Sinaita, 'Ὁδηγός, ed. Gretser, Ingolst. 1606, p. 269.

## IX.

## CAINAN SON OF ENOS.

"*And Seth lived an hundred and five years, and begat Enos: and Seth lived after he begat Enos eight hundred and seven years, and begat sons and daughters: and all the days of Seth were nine hundred and twelve years: and he died. And Enos lived ninety years, and begat Cainan.*"[1]

Alexander wrote many epistles to Aristotle, his preceptor, in which he narrated what had befallen him in India. Amongst other things he wrote: "After I had entered the Persian region, which is a province of India, I arrived at some islands of the sea, and there I found men, like women, who fed on raw fish, and spake a language very like Greek; they said to me that there was in the island the sepulchre of a most ancient king, who was called Cainan, son of Enos, and who ruled the whole world, and taught men all kinds of knowledge, and had demons and all kinds of evil spirits under his control. He, by his wisdom, understood that the ever-blessed God would bring in a flood in the times of Noah; wherefore he engraved all that was to take place on stone tables, which exist there to this day, and are written in Hebrew characters. He wrote therein that the ocean would, in that age, overflow a third part of the world, which took place in the lifetime of Enos, the son of Seth, who was the son of Adam, our first parent.

"In the same island, Cainan built a most extensive city,

[1] Gen. v. 6–9.

surrounded with walls; and a great marble citadel, in which he treasured jewels and pearls, and gold and silver in great abundance.

"Moreover, he erected a tower, very lofty, over a sepulchre for himself, to serve as his monument. This tower can be approached by no man; for it was built by astronomical art under the seven planets, and with magical skill, so that every one who draws near the wall is struck down with sudden death."[1]

[1] Pseudo Josephus Gorionides; ed. Clariss. Breithauptius, lib. ii. c. 18, p. 131.

## X.

## ENOCH.

### 1. THE TRANSLATION OF ENOCH.

ENOCH, or Edris,[1] as he is called by the Arabs, was born in Hindostan, but he lived in Yemen. He was a prophet. In his days men worshipped fire, being deceived by Eblis. When God sent Enoch to his brethren to turn them from their false worship, they would not believe him.

Idolatry began in the times of Jared, son of Mahalaleel, and it spread to such an extent that, when Noah was born, there were not eighty persons who worshipped the true, and living, and only God. Jared fought Satan, the prince of demons, and captured him, and led him about in chains wherever he went.

Enoch knew how to sew, and was an accomplished tailor. He was the first to put pen to paper; he wrote many books. He had in his possession the books of Adam, and for ten years, instead of sleeping, he spent the night in reading them.

He instructed men in the art of making garments; Enoch showed them how to cut out the skins to the proper shape, and to sew them together; and how to make shoes to protect their feet.

[1] I give the Arabic legend. The account in Jasher is different. Enoch retired from the world, and showed himself only at rare intervals, when he gave advice to all who came to hear his wisdom. He was taken up to heaven in a whirlwind, in a chariot with horses of fire. (Yaschar, pp. 1094-1096.)

And then, when the people had derived this great blessing from him, they were ready to listen to his books; and he read to them the books of Adam, and endeavoured thereby to bring them back to the knowledge of the true God.

When he had spent many years in prayer, the Angel of Death desired to make a compact of friendship with him. He took on him a human form and approached him, saying, "I am the Angel of Death, and I desire thy friendship. On account of thy great piety, thou mayest make me a request which I shall accomplish."

Enoch answered, "I desire that thou shouldst take my soul."

The angel replied, "I have not come to thee for this purpose; thy time is not yet arrived at its appointed close."

Then Enoch said, "It is well; but take my soul away for a little space, and then return it to my body, if God so wills."

The angel said, "I cannot do this without God's consent." But he presented the supplications of Enoch before Allah, and God, knowing what was the design of Enoch, granted the prayer.

Then Azrael bore away the soul of Enoch, and at the same instant the Eternal One restored it to him. After this, Enoch continued to praise and pray to God; and the Angel of Death became his friend, and often came to visit him.

Years passed, and Enoch said one day to the angel, "Oh, my friend! I have yet a request to make."

Azrael answered, "If I can grant it, I will do so readily."

Enoch said, "I would see Hell, for I have undergone death, and I know its sensations. I would know now the torments of the lost."

But the angel answered, "This I cannot grant without permission from the Almighty."

God heard the prayer of Enoch, and He suffered Azrael to accomplish what the prophet had desired. Then the Angel of Death bore away Enoch, and showed him the seven stages of Hell, and all the torments inflicted there on sinners: after that he replaced him where he was before.

After some while had elapsed, Enoch again addressed Azrael, and said, "I have another request to make."

The angel answered, "Say on."

Then said Enoch, "I desire to see the Paradise of God, as I have seen Hell."

Azrael replied, "I cannot grant thy petition without the consent of God."

But the All-Merciful, when he heard the request of his servant, consented that it should be even as he desired. So the angel bore Enoch into Paradise. And when they had reached the gates, the keeper, Ridhwan, refused to open, saying to Enoch, "Thou art a man, and no man can enter Paradise who has not tasted death."

Then Enoch replied, "I also have tasted death; the soul that I have will dwell eternally with me; God has resuscitated me from death."

Ridhwan, however, said, "I cannot do this thing and admit thee without the order of God."

Then the order arrived from Allah, and the angel of the gate refused no more; so Enoch entered; but before Enoch and Azrael passed the gates, Ridhwan said to the prophet, "Go in, and behold Paradise, but be speedy and leave it again, for thou mayst not dwell there till after the Resurrection."

Enoch replied, "Be it so;" and he went in and viewed Paradise, and came out, as he had promised; and as he passed the threshold of the door he turned and said to the angel, "Oh, Ridhwan! I have left something in there; suffer me to run and fetch it."

But Ridhwan refused; and a dispute arose between them.

Enoch said, "I am a prophet; and God has sent me thirty books, and I have written them all, and I have never revolted against God. In those books that God sent me, I was promised Paradise. If it be necessary that I should have undergone death, I have undergone it. If it be necessary that I should have seen Hell, I have seen it. Now I am come to Paradise, and that is my home; God has promised it to me, and now that I have entered I will leave it no more."

The dispute waxed hot, but it was terminated by the order of God, who bade Ridhwan open the gate and re-admit Enoch into Paradise, where he still dwells.[1]

### 2. THE BOOK OF ENOCH.

The Book of Enoch, quoted by S. Jude in his Epistle, and alluded to by Origen, S. Augustine, S. Clement of Alexandria, and others of the Fathers, must not be passed over.

The original book appears from internal evidence to have been written about the year 110 B.C.[2] But we have not the work as then written; it has suffered from numerous interpolations, and it is difficult always to distinguish the original text from the additions.

The book is frequently quoted in the apocryphal "Testament of the Twelve Patriarchs," which is regarded as canonical by the Armenian Church, but the references are for the most part not to be found in the text. It was largely used by some of the early Christian writers, either with acknowledgment or without. The monk George Syncellus, in the eighth century, extracted portions to compose his Chronography. This fragment in Syncellus was all that was known of the book in the West till last century. The Jews, though remembering the work, had lost it in Hebrew; but it was alluded to by the Rabbis down to the thirteenth century, and it is referred to in the Book Sohar, though the writer may not have read the book of Enoch. Bruce, the African traveller, was the first to bring it to Europe from Abyssinia in two MSS., in the year 1773.

---

[1] Tabari, i. c. xxxv.
[2] Dillmann, Das Buch Enoch; Leipzig, 1853. Ewald, in his "Geschichte der Volks Israel" (iii. 2, pp. 397-401), attributes it to the year 130 B.C.

Much attention was not, however, paid to it till 1800, when De Sacy in his "Magasin Encyclopédique," under the title "Notice sur le Livre d'Enoch," gave some account of the work. In 1801, Professor Laurence gave to the public an English translation, accompanied by some critical remarks. Since then, the book has been carefully and exegetically examined. The version we now have is Ethiopic.

The Book of Enoch consists of five divisions, or books, together with a Prolegomena and an Epilegomena.

After the introduction (caps. 1—5), which describes the work as the revelation of the seer Enoch concerning the future judgment and its consequences, with warnings to the elect as to the signs; the *First* part (caps. 6—16) opens with an account of the fall of the Angels, their union with the daughters of men, and the generation of the Giants. Connected with this, and divided from it by no superscription or sign of change of subject, is an account of a journey made by Enoch, in the company of the angels, over the earth and through the lower circles of heaven, during which he is instructed in various mysteries hidden from the knowledge of men, and a great deal of this wondrous information is communicated to the reader.

This description of a journey, which is itself divided into two parts, unquestionably belongs to the original book, and the historical portion, narrating the procreation of the Giants, is an interpolation.

The *Second* portion of the book (caps. 37—71), with its own special superscription and introduction, is called "The Second History of Wisdom." It continues the history of the voyage. The first portion contained the description of the mysterious places and things in the earth and in the lower heaven; the second portion contains an account of the mysteries of the highest heaven, the angel-world, the founding of the kingdom of the Messias, and the signs of His coming.

The close of this portion contains prophecies of Noah's Flood, and accounts of the fall of the Angels, their evil life and their punishment. The whole account of the Flood, which comes in without rhyme or reason, is also a manifest interpolation.

The *Third* portion (caps. 72—82), also under its own heading, is on "The Revolution of the Lights of Heaven," and describes the motions of the planets, the duration of the seasons, and the number of the days of the months, and the great winds of heaven. With this part the voyage of Enoch closes.

The *Fourth* part (caps. 83—91), which has no superscription, but which is generally designated as "The Book of the Dream History," contains the visions shown Enoch in his youth, which, in a series of pictures, gives the history of the world till the end of time. This part closes with some words of advice from Enoch to his sons.

The *Fifth* and last part (caps. 92—105) is "The Book of Exhortation," addressed by Enoch to his family against sin in all its forms, under all its disguises, and concludes with an account of certain presages which should announce the birth of Noah.

The Talmudic writers taught that Enoch at his translation became a chief angel, and that his name became Metatron. In the Chaldee version of Jonathan on the words of Genesis v. 24, it is said, "And Enoch served before the Lord in truth, and was not among the inhabitants of the earth, for he was translated above into the firmament, through the word of the Lord; and He called him by the name of Metatron (the great writer)." And in Rabbi Menachem's Commentary on the Five Books of Moses, it is written, "The Rabbi Ishmael relates that he spoke to the Metatron, and he asked him why he was named with the name of his Creator and with seventy names, and why he was greater than any prince, and higher than any angel, and dearer than any servant, and more honoured than all the host, and more excellent in greatness, in power, and dominion than all the mighty ones. Then he answered and said, 'Because I was Enoch, son of Jared. This is what the holy, ever-blessed God wrought,—when the races of the Flood (*i.e.* the sinners who lived at the time when the Flood came) sinned, and did unrighteously in their works, and had said to God, "Depart from us,"— He took me from that untoward generation into the highest heaven, that I might be a witness against that generation. And after the ever-blessed God had removed me that I should stand before the throne of His Majesty, and before the wheels of His chariot, and accomplish the requirements of the Most High, then my flesh became flame, and my arteries fire, and my bones juniper ashes, and the light of my eyelids became the flashing of lightning, and my eyeballs torches of fire, and the hair of my head was a flame, and all my limbs were fiery, burning wings, and my body became burning fire; and by my right hand flames were cleft asunder; and from my left hand burnt fiery torches; but around me blew a wind, and storm, and tempest; and before and behind me was the voice of a mighty earthquake.'"

The Rabbi Ishmael gives further particulars which are enshrined in the great Jalkut Rubeni.[1]

The Rabbi Ishmael, according to this book, received in addition these particulars from the lips of Enoch. He was carried to heaven in a chariot of fire by horses of fire; and when he entered into the presence of God, the Sacred Beasts, the Seraphim, the Ōsannim, the Cherubim, the wheels of the chariot, and all the fiery ministers recoiled five thousand three hundred and eighty miles at the smell of him, and cried aloud, "What a stink is come among us from one born of a woman! Why is one who has eaten of white wheat admitted into heaven?"

Then the Almighty answered and said, "My servants, Cherubim and Seraphim, do not be grieved, for all my sons have rejected my sovereignty and adore idols, this man alone excepted; and in reward I exalt him to principality over the

---

[1] Fol. 26, col. 2.

angels in heaven." When Enoch heard this he was glad, for he had been a simple shoemaker on earth; but this had he done, at every stitch he had said, "The name of God and His Majesty be praised."

The height of Enoch when a chief angel was very great. It would take a man five hundred years to walk from his heel to the crown of his head. And the ladder which Jacob saw in vision was the ladder of Metatron.[1] The same authority, above quoted, the Rabbi Ishmael, is reported to have had the exact measure of Enoch from his own lips; it was seven hundred thousand times thousand miles in length and in breadth.[2]

The account in the Targum of Palestine is simply this. "Enoch served in the truth before the Lord; and behold, he was not with the sojourners of the earth; for he was withdrawn, and he ascended to the firmament by the Word before the Lord, and his name was called Metatron, the Great Saphra."[3]

Whether the Annakos, or Nannakos of whom Suidas wrote, is to be identified with Enoch, I do not venture to decide. Suidas says that Nannak was an aged king before Deucalion (Noah), and that, foreseeing the Deluge, he called all his subjects together into the temple to pray the gods with many tears to remit the evil.[4] And Stephanos, the Byzantine lexicographer, says that Annakos lived at Iconium in Phrygia, and that to weep for Annak, became a proverb.

[1] Jalkut Rubeni, fol. 27, col. 4.   [2] Ibid., fol. 107, col. i.
[3] Targums, ed. Etheridge, i. p. 175.   [4] Suidas, Lexic. s. v. Nannacos.

## XI.

## THE GIANTS.

THE Giants, say the Cabbalists, arose thus.

Aza and Azael, two angels of God, complained to the Most High at the creation of man, and said, "Why hast Thou made man who will anger Thee?"

But God answered, "And you, O angels, if you were in the lower world, you, too, would sin." And He sent them on earth, and then they fell, as says the Book of Genesis, "*And it came to pass that the sons of God saw the daughters of men that they were fair, and they took them wives of all which they chose.*" After they had sinned, they were given bodies of flesh; for an angel who spends seven days on earth becomes opaque and substantial. And when they had been clothed with flesh and with a corrupt nature, then they spake the word "Shem hamphorasch," and sought to regain their former place, but could not; and were cast out into mountains, there to dwell. From these angels descend the sons of the giants and the Anakim, and from their seed also spring the devils.[1] The Rabbi Eliezer says that the giants sprang from the union of the angels with the daughters of Cain, who walked about in immodest clothing and cast their eyes around with bold glances. And the book Zeena-ureena, in the Parascha Chykkath, says that Og sprang from this connection, and that Sammael, the angel, was the parent of Og, but that Sihon was the son of the same angel

[1] Nischmath Chajim, fol. 116, col. i.

who deceived the wife of Ham when she was about to enter the ark.¹

The account in the Book of Enoch is as follows:—

"Hear and fear not, Enoch, thou righteous man, and writer of righteousness, come hither and hear my words: Go speak unto the Watchers of Heaven, and say unto them, Ye shall pray for men and not men for you. Why have ye forsaken the high and holy and eternal heaven, and have joined yourselves to women, and polluted yourselves with the daughters of men, and have taken to you wives, and have become the fathers of a giant race? Ye, who were spiritual, holy, and enjoying eternal life, have corrupted yourselves with women, and have become parents of children with flesh and blood; lusting after the blood of men, ye have brought forth flesh and blood, like those who are mortal and perishable. Because men die, therefore did I give unto them wives, that they might have sons, and perpetuate their generation. But ye are spiritual and in the enjoyment of eternal life. Therefore gave I not to you wives, for heaven is the abode of the spirits. And now the giants, who are born of flesh and blood, shall become evil spirits, and their dwelling shall be on the earth. Bad beings shall proceed from them. Because they have been generated from above, from the holy Watchers have they received their origin, therefore shall they be evil spirits on the earth, and evil spirits shall they be called. And the spirits of the giants, which mount upon the clouds, will fail and be cast down, and do violence, and cause ruin on the earth and injury; they shall not eat, they shall not thirst, and they shall be invisible."²

Among the Oriental Christians it is said, that Adam having related to the children of Seth the delights of Paradise, several of them desired to recover the lost possession. They retired to Mount Hermon and dwelt there in the fear of the Lord; living in great austerity, in hope that their penitence

---

¹ Eisenmenger, i. p. 380.
² Das Buch Henoch, von Dillmann, Leipz. 1853, c. xv. p. 9.

would recover Eden. But the Canaanites dwelt round them on all sides, and the sons of Seth, becoming tired of celibacy, took the daughters of the Canaanites to wife, and to them were born the giants.[1]

Others say that the posterity of the patriarch Seth were those called the "Sons of God," because they lived on Mount Hermon in familiar discourse with the angels. On this mountain they fed only on the fruit of the earth, and their sole oath was, "By the blood of Abel."[2]

Among the giants was Surkrag, of whom we have already related a few particulars. He was not of the race of men, nor of the posterity of Adam. According to the Mussulman account he was commander of the armies of Soliman Tchaghi, who reigned over the earth before the time of Gian ben Gian, who succeeded him and reigned seven thousand years. The whole earth was then in the power of the Jins. Gian ben Gian erected the pyramids of Egypt.

Surkrag obeyed God, and followed the true religion, and would not suffer his subject Jins to insult or maltreat the descendants of Adam. He reigned on Mount Kaf, and allied himself, according to Persian authorities, with Kaïumarth, the first king of the world, whom some Persian writers identify with Adam, but others suppose to be the son of Mahalaleel, and cotemporary with Enoch. Ferdussi, the author of the Schah-Nâmeh, speaks of him as the first who wore a crown and sat on a throne, and imposed a tribute on his subjects. He says that this monarch lived a thousand years, and reigned five hundred and fifty years. He was the first to teach men to build houses.

But if Kaïumarth was the first man to reign, he was the first also to weary of it; for he abdicated his sovereignty and retired into his former abode, a cave, after having surrendered his

[1] Abulfaraj, p. 6.
[2] Eutych., Patriarcha Alex., Annales ab Orbe Condito, Arabice et Lat., ed. Selden; London, 1642, i. p. 19.

authority to his son Siamek. Siamek having been killed, Kaïumarth re-ascended his throne to revenge his death. After having recovered the body of his son, he buried him with great honours, and kindled over his grave a great fire, which was kept perpetually burning, and this originated the worship of fire among the people of Iran.

Kaïumarth overcame the giant Semendoun, who had a hundred arms; his son, Huschenk, also overcame a giant who had three heads, mounted on an animal with twelve legs. This animal, named Rakhsche, was found by him in the Dog Isle, or the New Continent, and was born of the union of a crocodile and an hippopotamus, and it fed on the flesh of serpents. Having mastered this beast, Huschenk overcame the Mahisers, which have heads of fish and are of great ferocity. After having extended his conquests to the extremities of the earth, Huschenk was crushed to death by a mass of rock which the giants, his mortal enemies, hurled against him.[1]

According to Tabari, Huschenk was the son of Kaïumarth, who was the son of Mahalaleel. He was the first man to cut down trees and to make boards, and fashion them into doors to close the entrance to houses. He also discovered many precious stones, such as the topaz and the jacinth. He reigned four hundred years.[2]

He was succeeded by Tahmourath, who taught men to saddle and bridle horses; he was also the first man to write in Persian characters; he figures as a great hero in Iranian fable. According to the story in Persia, he was carried by the Simorg to the mountain of Kaf. 'Now the Simorg is a wondrous bird, speaking all languages, and eminently religious.

According to the Kaherman Nâmeh, the bird Simorg, being asked its age, replied, "This world has been seven times peopled, and seven times made void of living beings. The generation of Adam, in which we now are, will last seven

---
[1] D'Herbelot, s. v. Surkrag and Kaïumarth.
[2] Tabari, c. xxxvii.

thousand years, which form a cycle, and I have seen twelve of these revolutions. How many more I shall see is unknown to me."

The same book informs us that the Simorg was a great friend of the race of Adam, and a great enemy to the demons and Jins. He knew Adam personally, and had done obeisance to him, and enjoyed the same religion as our first fathers. He foretold to Tahmourath all that was to take place in the world, and plucking from his bosom some feathers, he presented them to him, and from that time all great captains and men of war wear feather crests.

Tahmourath having been transported by the bird to the mountains of Kaf, he assisted the Peris, who were at war with the Jins. Argenk, the giant, finding that the Peris were gaining the mastery, with the assistance of Tahmourath, sent an embassy desiring peace; but the ambassador, Imlain, abandoned the party of the Jins and assisted Tahmourath to obtain complete mastery in the mountains of Kaf, and to overcome not only the giant Argenk, but also Demrusch, a far more terrible monster. Demrusch lived in a cavern guarding a vast treasure, which he had amassed in Persia and India. He had also carried off the Peri Mergian. Tahmourath slew Demrusch and released Mergian.

According to the Persian story, Tahmourath was the first to cultivate rice, and to nourish silk-worms in the province of Tabristan.[1]

To return to Tabari.

Djemschid was the brother of Tahmourath; he was the first man to forge arms, and he is probably to be identified with Tubal-cain. He introduced also the use of pigments, and he discovered pearls, and also to dig for lime, vermilion, and quicksilver; he likewise compounded scents, and cultivated flowers. He divided all men into four classes,—soldiers, scribes, agriculturists, and artisans. At the head of all he placed the

[1] D'Herbelot, s. v. Tahmourath.

learned, that they might guide the affairs of men, and set them their tasks and instruct them in what they were to do.

Then Djemschid asked the wise men, "What must a king do to secure his throne?"

They answered, "He must reign in equity."

Consequently, Djemschid instituted justice; and he sat the first day of every month with his wise men, and ministered righteous judgments. For seven hundred years he continued this practice; and in all that time no rebellion broke out, no afflictions troubled him, nor was his reign in any way menaced.

One day, whilst Djemschid was taking his siesta alone in his chamber, Eblis entered by the window, and Djemschid asked, "Who art thou?" Now he thought he was one of those who waited without till he should come forth to administer justice. Eblis entered into conversation with Djemschid, and said, "I am an angel, and I have descended from heaven to give thee counsel."

"What counsel dost thou offer?" asked the king.

Eblis replied, "Tell me, who art thou?"

He answered, "I am one of the sons of Adam."

"Thou mistakest," said the Evil One: "thou art not a man. Consider, since thou hast reigned, has anything failed thee? Hast thou suffered any affliction, any loss, any revolt? If thou wert a son of Adam, sorrow would be thy lot. Nay, verily, thou art a god!"

"And what sign canst thou show me of my divinity?"

"I am an angel. Mortal man cannot behold an angel, and live."

Then he vanished. Djemschid fell into the snare of pride.

Next day he caused a great fire to be lighted, and he called together all men and said to them, "I am a god, worship me; I created heaven above and earth beneath; and those that refuse to adore me shall be consumed in the fire."

Then from fear of him many obeyed; and the same hour revolt broke out.

There was a man named Beyourasp who stirred up the people, and led a great army against Djemschid, and overcame him, and took from him his kingdom, and sawed the king asunder from the head to the feet.[1]

[1] Tabari, caps. xxxix. xl.

XII.

## LAMECH.

"*Methusael begat Lamech. And Lamech took unto him two wives: the name of the one was Adah, and the name of the other Zillah. And Adah bare Jabal: he was the father of such as dwell in tents, and of such as have cattle. And his brother's name was Jubal: he was the father of all such as handle the harp and organ. And Zillah, she also bare Tubal-cain, an instructor of every artificer in brass and iron: and the sister of Tubal-cain was Naamah. And Lamech said unto his wives, Adah and Zillah, Hear my voice; ye wives of Lamech, hearken unto my speech: for I have slain a man to my wounding, and a young man to my hurt. If Cain shall be avenged seven-fold, truly Lamech seventy and seven-fold.*"[1]

The speech of Lamech points to a tradition unrecorded in the Sacred Text, with which the Israelites were probably well acquainted, and which therefore did not need repetition; or else, there has been a paragraph dropped out of the original text. The speech is sufficiently mysterious to raise our curiosity. Whom had Lamech slain? and why should Lamech be avenged?

The Targums throw no light on the passage, merely paraphrasing it, without supplying the key to the speech of Lamech.[2] But Rabbinic tradition is unanimous on its signification. The book Jasher says that in those days men did not

[1] Gen. iv. 18–24.    [2] Targums, ed. Etheridge, i. p. 173.

love to have children, therefore they gave their wives drink to make them sterile. Zillah had taken this drink, and she was barren till in her old age she bare Tubal-cain and Naamah. Now Lamech became blind in his old age, and he was led about by the boy Tubal-cain. Tubal-cain saw Cain in the distance, and supposing from the horn on his forehead that he was a beast, he said to his father, "Span thy bow and shoot!" Then the old man discharged his arrow, and Cain fell dead.

But when he ascertained that he had slain his great ancestor, he smote his hands together, and in so doing, by accident struck his son and killed him. Therefore his wives were wroth and would have no communication with him. But he appeased them with the words recorded in Genesis.[1] The same story is told in the book of the "Combat of Adam."

Some Jewish writers adopt a tradition that Tubal-cain was not slain, but was severely injured by his father; according to some, he was lamed. Connecting this tradition with his name, a striking analogy springs up between him and the Vulcan of classic antiquity, and the Völundr of Norse mythology. Both were lame, both were forgers of iron, and the names Vulcan and Völundr bear some affinity to Tubal-cain; for, cutting off Tu, we have Balcain or Vulcan. A very learned and exhaustive monograph on Völundr has been written by MM. Depping and Michel.[2]

Tubal is said by Tabari to have discovered the art of fermenting the juice of the grape, as well as that of music. Eblis deceived the young man, who was full of gaiety, and taught him many things, amongst others how to make wine. Tubal took grapes and crushed them, and made must, and let it grow bitter. Then he took it and put it in a glass jug. He made flutes, lutes, cymbals, and drums. When he began to drink the

---

[1] Yaschar, tr. Drach, p. 1092; the same in Midrash Jalkut, c. 38; Midrash, Par. Bereschith, fol. 2; Rabbi Raschi on Genesis; &c. &c.
[2] Véland le Forgeron; Paris, 1833. There is an English translation by Wright.

wine he had made, he jumped and danced. All the sons of Cain looked on, and, pleased with his merriment, they also drank and played on the instruments Tubal had made.[1]

Naamah, the sister of Tubal-cain, became the wife of the devil Schomron, by whom she became the mother of Asmodeus.[2]

[1] Tabari, i. c. xxi.   [2] Eisenmenger, ii. p. 416.

XIII.

## METHUSELAH.

It is related that an angel appeared to Methuselah, who was then aged five hundred years, and lived in the open air, and advised him to build a house. The Patriarch asked how long he had to live. "About five hundred years more," answered the angel. "Then," said Methuselah, "it is not worth taking the trouble for so short a time."[1]

"Methuselah," says the Midrash, "was a thoroughly righteous man. Every word that fell from his lips was superlatively perfect, exhausting the praises of the Lord. He had learnt nine hundred chapters of the Mischna. At his death a frightful thunder was heard, and all beasts burst into tears. He was mourned seven days by men, and therefore the outbreak of the Flood was postponed till the mourning was over."[2]

Eusebius says, "He lived longer than all who had preceded him. He, according to all editions (of the LXX.), lived fifteen years after the Deluge, but where he was preserved through it is uncertain."[3]

But the general opinion of the Jews follows the Midrash. The Rabbi Solomon says, he died seven days before the Flood; and the Pirke of Rabbi Eliezer and the Jalkut confirm this opinion. He is said to have pronounced three hundred and

---

[1] Colin de Plancy, p. 102.
[2] Midrash, fol. 12; so also Targum of Palestine, Etheridge, i. p. 179.
[3] Chron. Græc., ed. Scaliger, Lugd. Batav. 1606, p. 4.

thirty parables to the honour of the Most High. But the origin of this is to be traced to the Cabbalists, who say that, by transposition of the letters of his name, the anagram "He who prophesied in parables" can be read.[1]

He had a sword inscribed with the Schem hammphorasch (the Incommunicable Name), and with it he succeeded in slaying a thousand devils.[2]

[1] Fabricius, i. p. 225.   [2] Eisenmenger, i. p. 651.

XIV.

## NOAH.

THE earth being filled with violence, God resolved on its destruction, but Noah, the just, He purposed to save alive.

On the words of Genesis, "*All flesh had corrupted his way upon the earth,*" the Rabbi Johanan taught that not only was the race of men utterly demoralized, but also all the races of animals.[1] Noah and his family, and one pair of all the beasts of earth, were to be saved in the ark, but of every clean beast seven were to enter in. Falsehood hastened to the ark and asked to be admitted; Noah refused. "I admit the animals only in pairs," said he.

Then Falsehood went away in wrath, and met Injustice, who said—

"Why art thou so sad?"

"I have been refused admittance into the ark, for I am single," said Falsehood; "be thou my companion."

"See, now," answered Injustice, "I take no companionship without prospect of gain."

"Fear not," said Falsehood, "I will spread the toils and thou shalt have the booty."

So they went together to the ark, and Noah was unable to refuse them admission. And when the Flood was passed and the beasts went forth out of the ark, Falsehood said angrily,

[1] Talmud, Tractat. Sanhedrin, fol. 108, col. 1. So also the Book Yaschar, p. 1097.

"I have done my work and have caused evil, but thou hast all the plunder; share with me."

"Thou fool!" answered Injustice, "dost thou forget the agreement? Thine it is to spread the net, mine alone to take the spoil."[1]

At the time of the Deluge the giants were not all drowned, for Og planted his foot upon the fountains of the great deep, and with his hands stopped the windows of heaven, or the water would have risen over his head. The Rabbi Eliezer[2] said that the giants exclaimed, when the Flood broke out, "If all the waters of the earth be gathered together, they will only reach our waists; but if the fountains of the great deep be broken up, we must stamp them down again." And this they did, but God made the waters boiling hot, and it scalded them so that their flesh was boiled and fell off their bones.[3] But what became of Og in the Deluge we learn from the Talmud.[4] He went into the water along with a rhinoceros[5] beside the ark, and clung to it; now the water round the ark was cold, but all the rest was boiling hot. Thus he was saved alive, whereas the other giants perished.

According to another authority, Og climbed on the roof of the ark; and on Noah attempting to dislodge him, he swore that, if allowed to remain there, he and his posterity would be the slaves of the sons of Noah. Thereupon the patriarch yielded. He bored a hole in the side of the vessel, and passed through it every day the food necessary for the giant's consumption.[6]

It is asserted by some Rabbinic writers that the Deluge did not overflow the land of Israel, but was partial; some say the

---

[1] Jalkut, Genesis, fol. 14a.
[2] Jalkut Shimoni, Job. fol. 121, col. 2.
[3] Eisenmenger, i. p. 385. The Targum of Palestine says the water was hot (i. p. 179).
[4] Tractat. Sevachim, fol. 113, col. 2.
[5] Or, a unicorn; the Hebrew word is Reém.
[6] Midrash, fol. 14.

Holy Land was alone left dry, and a rhinoceros had taken refuge on it and so escaped being drowned. But others say that the Land of Israel was submerged, though all agree that the rhinoceros survived without having entered the ark. And they explain the escape of the rhinoceros in this manner. Its head was taken into the ark, and it swam behind the vessel. Now the rhinoceros is a very large animal, and could not be admitted into the ark lest it should swamp it. The Rabbi Jannai says, he saw a young rhinoceros of a day old, and it was as big as Mount Tabor; and Tabor's dimensions are forty miles. Its neck was three miles long, and its head half a mile. It dropped dung, and the dung choked up Jordan. Other commentators object that the head was too large to be admitted into the ark, and suppose that only the tip of its nose was received. But as the ark swayed on the waters, Noah tied the horn of the rhinoceros to the side of the vessel, lest the beast's nose should slip off in a lurch of the ark, and so the creature perish.

All this is from the Talmud.

Let us now turn to some of the Mussulman legends of Noah. His history is briefly related in the Koran, in the chapter entitled "Hud."

"Noah built the ark with our assistance and that of the angels, following the knowledge we revealed to him, and we said to him: Speak no more in behalf of the sinners; they shall all be drowned.

"Whilst Noah was building his ark, all those who passed by mocked him; but he said to them: Though you rail at me now, the time will come when I shall rail at you; for you will learn to your cost, Who it is that punishes the wicked in this world, and reserves for them a further punishment in the world to come."

In the annals of Eutychius of Alexandria, who wrote in Egypt in the tenth century, and who probably quoted from apocryphal documents now perished, we read that, before the

Flood broke out, Noah made a bell of plane wood, about five feet high, which he sounded every day, morning, noon, and evening. When any one asked him why he did so, he replied, "To warn you that God will send a deluge to destroy you all."

Eutychius adds some further particulars.

"Before they entered the ark," says he, "Noah and his sons went to the cave of Elcanuz, where lay the bodies of Adam, Seth, Cainan, Mahalaleel, Jared, Methuselah, and Lamech. He kissed his dead ancestors, and bore off the body of Adam together with precious oblations. Shem bore gold; Ham took myrrh; and Japheth incense. Having gone forth, as they descended the Holy Mount they lifted their eyes to Paradise, which crowned it, and said, with tears, 'Farewell! Holy Paradise, farewell!' and they kissed the stones and embraced the trees of the Holy Mount."[1]

Ibn Abbas, one of the commentators on the Koran, adds, that Noah being in doubt as to the shape he was to give to the ark, God revealed to him that it was to be modelled on the plan of a bird's belly, and that it was to be constructed of teak wood. Noah planted the tree, and in twenty years it grew to such a size that out of it he was able to build the entire ark.[2]

To return to the Koran.

"When the time prescribed for the punishment of men was arrived, and the oven began to boil and vomit, we said to Noah: Take and bring into the ark two couples of every kind of animal, male and female, with all your family, except him who has been condemned by your mouth, and receive the faithful, and even the unbelievers; but few only will enter."

The interpreters of the Koran say that the ark was built in two years. They give it the dimensions mentioned in Genesis: —three stages, that on the top for the birds, the middle one for the men and the provisions, whilst the beasts occupied the

[1] Eutych., Patriarcha Alex., ed. Selden, i. p. 36.
[2] Tabari, p. 108.

hold. The sign of the outburst of the Flood was that water flowed out of the burning oven of Noah's wife. Then all the veins and arteries of the earth broke and spirted out water. He who was excluded was Canaan, the son of Ham, whom he had cursed. But Abulfeda says that it was Jam, a fourth son of Noah, who was excluded from the ark.[1] The Persians say that Ham incurred his father's malediction as well, and, for that, he and his posterity became black and were enslaved; but that Noah, grieved for his son's progeny, prayed God to have mercy on them, and God made the slave to be loved and cherished by his master.

The Koran says, "Noah having entered the ark with his wife (Noema, daughter of Enoch, according to the Yaschar; Noria, according to the Gnostics; Vesta, according to the Cabbalists), and his three sons, Shem, Ham, and Japheth, and their wives, the three daughters of Eliakim, son of Methuselah, he said to those who dwell on the earth, 'Embark in the name of the Lord.'

"And whilst he thus spake, the ark advanced or halted, according to his order, in the name of God."

But the Yaschar says that the ungodly dwellers on the earth, finding the Flood rising, hastened in such crowds to the ark, that they would have overfilled it, had not the lions and other animals within defended the entrance and repulsed them.[2]

According to some Oriental traditions, Noah embarked at Koufah; according to others, near where Babylon was afterwards erected; but some say in India; and some affirm that in the six months during which the Deluge lasted, the ark made the circuit of the world.[3]

Noah, seeing that his grandson Canaan was not on board, called to him, and said, "Embark, my child, and do not remain among the ungodly."

[1] Abulfeda, p. 17.     [2] Yaschar, p. 1100.
[3] Colin de Plancy, p. 110.

But Canaan replied, "I will ascend the mountains, and shall be safe there."

"Nothing can save thee to-day but the mercy of God," said Noah.

Whilst thus speaking, a wave rushed between them and submerged Canaan.

After forty days, the ark swam from one end of the earth to the other, over the highest mountains. Over Mount Kubeis, chosen by God in which to preserve the sacred black stone of the Kaaba, the ark revolved seven times.[1]

Tabari says that Noah had four sons, and that of these Canaan was the youngest, and that the three elder believed in his mission, but his wife and Canaan laughed at his predictions. The animals that were brought into the ark were collected and wafted to it by the wind. When the ass was about to enter, Eblis (Satan) caught hold of its tail. The ass came on slowly; Noah was impatient, and exclamed, "You cursed one, come in quick."

When Eblis was within, Noah saw him, and said, "What right have you in here?"

"I have entered at your invitation," answered the Evil One. "You said, 'Cursed one, come in;' I am the accursed one."

When six months had passed, the ark rested on the surface of the water above Djondi,[2] and the rain ceased to fall, and God said to the earth, "Suck in the water;" and to the sky, "Withhold thy rains." The water abated; and the ark lodged on the top of the mountain.

"There left the ark two sorts of animals which had not entered it—the pig and the cat. These animals did not exist before the Deluge, and God created them in the ark because it was full of filth and human excrements, which caused a great stench. The persons in the ark, not being able to endure any longer the smell, complained to Noah. Then Noah passed his

---

[1] Weil, p. 45. [2] Ararat.

## NOAH.

hand down the back of the elephant, and it evacuated the pig. The pig ate all the dung which was in the ark, and the stench was no more.

"Some time after the rats gave great annoyance. They ate the food, and befouled what they did not eat. Then the voyagers went to Noah, and said to him, You delivered us in our former difficulty, but now we are plagued with rats, which gnaw our garments, eat our victuals, and cover everything with their filth. Then Noah passed his hand down the back of the lion, who sneezed, and the cat leaped out of its nose. And the cat ate the rats.

"When Noah had left the ark, he passed forty days on the mountain, till all the water had subsided into the sea. All the briny water that is there is what remains from the Flood.

"Noah said to the raven, Go and place your foot on the earth and see what is the depth of the water. The raven departed; but, having found a carcase, it remained to devour it, and did not return. Noah was provoked, and he cursed the raven, saying, May God make thee contemptible among men, and let carrion be thy food!

"After that Noah sent forth the dove. The dove departed, and, without tarrying, put her feet in the water. The water of the Flood scalded and pickled the legs of the dove. It was hot and briny, and feathers would not grow on her legs any more, and the skin scaled off. Now, doves which have red and featherless legs are of the sort that Noah sent forth. The dove returning showed her legs to Noah, who said, May God render thee well-pleasing to men! For that reason the dove is dear to men's hearts."[1]

Another version of the story is this. Noah blessed the dove, and since then she has borne a neck-ring of green feathers; but the raven, on the other hand, he cursed, that its flight should be crooked, and never direct like that of other birds.[2] This is also a Jewish legend.[3]

[1] Tabari, c. xli.     [2] Weil, p. 45.     [3] Midrash, fol. 15.

After that, Noah descended the mountain along with the eighty persons who had been saved with him, and he found that not a house was left standing on the face of the earth. Noah built a town consisting of eighty houses,—a house apiece for all who had been saved with him.[1]

Fabricius, in his collection of apocrypha of the Old Testament, has published the prayer that Noah offered daily in the ark, beside the body of Adam, which he bore with him, to bury it on Golgotha.

"O Lord, Thou art excellent in truth, and nothing is great beside Thee; look upon us in mercy; deliver us from this deluge of water for the sake of the pangs of Adam, the first man whom Thou didst make; for the sake of the blood of Abel, the holy one; for the sake of just Seth, in whom Thou didst delight; number us not amongst those who have broken Thy commandments, but cover us with Thy protection, for Thou art our deliverer, and to Thee alone are due the praises uttered by the works of Thy hands from all eternity." And all the children of Noah responded, "Amen, O Lord."[2]

Noah is said to have left the ark on the tenth day of the first month of the Mussulman year, and to have instituted the fast which the Mahommedans observe on that day, to thank God for his deliverance.

According to the Book of Enoch, the water of the Flood was transformed by God into fire, which will consume the world and the ungodly, at the consummation of all things.[3]

The Targum of Palestine says that the dove plucked the leaf she brought to Noah from off a tree on the Mount of Olives.[4]

The Book Jasher supplies an omission in Genesis. In Genesis it is said of Lamech, on the birth of Noah, "*He called his name Noah; saying, This same shall comfort us concerning our work and toil of our hands, because of the ground which the Lord hath cursed;*"[5] but Noah signifies *rest*, not *comfort*. The Book

---

[1] Tabari, p. 113.
[2] Fabricius, i. pp. 74, 243.
[3] Ed. Dillmann, c. 67.
[4] Ed. Etheridge, i. p. 182.
[5] Gen. v. 20.

Jasher says that Methuselah called the child Noah, *rest*, because the land rested from the curse; but Lamech called him Menahem, *comfort*, for the reason given in the text of Genesis. The sacred writer has given one name with the signification of the other.[1]

[1] In the Midrash Rabba, this want of connection between the name and the signification is remarked upon, and Solomon Jarki in his commentary says that, for the meaning assigned, the name ought to have been, not Noah, but Menahem.

## XV.

## HEATHEN LEGENDS OF THE DELUGE.

ARARAT has borne this name for three thousand years. We read in the Book of Genesis that "*the ark rested, in the seventh month, on the seventeenth day of the month, upon the mountains of Ararat.*" In passages of the Old Testament, as in Isaiah xxxvii. 38 and 2 Kings xix. 37, mention is made of a land, in Jeremiah li. 27 of a kingdom, of Ararat; and we are likewise informed by Moses of Chorene, the first authority among Armenian writers, that an entire country bore this name after an ancient Armenian king, Arai the Fair, who lived about 1750 years before Christ. He fell in a bloody battle with the Babylonians on a plain in Armenia, called after him Arai-Arat, the Fall of Arai.

Before this event the country bore the name of Amasia, from its sovereign, Amassis, the sixth in descent from Japheth, who gave the name of Massis to the mountain. This is still the only name by which it is known to the Armenians; for, though it is called Ararat in the Armenian edition of the Old Testament, yet the people call it Massis, and know no other name for it. The Mussulmans call it Agridagh, the strong mountain. The name by which it is known to the Persians is Kuhi-Nuh, the mountain of Noah, or Saad-dagh, the Blessed Mountain.[1]

[1] Buttmann, Ueber der Mythus d. Sündfluth, Berlin, 1819; Lüken, Die Traditionen des Menschengeschlechts, Münster, 1856; Bryant, Of the Deluge, in Ancient Mythology, London, 1775, &c.

## THE DELUGE.

But tradition is not at one as to the peak on which the ark rested, or from which Noah descended, as we shall presently see. Ararat is 17,210 feet in altitude above the sea, and 14,320 feet above the plain of the Araxes. On the northeastern slope of the mountain, even from a distance, may be seen a deep, gloomy chasm, which gives the appearance as if the mountain had been rent asunder at the top : this was probably at some remote period the volcanic vent, for the mountain is composed of tufa, scoria, and erupted matter. It shoots up in one rigid crest, and then sweeps down towards Little Ararat, the second summit, which stands 13,000 feet above the sea.[1]

The people of the neighbourhood point to a step on the mountain side, covered with perpetual snow and glacier, and where, say they, the ark rested; and to a town near Ararat named Naktschiwan, or "the first outgoing" of Noah from the ark. This etymological interpretation is probably as questionable as that of Ararat given by Moses of Chorene; it is true the city is ancient, for it was severely injured by an earthquake in the reign of Astyages the Median, in the sixth century before Christ. It is called Naxuana by Josephus,[2] and he says it was so called because there Noah first descended from the ark, and that remains of the ark were there to be seen carefully preserved. And there, says the Armenian historian Vartan, is also the tomb of Noah. Nicolas of Damascus, in his History of Syria, Berosus the ancient Babylonian writer, and other heathen historians, tell a similar tale; and we learn that relics of the ark were distributed thence, and were regarded with the utmost reverence, as amulets.

Nicolas of Damascus, who wrote in the reign of Augustus, says, "There is beyond the Minyadian land a great mountain in Armenia, Baris by name (perhaps for Masis), on which, as the tradition says, some one sailing over it in an ark, lodged on the topmost peak. The remains of the wood continued to

[1] Parrot, Journey to Ararat, English Trans. Lond. 1845.
[2] Joseph. Antiq., i. 3; see also Ptolem. Geogr. vi. 2.

exist long. Perhaps this may be the same as he of whom Moses, the Jewish historian, has written."[1]

The story quoted by Eusebius from an ancient writer named Molo, gives a form of the Syrian tradition. "After the Deluge, the man who with his sons escaped the flood, went out of Armenia, after he had been driven out of his inheritance by the violence of the natives. He came thence into the mountains of Syria, which were then uninhabited."[2] And with this agrees a curious allusion in Lucian, who was himself a Syrian. He says that there was in Syria, in the city Hierapolis, a religious festival, and a very ancient temple, connected "with the popular story of Deucalion the Scythian, who lived at the time of the great Deluge." It is curious that he should give to the Syrian Noah the Greek name, and that he should speak of him as not a native, but as coming from the East, from Scythia. He says: "Of this Deucalion have I heard in Greece, what the Greeks relate. The story is this: The present race of men is not the first, for that perished. This is the second race which sprang from Deucalion, and was very numerous. The earlier generation was very evil, and violated the Divine law. They neither kept oaths nor showed hospitality; they took not the stranger in, nor protected him when he sought protection; therefore a terrible destruction fell upon them. Much water gushed out of the earth, great rains poured down, and the sea rose and overwhelmed the earth. Deucalion alone of all men was preserved to another generation on account of his wisdom and piety. He was thus saved. He went into a great ark which he had built, along with his wife and children. Then came to him, pair by pair, cows, horses, lions, serpents, and all kinds of animals which are nourished on earth, and he took them all in. They did not hurt him, for Zeus ordained a great friendship among them. So they all sailed in the ark as long as the flood lasted. This is the Greek story of Deucalion.

"But very wonderful is the confirmation of the history as it

[1] Joseph. Antiq., i. 4.   [2] Euseb. Præp. Evang. ix. 19.

is related in Hierapolis. In the neighbourhood of that city a great chasm opened which engulphed all the waters of the Flood. Thereupon Deucalion erected altars, and dedicated a temple to Here (Atergatis) over the chasm. I have seen this; it is very small: whether it was once large but has since become smaller, I cannot say; but I saw that it was small. For the confirmation of the history the following takes place: twice in the year the sea-water is brought into the temple. Not only do the priests bear it, but all Syria and Arabia, and many from beyond Euphrates, come and carry water. They pour it out in the temple; then it runs down into the chasm, and, though it may be very small, it takes in all the water poured into it. This they do, say they, because Deucalion instituted this rite as a memorial of his deliverance, and of the mercy of God."[1]

Equally fully has the Babylonian tradition reached us from the Chaldee history of the old priest of Bel, Berosus (B.C. 260). The Chaldees had placed ten kings at the head of this mystic history, which answer to the ten generations in Genesis before the Flood. The last of these patriarchs was called Xisuthrus, who is the same as the Biblical Noah. Berosus relates the story of the Deluge thus: "Under the reign of Xisuthrus there was a great flood. Kronos (*i.e.* Bel) appeared to Xisuthrus in a dream, and warned him that all men would be destroyed by a deluge on the 15th of the month Dæsios, and he commanded him to write down all the learning and science of men, and to hide it in the sun-city Siparis, and then to build a ship and to enter it along with his family and relatives and nearest friends, and to take into it with him food and drink, and beasts and winged fowl. When he was asked whither he was about to sail, he was bidden reply: To the gods, to pray them that men may prosper. He obeyed; and made an ark five stadia long and two wide, laid in what was commanded, and sailed with his wife and child and relatives. When the flood abated,

[1] Lucian, De Dea Syra, c. 12, 13.

Xisuthrus sent out a bird which, as it found no food nor ground on which to perch, returned to the ship. After a day, he sent out another bird; this came back with mud on its feet. The third bird he sent out did not return. So Xisuthrus knew that the land appeared, and he broke a hole in the ship and saw that the ship was stranded on a mountain; so he disembarked with his wife and daughter and steersman; and when he had adored the earth, raised an altar, and offered to the gods, he vanished. Those who remained in the ship also went out, when they saw that Xisuthrus did not return, to seek Xisuthrus, and they called him by name. But Xisuthrus appeared again no more, only his voice was heard bidding them fear God, and telling them that he was taken to dwell with the gods, because he was pious. The same honour was accorded to his wife and daughter and to the steersman." This refers to their being set in the sky as constellations: Xisuthrus as the water-bearer, the virgin, and steersman still occupy their places there. "He bade them," continues Berosus, "return to Babylon, and, as Fate decreed, take his writings out of Siparis, and from them instruct men. The place where they found themselves was Armenia. Some fragments of the ship remain on the mountains of the Kordyæans in Armenia, and some take away particles and use them as amulets."[1]

Eusebius has preserved a fragment of another Babylonian writer, Abydenos, which gives the same story precisely.[2]

Another Chaldee tradition preserved by Cassian is that, before the Flood, Ham concealed in the ground treatises of witchcraft and alchemy, and that, when the water abated, he recovered them.[3] According to Berosus also, Xisuthrus had three sons,—Zerovanos, Titan, and Japetosthes. Zerovanos is the same as Zoroaster.

[1] Georg. Syncellus, Chronographia, p. 29, B., ed. Bonn; or Cory's Ancient Fragments, p. 26 et seq.
[2] Præp. Evang. ix. 12; see also S. Cyril contra Julian, i.
[3] Bochart, Geogr. Sacra, p. 231.

## THE DELUGE.

From Phrygia also come to us traces of a Diluvian tradition. A number of coins of Apamea, a city of Phrygia, between the rivers Mæander and Marsyas, of the period of Septimius Severus and the following emperors, possibly bear reference to this event.[1] One, a coin of Philip, bears on the reverse something like a box, containing a man and woman; on the panel of the box, under the man, is written "Noe," the dove is bringing the olive branch, and the raven is seated on the edge of the box above the head of the female figure. The same two persons are also represented on dry land, with the right hand uplifted in the attitude of prayer. Another coin with the same subject, on the reverse has, inscribed on the ark, NHTΩN.

To elucidate these coins, reference is made to a passage in the Sibylline Oracles to this effect: "In Phrygia lies steep, to be seen from afar, a mountain, named Ararat. . . . Therefrom streams the river Marsyas; but on its crest rested the ark (κιβωτός) when the rain abated."[2] As the ancient name of Apamea seems to have been Kibotos, it is not unlikely that the Sibylline writer mixed together in those lines the Mosaic and the Phrygian traditions.

It must, however, be admitted that it is quite as probable that the box represents a temple, and the two figures tutelary deities, and that the "Noe" is a contraction for "Neocoros," the most important title assumed by Greek cities, and often recorded on their coins.

The ancient Persian account in the Bundehesch is this:—
"Taschter (the spirit ruling the waters) found water for thirty days and thirty nights upon the earth. Every water-drop was as big as a bowl. The earth was covered with water the height of a man. All idolaters on earth died through the rain; it penetrated all openings. Afterwards a wind from heaven divided the water and carried it away in clouds, as souls bear

---

[1] Ekhel, Doctrina Numm. Vet. iii. p. 132 et seq.; see also Bryant's New System of Ancient Mythology, Lond. 1775, i. note 3.
[2] Orac. Sibyll, i. v. 260, 265-7. Ed. Fiedlieb.

bodies; then Ormuzd collected all the water together and placed it as a boundary to the earth, and thus was the great ocean formed."[1]

The ancient Indian tradition is, "that in the reign of the sun-born monarch Satyavrata, the whole earth was drowned, and the whole human race destroyed by a flood, except the pious prince himself, the seven Rishis and their several wives." This general *pralaya*, or destruction, is the subject of the first Purana, or sacred poem; and the story is concisely told in the eighth book of the Bhagavata, from which the following is an abridged extract:—" The demon Hayagriva having purloined the Vedas from Brahma whilst he was reposing, the whole race of men became corrupt, except the seven Rishis and Satyavrata. This prince was performing his ablutions in the river Critamala, when Vishnu appeared to him in the shape of a small fish, and after several augmentations of bulk in different waters, was placed by Satyavrata in the ocean, when he thus addressed his amazed votary:—'In seven days all creatures who have offended me shall be destroyed by a deluge; but thou shalt be secured in a capacious vessel miraculously formed. Take, therefore, all kinds of medicinal herbs and esculent grain for food, and, together with the seven holy men, your respective wives, and pairs of all animals, enter the ark without fear; then shalt thou know God face to face, and all thy questions shall be answered.' Saying this, he disappeared; and, after seven days, the ocean began to overflow the coasts, and the earth to be flooded by constant showers, when Satyavrata, meditating on the Deity, saw a large vessel moving on the waters: he entered it, having in all respects conformed to the instructions of Vishnu, who, in the form of a large fish, suffered the vessel to be tied with a great sea-serpent, as with a cable, to his measureless horn. When the deluge had ceased, Vishnu slew the demon and recovered the Vedas, and instructed Satyavrata in divine knowledge."[2]

[1] Bundehesch, 7.
[2] On the Chronology of the Hindus, by Sir W. Jones; Asiatic Researches, ii. pp. 116-7.

The Mahabharata says that the boat containing Manu and his seven companions rested on Mount Naubhandanam, the highest peak of the Himalayas; and the name Naubhandanam signifies "ships stranding."[1]

The Greek traditions are not early, and were probably borrowed from Semitic sources. We have seen the story told by Lucian in his book "De Dea Syra," but in his "Timon" he follows the more authentic Greek legend, and makes Deucalion escape in a little skiff (consequently without the animals), and land on Mount Lycoris.

We have also the same catastrophe somewhat differently related by Ovid. The world he represents "as confederate in crime," and doomed therefore to just punishment. Jupiter sends down rain from heaven, and rivers and seas gushing forth from their caves gather over the earth's surface, and sweep mankind away. Deucalion and his wife alone, borne in a little skiff, are stranded on the top of Parnassus. By degrees, the waters subside: the only surviving pair inquire of the gods how they may again people the desert earth. They are ordered, with veiled heads, to throw behind them the bones of their great mother. Half doubtful as to the meaning of the oracle, they throw behind them stones, which are immediately changed into men and women, and the earth spontaneously produces the rest of the animal creation.[2]

Apollodorus relates the matter thus:—"When Zeus determined to destroy the brazen race, Deucalion, by the advice of Prometheus, made a great ark, λάρναξ, and put into it all necessary things, and entered it with Pyrrha. Zeus then, pouring down heavy rains from heaven, overwhelmed the greater part of Greece, so that all men perished except a few who fled to the highest mountains. He floated nine days and nights in the sea of waters, and at last stopped on Mount Parnassus. Then Zeus sent Hermes to ask him what he wished, and he

---

[1] Bopp, Die Sündfluth; Berlin, 1829, p. 9.
[2] Ovid. Metam. i. 240 et seq.

solicited that mankind might be made again. Zeus bade him throw stones over his head, from which men should come, and said that those cast by Pyrrha should be turned into women."

Stephanus of Byzantium says that the tradition was that after the surface of the earth became dry, Zeus ordered Prometheus and Athene to make images of clay in the form of men; and when they were dry, he called the winds and made them breathe into each, and rendered them vital: and thus the earth after the Flood was repeopled.[1] Diodorus says, "In the Deluge, which happened in the time of Deucalion, almost all flesh died."[2]

The Chinese begin their dynasties with Jao, the last of the old race, whose words are thus recorded in the Schu-Kiug:— "The mighty waters of the flood spread themselves out, and overflowed, and drowned everything. The mountains disappeared in the deep, and the hills were buried beneath them. The foaming billows seemed to threaten heaven. All people were drowned."[3] An ancient inscription, which the Chinese attribute to Yu, the third patriarch after the Flood, and which at least dates from before Christ, refers to this event:—"The illustrious Emperor Jao said, sighing, 'Companions and counsellors! The great and little territories up to the mountain's peak, the homes of birds and wild beasts, were overflowed far and wide. Long had I forgotten my home; now I rest upon the mountain top of Jo-lu. . . . The trouble is over, and the misfortune is at an end; the streams of the south flow, clothes and food are before us. The world is at rest, and the flying rain cannot again destroy us.'"[4]

In one of the writings of the disciples of Tao-tse, the tradition takes a fuller form. Kung-Kung, a bad spirit, enraged at having been overcome in war, gave such a blow against one of the pillars of the sky with his head that he broke it; and the vault

---

[1] Steph. Byzant., s. voce Ικονιον.
[2] Diod. Sicul. lib. i.
[3] Mém. concernant les Chinois, i. p. 157.
[4] Klaproth, Inschrift. des Yu; Halle, 1811, p. 29.

of heaven fell in, and a tremendous flood overwhelmed the earth. But Niu-Noa overcame the water with wood, and made a boat to save himself, which could go far; and he polished a stone of five colours—the rainbow—and therewith he fastened the heavens, and lifted them up on a tortoise-shell. Then he killed the black dragon Kong-Kong, and choked the holes in heaven with the ashes of a pumpkin.[1] In the story of Jao there is also a faint trace of his connection with the rainbow, for he is said to have eyebrows coloured and shaped like rainbows.[2]

The Kamskadales say, "that in the remote ages when their great ancestor and God, Kutka, lived in Kamschatka, there was a mighty deluge. Many men were drowned therein, but some tried to save themselves in boats, but the waves overwhelmed them. Those who were saved were rescued on great rafts made of trees bound together, to which they retreated, taking food and their property with them. And that they might not drift out to sea, they anchored themselves with great stones, which they tied to the edges and let down into the water. And when the flood abated, they rested on the top of a high mountain."[3]

A Lapp tradition is that God once submerged the world, saving only one brother and sister alive, whom He placed on Mount Passeware. When all the water disappeared, the children separated to wander over the earth, and see whether they alone remained alive. They met after three years, and then separated again, for they recognized one another as brother and sister. After three years they met, but turned their backs on one another once more for the same reason. Again they met after the lapse of three years, and again they parted; but when they met again, after three years' further absence, they no longer recognized each other, and so they took one another in marriage; and of them all generations of men are come.[4]

[1] Mém. concernant les Chinois, ix. p. 383.
[2] Mart. Martinii, Hist. Sin. p. 26.
[3] Steller, Beschreibung v. Kamschatka; Frankf. 1774, p. 273.
[4] Serres, Kosmoganie des Moses. übersetzt von F. X. Stech, p. 149.

Among the Kelts, the Deluge formed a prominent feature, and the ark was connected with their most sacred religious rites.

A Welsh legend is this:—"One of the most dreadful of events was the outbreak of Llyn Llion, the sea of seas, which overwhelmed the world and drowned all men except Dwyan and Dwyvach, who escaped in a bare boat and colonized Britain. This ship was one of the three masterpieces of Hu, and was built by the heavenly lord, Reivion; and it received into it a pair of every kind of beast when the Llyn Llion burst forth." This Reivion is the same as Hu Cadarn, the discoverer of the vine; and it is said of him that "he built the ark laden with fruit, and it was stayed up in the water, and carried forward by serpents;" and of the rainbow it was said, that the Woman of the silver wheel, Arianrhod, to control the wizards of night and evil spirits of tempest, and out of love to the Britons, "wove the stream of the rainbow,—a stream which drives the storm from the earth, and makes its former destruction stay far from it, throughout the world's circle."[1]

The Norse legend in the younger Edda is, "Bör's sons (Odin, Vilj, and Ve) slew the giant Ymir; and when he fell, so much blood (in poetic phraseology Ymir's blood signified water) ran out of the wounds, that the whole race of the giants was drowned in it, except one, who with his family escaped; this one is called Bergelmr. He got into a boat along with his wife, and was thus saved."[2]

The Lithuanian myth was this:—When Pramzimas, the most high God, looked out of his heavenly house upon the world through a window, he saw that it was filled with violence. Then he sent Wind and Water to devastate the earth, and this they did for twenty days and nights. Pramzimas looked on, and as he looked on, he ate nuts at his window, and threw the

---

[1] Davies, Mythology of the British Druids, London, 1809; and Celtic Researches, London, 1844: curious works on the Arkite worship and traditions of the Kelts.
[2] The prose Edda; Mallet, Northern Antiq., ed. Bohn, p. 404.

shells down. One shell fell on the top of a mountain, and some men, women, and beasts scrambled into it and were saved alive, while all the rest of the inhabitants of the world were drowned. When the flood drained away, the pairs in the nutshell left it, and were scattered over the earth. Only one aged couple remained, and they complained; then God sent them the rainbow to console them, and bade them jump over the bones of the earth. They jumped nine times, and nine pairs of living human beings started to life, and founded the nine races of Lithuanian blood.[1]

Among the negroes of Africa, traditions are faint, or have been little sought after and collected. The Jumala negroes say that once when the earth was full of cruelty and wickedness, the god Til destroyed it with fire, and that one man alone was saved alive, named Musikdgen, *i.e.* the mountain chief, because he was found without blame.

In America the crop of traditions is abundant.

The Kolosches, living in Russian America, say that the first dweller on the earth was Kitkhughia-si, and that he resolved to destroy all his children who sinned against him. Thereupon he brought a flood over the land, and all perished save a few who escaped in boats to the tops of mountains, where, say they, the remains of the boats, and the ropes which fastened them, remain to be seen.[2]

Among the Dog-rib Indians, Sir John Franklin found the story much more complete; and as this tribe lives near the Polar Sea, far from any mission stations, it is scarcely possible that the story can have been derived from Christian teachers. They say that Tschäpiwih, their great ancestor, lived on a track between two seas. He built a weir, and caught fish in such abundance that they choked the watercourse, and the water overflowed the earth. Tschäpiwih with his family entered his

---

[1] Grimm, Deutsche Mythol. ; Göttingen, 1854, p. 545.
[2] The same story precisely is told by the closely allied race of the Chippewas: Atherne Jones, Traditions of the North American Indians, London, 1830, ii. p. 9 et seq.

canoe, and took with him all kinds of beasts and birds. The land was covered for many days; at last Tschäpiwih could bear it no longer, so he sent out the beaver to look for the earth. But the beaver was drowned. Then he sent out the musk-rat, which had some difficulty in returning, but it had mud on its paws. Tschäpiwih was glad to see the earth, and moulded it between his fingers, till it became an island on the surface of the water, on which he could land.[1]

The Pacullies, on the west coast of New Georgia, say that at the Deluge one man and one woman were saved by escaping into a cave; and they add that when the earth was drowned, a water rat dived for it and brought it to the surface again.[2]

A Caddoque tradition is, that Sakechah was a great hunter. One night he saw in vision the Master of Life, who spoke to the dreamer these words:—

"The world is getting very wicked, Sakechah."

"I know it," answered the hunter.

"I hear no longer the voices of men supplicating me for favours; they no longer thank me for what I send them. I must sweep, wash, and purify the earth; I must destroy all living creatures from off the face of it."

Then Sakechah said, "What have I done, Master of Life, that I should be involved in this general destruction?"

The Master answered, "No, Sakechah, thou hast been a good servant; I will except thee from the general doom. Go now, cut thee a hemlock, knock off the cones, and bring them, together with the trunk and leaves, to the bottom of the hill Wecheganawan. Burn them in a fire made of the dry branches of the oak, kindled with the straw of wild rice. When the heap is reduced to ashes, take the ashes and strew them in a circle round the hill. Nothing need be gathered within the circle, for the living creatures will of themselves retreat to it for safety; but when this is done, take the trunk of the hem-

[1] Lütke, Voyage autour du Monde, i. p. 189.
[2] Braunschweig, Die alten amerik. Denkmäler; Berlin, 1840, p. 18.

lock, and strike it into the earth at the spot where the large tuft of grass is growing on the barren hill. There lies the great fountain of waters; and when the staff is struck into the earth the fountain shall burst forth, and the earth be swept and washed and purified by the great deluge that shall overwhelm it. Sakechah and his family shall alone, of all the inhabitants of the earth, be saved; and the creatures he assembles around him on the hill Wecheganawan be alone those exempted from the all-sweeping destruction."

The hunter obeyed. He took the staff and stuck it deep into the earth at the place indicated, and the great fountain was broken up, and the waters burst forth in a mighty volume. Slowly the element began to cover the earth, while the hunter and his family looked on. Now the low grounds appeared but as they appear in the season of showers; here a little water, and there a little water; soon they became one vast sheet. Now a little hill sank from view, then the tops of the trees disappeared; again a tall hill hid its head. At length the waves rose so high that Sakechah could see nothing more; he stood as it were in a well. The waters were piled up on every side of him, restrained from harming him, or his, or the beasts that had clustered around him, by the magic belt of hemlock ashes.

"Sakechah!" said the Master of Life, "when the moon is exactly over thy head, she will draw the waters on to the hill. She is angry with me because I scourged a comet. I cannot prevent her revenge unless I destroy her, and that I may not do, as she is my wife. Therefore bid every living creature that is on the hill take off the nail from the little finger of his right hand, if a man; if a bird, or beast, of the right foot or claw. When each has done this, bid him blow in the hollow of the nail with the right eye shut, saying these words, 'Nail become a canoe, and save me from the wrath of the moon.' The nail will become a large canoe, and in this canoe will its owner be safe."

The Great Spirit was obeyed, and shortly every creature was

floating in a boat on the surface of the water. And, lest they should be dispersed, Sakechah bound them together by thongs of buffalo-hide.

They continued floating for a long time, till at last Sakechah said, "This will not do—we must have land. Go," said he to a raven that sat in his canoe near him, "fetch me a little earth from the bottom of the abyss. I will send a female, because women are quicker and more searching than men."

The raven, proud of the praise bestowed on her sex, left her tail feathers at home, and dived into the abyss. She was gone a long time, but, notwithstanding her being a woman, she returned baffled of her object. Whereupon Sakechah said to the otter, "My little man, I will send you to the bottom, and see if your industry and perseverance will enable you to accomplish what has been left undone by the wit and cunning of the raven." So the otter departed upon his dangerous expedition. He accomplished his object. When he again appeared on the earth, he held in his paw a lump of black mud. This he gave into the hands of Sakechah; and the Great Master bade him divide the lump into five portions; that which came out of the middle of the lump he was commanded to mould into a cake and to cast into the water: he did so, and it became dry land, on which he could disembark; and the earth thus formed was repeopled from his time. No matter whether the men of the earth be red or white, all are descended from Sakechah.[1]

The Iroquois tell a very similar story, differing from the above in merely few trivial particulars. According to the tradition of the Knistineaux on the Upper Missouri, all men perished in the Deluge except one woman, who caught the leg of a bird which carried her to the top of a rock, where she was confined of twins, of whom the earth was peopled.[2]

[1] Atherne Jones, Traditions of the N. American Indians, ii. 21-33.
[2] Catlin, Letters and Notes on the Manners, &c., of the N. American Indians; London, 1841.

The Appalachian tribe in Florida is a relic of a more ancient nation than the North American Indian tribes. They relate that the lake Theomi burst its bounds, and overflowed the earth, and stood above the top of the highest mountains, saving only the peak Oldamy, on which stood a temple to the sun. Those men who had succeeded in reaching this temple were saved, but all the rest of mankind perished.[1]

According to the Cherokees, a dog foresaw the destruction that was coming on the earth. It went every day to the bank of a river and howled; and when its master rebuked it, it revealed to him what was about to take place. The man therefore built a boat and entered it with his family, and he alone of all mankind was saved.[2]

If we turn to Central America, we find that there also traditions of the Flood abounded.

The ancient inhabitants of Mexico related the event as follows:—

There was a great deluge which destroyed all men and beasts, save Coxcox and his wife Chichequetzal, who escaped in a cyprus trunk and landed on Mount Colhuacan, where they became parents of many children, who, however, were all dumb. Then appeared a dove, which seated itself on a high tree, and taught them language. But as none of them understood the speech of the other, they separated and dispersed over the world. Fifteen heads of families, however, had the good fortune to speak the same language. These lived together in the same place, but at last they moved, and after 104 years of wanderings they settled in Aztlan. Thence they journeyed to Chiapultepeque, and then returned to the Mount Colhuacan and settled in Mexico.[3]

There was a story of similar description connected with the ancient city of Cholula in the modern province of Puebla.

[1] Mayer, Mytholog. Taschenbuch; Weimar, 1811, p. 245.
[2] Schoolcraft, Notes on the Iroquois; New York, 1847, p. 358.
[3] Müller, Geschichte des amerikanischen Urreligionen, Basle, 1855, p. 515; Lüken, Die Traditionem des Menschengeschlechts, p. 223.

"Before the great flood in the year 4,008 after the creation of the world, the land Anaknac (Mexico) was peopled with giants. All those who did not perish, with the exception of seven, escaped into holes, and were transformed into fish. When the deluge was over, one of these giants, Xelhuaz by name, the builder, went to Cholula, and built a pyramid on Mount Tlalok, to commemorate his having been saved thereon along with his six brothers."[1]

The inhabitants of Mechoacan related that, on account of the iniquity of men, a flood was sent to sweep them all away; but a priest, named Tezbi, along with his wife and children, were saved in a box of wood into which they had entered along with all kinds of seeds and animals. After some time Tezbi, wearying of his confinement, sent forth the vulture, which however did not return to him; then he sent forth other birds, but they did not come back; finally, he sent out the Colibri, which returned with a branch in its beak.[2] And of this event they had paintings in their temples which they showed to the white men who arrived amongst them.

The Indians in Cuba told a similar story, so did those at St. Domingo and the Antilles.[3]

Nor is South America without a rich crop of similar legends. Humboldt says, "This belief (in a deluge) is not found merely among the Tamanaks, but is a portion of a whole system of historical traditions of which the scattered accounts are to be gathered from the Maipures of the Great Cataract, the Indians of Rio-Crevato, which pours into the Cauca, and almost from all the races in the Upper Orinoko."[4]

This is the tradition of the Tamanaks. "At the time of our ancestors the whole earth was overflowed. Then two persons alone were saved, a man and a woman, who remained on

---

[1] Humboldt, Anh. des Cordilleren, i. p. 42.
[2] Antonio de Herrera, Hist. general de los Hechos, &c.; Madrid, 1601, iii. c. 10. [3] Compare Lüken and Müller.
[4] Humboldt, Reise in die Aequinoctial Gegenden, iii. pp. 406-7.

Mount Tamanaku, which is not far from the Cucivero river, where our ancestors formerly dwelt. They lamented sore over the loss of their friends and relations, and as they wandered sadly about the mountain they heard a voice which told them to cast the kernels of the nuts of the *Palma Mauritia* backwards over their shoulders. They did so, and out of the nuts cast by the woman rose females, and out of those cast by the man sprang males."[1]

The Peruvians related that their first king and founder of their nation, Manco Capak, along with his wife Mama Ocllo, after the great deluge left their land, and came from the holy island in the lake Titicaca, on which the sun cast its first beam when the flood drained away.[2]

A Brazilian legend is that the Evil Spirit Arbomoku, and the spirits of the air, made a compact together to destroy mankind. The former opened all the fountains of the earth, the latter poured the clouds upon the ground and inundated it, so that only one mountain-top appeared above the water, and on that took refuge two persons, a brother and a sister, from whom all the new generations sprang.[3]

---

[1] Nachrichten aus dem Lande Guiana, v. Salvator Gili; Hamb., 1785, p. 440-1, quoted by Lüken.
[2] Garcilasso de la Vega, Hist. des Yncas; Amst., i. pp. 73 and 326.
[3] Ausland, Jan. 1845, No. 1.

## XVI.

## THE PLANTING OF THE VINE.

BOWED under his toil, dripping with perspiration, stood the patriarch Noah, labouring to break the hard clods. All at once Satan appeared and said to him,—

"What new undertaking have you in hand? What new fruit do you expect to extract from these clods?"

"I plant the grape," answered the patriarch.

"The grape! proud plant, most precious fruit! joy and delight to men! Your labour is great; will you allow me to assist you? Let us share the labour of producing the vine."

The patriarch in a fit of exhaustion consented.

Satan hastened, got a lamb, slaughtered it, and poured its blood over the clods of earth. "Thence shall it come," said Satan, "that those who taste of the juice of the grape, shall be soft-spirited and gentle as this lamb."

But Noah sighed; Satan continued his work; he caught a lion, slew that, and poured the blood upon the soil prepared for the plant. "Thence shall it come," said he, "that those who taste the juice of the grape shall be strong and courageous as the lion."

Noah shuddered. Satan continued his work; he seized a pig and slaughtered it, and drenched the soil with its blood. "Thence shall it come," said he, "that those who drink of the juice of the grape in excess, shall be filthy, degraded, and bestial as the swine."[1]

[1] Jalkut Genesis, fol. 16a.

# THE VINE.

The Mussulman tradition is somewhat similar.

"When Ham had planted the vine, Satan watered it with the blood of a peacock. When it thrust forth leaves, he sprinkled it with the blood of an ape; when it formed grapes, he drenched it with the blood of a lion; when the grapes were ripe, he watered it with the blood of a swine.

"The vine, watered by the blood of these four animals, has assumed these characters. The first glass of wine makes a man animated, his vivacity great, his colour is heightened. In this condition he is like the peacock. When the fumes of the liquor rise into his head, he is gay, leaps and gambols as an ape. Drunkenness takes possession of him, he is like a furious lion. When it is at its height, he is like the swine: he falls and grovels on the ground, stretches himself out, and goes to sleep."[1]

Mohammed, to justify his forbidding his disciples to drink wine, cites the history of the two angels, Arot and Harot.

"God," says he, "charged them with a commission on the earth. A young lady invited them to dinner, and they found the wine so good that they got drunk. They then remarked that their hostess was beautiful, and they were filled with love which they declared to her. This lady, who was prudent, replied that she would only listen to their protestations when she knew the words by which they were enabled to ascend to heaven. When she had learned these words, she mounted to the throne of God, who, as a reward for her virtue, transformed her into a shining star (the Morning Star), and condemned the two drunken angels to await the day of judgment, suspended by their heels in the well of Babel, near Bagdad, which Mussulman pilgrims visit."

According to Tabari,[2] Ham, for having laughed at his father's drunkenness, was cursed by Noah, that his skin should become black, as well as all the fruits which were to grow in the land he should inhabit, and thus the purple grape arose. It was

[1] Colin de Plancy, p. 121.  [2] Tabari, i. c. xli.

the white grape that Ham transplanted, but it blackened in his hands.

Abulfaraj relates that after the Deluge, Noah divided the habitable world between his sons. He gave to Ham the country of the Black, to Shem that of the Brown, and to Japheth that of the Red.[1] Noah also, he continues, said to his son Shem, "When I am dead, take the bier of our father Adam from the ark, and, together with your son Melchizedek, who is a priest of the Most High, go with the body of Adam whither an angel shall guide you."

This they did; and an angel directed them to mount Breitalmakdes (Jerusalem), where they deposited the bier on a certain hill, and instantly it sank out of their sight into the ground. Then Shem returned to his home, but not so Melchizedek, who remained to guard the body of Adam: and he built there a city called Jerusalem, and he was called Melek Salim, the King of Peace, and there he spent the rest of his life in the worship of God; he touched not women, nor shed blood, but offered to God oblations of bread and wine.[2]

Eutychius, the Egyptian patriarch of Alexandria, in his Annals, which are rife with Oriental traditions, gives a fuller account of the same incident.

When Noah was near his death, he bade Shem take the body of Adam, and go with Melchizedek, son of Peleg, whither the angel of the Lord should lead. "And," said he, "thou shalt enjoin on Melchizedek to fix his habitation there, to take to him no wife, and to spend his life in acts of devotion, for God has chosen him to preserve His true worship. He shall build himself no house, nor shall he shed blood of beast, or bird, or any animal; nor shall he offer there any oblation save bread and wine; and let the skins of lions be his only vesture; he shall remain alone there; he shall not clip his hair, or pare his nails; for he is a priest of the Most High. The angel

---

[1] Hist. Dynastiarum, ed. Pocock; Oxon., 1663, p. 9.
[2] Ibid., p. 10.

of God shall go before you, till ye come to the place where ye shall bury the body of Adam, and know that that place is the middle of the world." Now Noah died on Wednesday, at the second hour, in the second month of Ayar, which is the same as Bashnes, in the nine hundred and fiftieth year of his age. And this year Shem was aged forty-five. The sons of Noah buried him, and bewailed him forty days.[1]

The wife of Noah is said by some to have been called Bath-Enos, or the daughter of Enos; but the Rabbi Gedaliah says her name was Noema; others say it was Tethiri, or Tithœa, the nurse of men, as Eve was the mother of men. The Gnostics called her Noria. She is, however, generally supposed by the Rabbis to have been Naamah, the sister of Tubal-cain.[2] But Eutychius, of Alexandria, says she was called Haical, and was the daughter of Namus, son of Enoch; and that the wives of Shem, Ham, and Japheth were the three daughters of Methuselah. Shem's wife was named Salith; the wife of Ham, Nahlath; and the wife of Japheth, Arisivah.[3]

The nurse of Noah was an important personage, and must not be forgotten. She was named Sambethe, and was the first Sibyl. Suidas, the grammarian, says, "The Chaldee Sibyl, named Sambethi by the Hebrews, and identified with the Persian Sibyl, was of the race of Noah. She foretold those things which were to befall Alexander of Macedon. She also predicted the coming of the Lord Christ, and many other things, through divine inspiration."[4]

[1] Eutychius, Patr. Alex., Annal., t. i. p. 44.
[2] Bereschith Rabba, fol. 22, col. 4.
[3] Eutych. Annal., ed. Selden, i. p. 35.
[4] Suidas, Lexic. s. v. Σίβυλλα.

## XVII.

## THE SONS OF NOAH.

HAM, the accursed, the third son of Noah, was the inventor or the preserver of magic. As we have already seen, he buried the books of magic which existed in the world, before the Deluge swept over the globe; and when it abated he exhumed them. Cerco d'Ascoli, in the fourth chapter of his "Commentary on the Sphere of Sacrabosco," declares that he had seen a book of magic which had been composed by Ham, "which contained the elements and practice of necromancy." Certain it is that apocryphal books of alchemy and conjuration of spirits existed in the Middle Ages, which purported to have been composed by Ham.

Ham was turned black, according to the Talmud, because he did not maintain himself in perfect continence whilst in the ark;[1] other authorities say his skin became sooty in consequence of his scoffing at his father's drunkenness; and Japheth, for having smiled, says the Mussulman, lost the gift of prophecy from his family.[2]

Berosus supposed that Ham was the same as Zoroaster.

Japheth, according to Khondemir, was given by his father all the land to the east and north of Ararat; he was the progenitor of the Turks, the Sclaves, of Gog and Magog, says Tabari. Before he started with his family to people these countries, Noah gave him a stone, on which was written the great name

[1] Tract. Sanhedrin, fol. 108, col. 2.
[2] Tabari, i. p. 115.

of God. The Turks say that, by means of this stone, Noah was able to guide the course of the ark without sail or oars. The Turks have similar stones, which, they pretend, came by a process of generation from the parental stone given to Japheth.[1] He is said by the Mussulmans to have had eleven male children: Sin or Tchin, the father of the Chinese; Scklab, the ancestor of the Sclavonian races; Manschug or Magog, the parent of the Scythians and Kalmuks; Gomari, the father of the Franks; Turk and Khalos, the ancestors of the Turks; Khozaz, from whom the Khozarans trace their pedigree; Rus, father of the Russians; Souffan, Ghoy, and Tarag, from whom the Turcomans derive.

Ilak, son of Turk, discovered the use of salt by having let fall a piece of meat he was eating on the ground covered with saline deposit.

Of Shem the Rabbis have somewhat to say. " I have found in the Midrash that the Rabbi Johanan, son of Nuri, said : ' The holy, ever-blessed God took Shem, son of Noah, and consecrated him priest of the Most High, that he should minister before Him; and He let his Majesty dwell with Him, and He gave him the name Melchizedek, a priest of the Most High God, king of Salem. His brother Japheth learnt the law of him in his school, till Abraham came, who learnt it in the school of Shem. For this Abraham obtained, praying to God that his Majesty should remain and dwell in the house of Shem, wherefore it was said of him, *Thou art a priest for ever after the order of Melchizedek.*'"[2]

Shem learned his knowledge from the Book of Wisdom which Raphael, the holy angel, gave to Adam; but Shem's instructor was the angel Jophiel.[3]

The Rabbi Gerson writes in his book called "Sepher geliloth erez Israel," that having travelled through the lands of Og, king of Bashan, he saw there a grave which measured

---

[1] Colin de Plancy, p. 124.   [2] Eisenmenger, i. pp. 318-9.
[3] Ibid., p. 376.

eighty ells, and it was indicated to him as the sepulchre of Shem.[1] A curious tradition that Shem, Ham, and Japheth fell asleep in a cave, and woke up at the Nativity of Christ, and that they were themselves the three wise men who came to adore Him, shall be mentioned more fully when we treat of the legends connected with the New Testament characters.

Shem is said to have received the priesthood instead of Noah, because Noah was bitten by the lion as he was leaving the ark, and, being suffused with blood, became incapable of receiving the priesthood.

Shem is believed to have written many books, and apocryphal writings of his exist.

[1] Eisenmenger, i. p. 395.

XVIII.

## RELICS OF THE ARK.

WE have already seen that Berosus relates how in his time portions of the ark were removed, and used as amulets. Josephus says that remains of the ark were to be seen at his day upon Ararat; and Nicolas of Damascus reports the same. S. Epiphanius writes: "The wood of the ark of Noah is shown to this day in the Kardæan (Koord) country."[1] And he is followed by a host of fathers. El Macin, in his History of the Saracens, relates that the Emperor Heraclius visited the relics after he had conquered the Persians, in the city of Thenia, at the roots of Ararat. Haithon, the Armenian, declares that upon the snows of Ararat a black speck is visible at all times: this is Noah's ark.[2] Benjamin of Tudela, in his Itinerary, says that all the wood was carried away by the Caliph Omar, in A.D. 640, and was placed by him in a temple or mosque he erected in an island formed by the Tigris. One of the beams is shown in the Lateran at Rome. In 1670, Johann Jansenius Strauss ascended to a hermit's cell on the side cf Ararat, to bind up the cœnobite's leg which was broken. The hermit's cell, said Strauss, was five days' journey up the mountain, athwart three clouds, and above a region of intolerable cold, in a calm warm atmosphere. From the account of the hermit, Herr Strauss learnt that the old man had dwelt there twenty-five years, and that he had felt there neither rain nor

[1] Adv. Hæres., lib. i.     [2] De Tartaris, c. 9.

winds. On the top of the mountain, fifteen Italian miles from the cell, through the clear air, was distinguishable the great vessel grounded in the snow. The hermit had reached it, and of one of its planks had cut a cross, which he exhibited to the German traveller.

In the town of Chenna, in Arabia Felix, says the traveller Prévoux, is a large building, said to have been erected by Noah; and a large piece of wood is exhibited through an iron grating, which is said to have formed a portion of his ark. There is also to be seen at Chenna a well, said to have been dug by the patriarch Jacob, of which the water is icy cold.

The Armenians say that a certain monk, Jacob, once ascended Ararat, and carried off a fragment of the ark, which he made afterwards into a cross, and this is preserved amongst the sacred relics of Etchmiadzin. When the Persian king, Abassus the Great, sent to inquire about the ark, the monks replied that it was in vain for him to attempt to reach it, on account of the precipices and glaciers, and innumerable difficulties of the way.[1]

---

[1] Reliquiæ Arcæ Noæ, in Fabricius, i. art. 33.

XIX.

## CERTAIN DESCENDANTS OF HAM.

WE shall follow certain Mussulman traditions for what follows. Ad, son of Amalek, therefore grandson of Ham, established himself in Arabia, where he became chief of the tribe of the Adites. He fell into idolatry. He had two sons named Schedad and Schedéd, who reigned over numerous subjects—one for two hundred and fifty, the other for three hundred years. They built a superb city, where houses were of sumptuous magnificence; the like of this city was never seen before, nor will be seen again. This city vanished when the tribe of the Adites was exterminated; as we shall relate when we give the legends attaching to Heber. The commentators of the Koran tell marvels of this wondrous city.

Under the Khalifate of Moawiyah, first of the Ommiades, an Arab of the desert, named Kolabah, going in quest of his camel in the plain of Aden, lighted on the gate of a beautiful city. He went in, but, being filled with fear, he did not remain there more time than sufficed for him to collect some of the stones of the street, and then he returned.

His neighbours, to whom he relates his adventure, repeated it to the Khalif, who ordered Kolabah to be brought before him. The Arab related frankly what he had seen, but Moawiyah would not give credence to the marvellous tale, till he had consulted his learned men, and especially the illustrious Al-Akhbar, who assured him that the story of the poor Arab was

solicited that mankind might be made again. Zeus bade him throw stones over his head, from which men should come, and said that those cast by Pyrrha should be turned into women."

Stephanus of Byzantium says that the tradition was that after the surface of the earth became dry, Zeus ordered Prometheus and Athene to make images of clay in the form of men; and when they were dry, he called the winds and made them breathe into each, and rendered them vital: and thus the earth after the Flood was repeopled.[1] Diodorus says, "In the Deluge, which happened in the time of Deucalion, almost all flesh died."[2]

The Chinese begin their dynasties with Jao, the last of the old race, whose words are thus recorded in the Schu-Kiug:— "The mighty waters of the flood spread themselves out, and overflowed, and drowned everything. The mountains disappeared in the deep, and the hills were buried beneath them. The foaming billows seemed to threaten heaven. All people were drowned."[3] An ancient inscription, which the Chinese attribute to Yu, the third patriarch after the Flood, and which at least dates from before Christ, refers to this event:—"The illustrious Emperor Jao said, sighing, 'Companions and counsellors! The great and little territories up to the mountain's peak, the homes of birds and wild beasts, were overflowed far and wide. Long had I forgotten my home; now I rest upon the mountain top of Jo-lu. . . . The trouble is over, and the misfortune is at an end; the streams of the south flow, clothes and food are before us. The world is at rest, and the flying rain cannot again destroy us.'"[4]

In one of the writings of the disciples of Tao-tse, the tradition takes a fuller form. Kung-Kung, a bad spirit, enraged at having been overcome in war, gave such a blow against one of the pillars of the sky with his head that he broke it; and the vault

---

[1] Steph. Byzant., s. voce Ικονιον.
[2] Diod. Sicul. lib. i.
[3] Mém. concernant les Chinois, i. p. 157.
[4] Klaproth, Inschrift. des Yu; Halle, 1811, p. 29.

extracted the brains and applied them to his cancers. The relief was instantaneous, and Dhohak felt, for the first time for many days, some hours of repose.

After this, every day two men were killed to form poultices for his ulcers. During the two hundred latter years of the life of Dhohak, the prisons were emptied to satisfy his requirement for fresh brains; and when no more criminals could be procured, it was made a tribute for his kingdom to render to him two men, each day, to be immolated to soothe his pain.

Now there was at Ispahan a blacksmith, named Kaveh, who had two beautiful sons, whom he loved more dearly than his own life. One day they were seized, carried before the king, and his shoulders were poulticed with their brains.

Kaveh was at work at his anvil when the news of the slaying of his sons reached him. He deserted his anvil; and uttering a piercing cry, he rushed into the streets, with his leathern apron before him, bitterly lamenting his loss, and calling for vengeance on the monarch. The people crowded about him, they plucked off his leather apron, and converted it into a standard.

The crowd gathered as it advanced. From every street men flowed to join the army, and shortly the blacksmith found himself at the head of a hundred thousand men.

They marched to Demavend, where was the palace of the tyrant. And Kaveh, before attacking it, thus addressed his soldiers, "I am not one to lead you against a king; you need a king to make war against a king."

"Well," said his followers, "we elect you to be our king."

"I am but a simple blacksmith, and am not fit to rule," answered Kaveh, "but there is a royal prince named Afridoun, the son of Djemschid, who has fled from the cruelty of Dhohak: choose him."

They agreed. The prince was found and invested with the

sovereignty; then a battle was fought, and Dhohak's army was routed, and the tyrant was slain.

When Afridoun mounted the throne, he named Kaveh governor of Ispahan. And when Kaveh was dead, the king asked his children to give him their father's leathern apron. Then, having obtained it, he placed it among his treasures, and whenever he went to battle he attached the smith's apron to a tall staff, and marched under that banner against his enemies.

In after years, this leathern apron was studded with precious stones, till Omar, despising it, ordered the old piece of leather to be burnt; but Yezdeguerd had already robbed it of its gems.[1]

Afridoun exercised the sovereignty during two hundred years. He was the first to study astronomy, and he founded the science of medicine. He was the first king to ride on an elephant. He had three sons, Tur, Salm, and Irad. He loved the third son, Irad, more than the two elder, and he gave him the sovereignty over Irad, Mosul, Koufa, and Bagdad.

After the death of Afridoun, Tur and Salm marched against Irad, defeated him and killed him, saying: "Our father has divided his inheritance unjustly. He has given to Irad the best portion, the centre of the world; as for us, we are cast out to its extremities."

On the death of Tur and Salm, the crown left this family, and passed to a king named Cush, who was of the sons of Ham, the son of Noah. Cush reigned forty years. After him Canaan ascended the throne. Cush and Canaan worshipped idols. It is said that Nimrod was the son of Canaan. When Canaan died, Nimrod succeeded him. Nimrod had a vizir named Azar (Terah), son of Nahor, son of Sarough (Serug), who was sixth in generation from Noah. This Azar was the father of Abraham, the friend of God.

From the time of the Deluge to the time of Abraham was

[1] Tabari, i. c. xlii. xliii.

three thousand years. During that period, there was no prophet save Hud (Eber), who was sent to the Adites, and Saleh, who was sent to the Thamudites.

We shall relate the history of Hud and of Saleh, and then return to that of Nimrod.[1]

[1] Tabari, i, c. xliii.

## XX.

## SERUG.

"*And Eber lived four and thirty years, and begat Peleg.*
"*And Peleg lived thirty years, and begat Reu. And Reu lived two and thirty years, and begat Serug. And Serug lived thirty years, and begat Nahor.*"[1]

Serug is said to have discovered the art of coining gold and silver money. In his days men erected many idols, into which demons entered and wrought great signs by them. Samiri was king of the Chaldees, and he discovered weights and measures and how to weave silk, and also how to dye fabrics. He is related to have had three eyes and two horns.

At the same time Apiphanus was king of Egypt. He built a ship, and in it made piratical descents upon the neighbouring people living on the shores of the Mediterranean Sea. He was succeeded by Pharaoh, son of Saner, and the kings after him assumed his name as their title.[2]

Nahor was the son of Serug. In the twenty-fifth year of his life, Job the Just underwent his trial, according to the opinion of Arudha the Canaanite. At that time Armun, king of Canaan, built the two cities Sodom and Gomorrah, and called them after the names of his two sons; but Zoar he named after his mother. At the same time, Murk or Murph, king of Palestine, built Damascus.[3]

[1] Gen. xi. 16, 18, 20, 22.   [2] Abulfaraj, Hist. Dynastiarum, p. 12.
[3] Ibid. p. 13.

## XX.

## THE PROPHET EBER.

"*Unto Shem, the father of all the children of Eber, the brother of Japheth the elder, even to him were children born.*

"*The children of Shem;—Elam, and Asshur, and Arphaxad, and Lud, and Aram.*

"*And the children of Aram;—Uz, and Hul, and Gether, and Mash.*

"*And Arphaxad begat Salah; and Salah begat Eber.*"[1]

According to some Mussulman writers, Oudh (Lud), the son of Shem, had a son named Ad; but, according to others, Ad was the son of Aram, son of Shem.

The tribes of Ad and Thamud lived near one another in the desert of Hedjaz, in the south of Arabia. The land of the people of Ad was nearer Mecca than the valley of Hidjr, and the valley of Hidjr is situated at the extremity of the desert on the road to Syria.

Never in all the world were there such great and mighty men as the Adites. Each of them was twelve cubits high, and they were so strong that if any of them stamped on the ground he sank up to his knees.

The Adites raised great monuments in the land which they inhabited. Wherever these Cyclopean edifices exist, they are called by the Arabs the constructions of the Adites.

God ordered the prophet Hud (Eber) to go to the Adites

[1] Gen. x. 21-24.

and preach to them the One true God, and turn them from idolatry. But the Adites would not hearken to his words, and when he offered them the promises of God, they said, "What better dwellings can He give us than those which we have made?" And when he spoke to them of God's threatenings, they mocked and said, "Who can resist us who are so strong?"

For fifty years did the prophet Hud speak to the Adites, and their reply to his exhortations is preserved in the Koran, "O Hud, you produce no evidence of what you advance; we will not abandon our gods because of your preaching. We mistrust your mission. We believe that one of our gods bears a hatred against you."

Hud replied, "I take God to witness, and you also be witnesses, that I am innocent of your polytheism."[1]

The words of the Adites, "We believe that one of our gods bears a hatred against thee," signified that they believed one of their gods had driven him mad.

During the fifty years that Hud's mission lasted, the Adites believed neither in God nor in the prophet, with the exception of a very few, who believed in secret.

At the end of that time God withheld the rain from heaven, and afflicted the Adites with drought. All the cattle of Ad died, and the Adites fainted for lack of water. For three years no rain fell.

Hud said to the Adites, "Believe in God, and He will give you rain."

They replied, "Thou art mad." But they chose three men to send to Mecca with victims; for the infidels believe in the sanctity of Mecca, though they believe not in the One true God.

But Eber said, "Your sacrifices will be unavailing, unless you first believe."

The three deputies started for Mecca with many camels, oxen, and sheep, as sacrifices. And when they reached Mecca

[1] Koran, Sura xi. verse 57.

they made friends with the inhabitants of that city, and were received with hospitality. They passed their days and nights in eating and drinking wine, and in their drunkenness they forgot their people, and the mission on which they had been sent. The inhabitants of Mecca ordered musicians to sing the afflictions of the Adites, to recall to the envoys the purpose of their visit. Then Lokman and Morthed, two of the deputies, declared to Qaïl, the third, that they believed in Allah; and they added, "If our people had believed the words of the prophet Hud, they would not have suffered from drought," and Lokman and Morthed were not drunk when they said these words.

Qaïl replied, "You do not partake in the affliction of our nation. I will go myself and will offer the victims."

He went and led the beasts to the top of a mountain to sacrifice them, and turning his face to heaven, he said, "O God of heaven, hearken unto my prayer, and send rain on my poor afflicted people."

Instantly there appeared three clouds in the blue sky: one was red, one was black, the third was white; and a voice issued from the clouds, saying, "Choose which shall descend upon thy people."

Then Qaïl said within himself, "The white cloud, if it hung all day over my nation, would not burst in rain; the red cloud, if it hung over them night and day, would not drop a shower; but the black cloud is heavy with water." So he chose the black cloud.

And a voice cried, "It is gone to fall upon thy people."

Qaïl returned full of joy, thinking he had obtained rain; but that cloud was big with the judgments of God. Qaïl told what he had done to his companions, Lokman and Morthed, but they laughed at him.

Now the cloud, when it arrived over the land of Ad, was accompanied by a wind. And the Adites looked up rejoicing, and cried, "The rain, the rain is coming!"

Then the cloud gaped, and a dry whirlwind rolled out from it, and swept up all the cattle that were in the land, and raised them in the air, spun them about, and dashed them lifeless on the ground.

But the Adites said, "Fear not; first comes wind, then comes rain." And they rushed out of their houses into the fields. Hud thought they were coming forth to ask his assistance; but they sought him not. Then the whirlwind caught them up and cast them down again. Now each of these men was like a palm-tree in stature, and they lay shattered and lifeless on the sand.

Hud was saved, along with those who had believed his word.

Now when the envoys at Mecca heard what had befallen their people, they went all three to the summit of the mountain, and Lokman and Morthed said to Qaïl, "Believe." But he answered, raising his face and hands to heaven: "O God of heaven, if thou hast destroyed my people, slay me also."

Then the whirlwind came, and rushed on him, and caught him up and cast him down, and he was dead.

But Lokman and Morthed offered their sacrifice, and a voice from heaven said, "What is your petition?"

Lokman answered: "O Lord, grant me a long life, that I may outlive seven vultures." Now a vulture is the longest-lived of all birds; it lives five hundred years.

And the voice replied, "However long thy life may be, death will close it."

Lokman said, "I know; that is true."

Then his prayer was granted. And Lokman took a young vulture and fed it for five hundred years, and it died; then he took a second, and at the expiration of five hundred years it died also; and so on till he had reached the age of three thousand five hundred years, and then he died also.

Morthed made his request, and it was, "O Lord, give me wheat bread," for hitherto in Ad he had eaten only barley bread. So Allah gave Morthed so much wheat, that he was able to make bread thereof all the rest of his life.

Hud lived fifty years with the faithful who had received his doctrine, and his life in all was one hundred and fifty years. The prophet Saleh appeared five hundred years after Hud; he was sent to the Thamudites.[1]

But there is another version of the story given by Weil.

Hud promised Schaddad, king of the Adites, a glorious city in the heavens, if he would turn to the true God. But the king said, "I need no other city than that I have built. My palace rests on a thousand pillars of rubies and emeralds; the streets and walls are of gold, and pearl, and carbuncle, and topaz; and each pillar in my house is a hundred ells long."

Then, at Hud's word, God let the city and palace of Schaddad fade away like a dream of the night, and storm and rain descended, and night fell, and the king was without home in the desert.[2]

Of Lokman we must relate something more. He was a great prophet; some say he was nephew of Job, whose sister was his mother; others relate that he was the son of Beor, the son of Nahor, the son of Terah.

One day, whilst he was reposing in the heat of the day, the angels entered his room and saluted him, but did not show themselves. Lokman heard their voices, but saw not their persons. Then the angels said to him,—

"We are messengers of God, thy Creator and ours; He has sent us unto thee to announce to thee that thou shalt be a great monarch."

Lokman replied, "If God desires what you say, His will can accomplish all things, and doubtless He will give me what is necessary for executing my duty in that position in which He will place me. But if He would suffer me to choose a state of life, I should prefer that in which I now am,"—now

---

[1] Tabari, i. c. xliv.; Abulfeda, Hist. Ante Islamica, pp. 19-21.
[2] Weil, pp. 47, 48.

Lokman was a slave,—"and above all would I ask Him to enable me never to offend Him; without which all earthly grandeur would be to me a burden."

This reply of Lokman was so pleasing to Allah, that He gave him the gift of wisdom to such a degree of excellence, that he became capable of instructing all men; and this he did by means of a great multitude of maxims, sentences, and parables to the number of ten thousand, each of which is more valuable than the whole world.[1]

When Lokman did not know anything with which others were acquainted, he held his tongue, and did not ask questions and thus divulge his ignorance.

As he lived to a great age, he was alive in the days of King David. Now David made a coat of mail, and showed it to Lokman. The sage had seen nothing like it before, and did not know what purpose it was to serve, but he looked knowing and nodded his head. Presently David put the armour upon him, and marched, and said, "It is serviceable in war." Then Lokman understood its object; so his mouth became unsealed and he talked about it.

Lokman used to say, "Silence is wisdom, but few practise it."[2]

Thalebi relates, in his Commentary on the Koran, that Lokman was a slave, and that having been sent along with other slaves into the country to gather fruit, his fellow-slaves ate them, and charged Lokman with having done so. Lokman, to justify himself, said to his master, "Let every one of us slaves be given warm water to drink, and you will soon see who has been the thief."

The expedient succeeded; the slaves who had eaten the fruit vomited it, and Lokman threw up only warm water.

The same story precisely is told of Æsop.

Lokman is always spoken of as black, with thick lips. He is regarded by the Arabs much as is Bidpay by the Indians, and Æsop by the Europeans, as the Father of Fable.

[1] Herbelot, Biblioth. Orientale, s. v. Lokman. [2] Tabari, i. p. 432.

## XXII.

## THE PROPHET SALEH.

THE prophet Saleh was the son of Ad, son of Aram, son of Shem, and is not to be confused with Saleh, son of Arphaxad.

The Mussulmans say that he was sent to convert the Thamudites.

The Thamudites were in size and strength like their brethren the Adites, but they inhabited the rocks, which they dug out into spacious mansions. They had in the midst of their land an unfailing supply of sweet and limpid water. They were idolaters. Saleh came armed with the command of Allah to these men, and he preached to them that they should turn from the worship of stocks and stones to that of the living God who made them.

Now Saleh had been born among the Thamudites, but he had never been an idolater. When he was young, the natives of the land had laughed at him, and said, "He is young and inexperienced; when he is old, and has grown wiser, he will adore our gods."

When Saleh grew old, he forbade the Thamudites to worship idols, and he spoke to them of the true and only God.

But they said, "What miracle can you work, to prove that your mission is from God?"[1]

Then he said, "Oh, my people, a she-camel that shall come from God shall be to you for a sign. Let her go and eat

[1] Koran, Sura xxvi. v. 153.

on the earth, and do her no injury, that a terrible retribution fall not upon you."[1]

Now Saleh had asked them what miracle they desired, and they had answered, "Bring out of the rock a camel with red hair, and a colt of a camel also with red hair; let them eat grass, and we will believe."

Saleh said to them, "What you ask is easy," and he prayed.

Then the rock groaned and clave asunder, and there came out a she-camel with her foal, and their hair was red, and they began to eat grass.

Then the Thamudites exclaimed, "He is a magician!" and they would not believe in him.

The camel went to the perpetual fountain, and she drank it up, so that from that day forward from their spring they could get no water, and they suffered from thirst.

The Thamudites went to Saleh and said, "We need water!"

Saleh replied, "The fountain shall flow one day for you, and one day for the camel."

So it was agreed that the camel should drink alternate days with the people of the land, and that alternate days each should be without water whilst the other was drinking.

Then Saleh said, for he saw that the people hated the camel and her foal, "Beware that you slay not these animals, for the day that they perish, great shall be your punishment."

The she-camel lived thirty years among the Thamudites, but God revealed to Saleh that they were bent on slaying the camel, and he said, "The slayer will be a child with red hair and blue eyes."

Now the Thamudites ordered ten midwives to attend on the women in their confinement, and if a child were born with the signs indicated by the prophet, it was to be destroyed instantly.

Nine children had thus been killed, and the parents conceived a deadly animosity against Saleh the prophet, and formed a design to slay him.

[1] Koran, Sura xi. v. 67.

One of the chiefs among the Thamudites had a son born to him with red hair and blue eyes, and the nurses would have destroyed it, but the nine men spake to the father of the child, and they banded together, and saved the infant.

Now when this child had attained the age of eleven, he became great and handsome; and each of the parents whose children had been put to death, when he saw him, said, "Such an one would have been my son, had not he been slain at the instigation of Saleh." And they combined to put the prophet to death. They said among themselves, "We will kill him outside the city, and returning, say we were elsewhere when he was murdered."

Having formed this project, they left the city and placed themselves under a rock, awaiting his exit from the gates. But God commanded the rock, and it fell and crushed them all.

Next day their corpses were recovered, but the Thamudites were very wroth, and said, "Saleh has slain our children, and now he slays our men;" and they added, "We will be revenged on his camel."

But no one could be found to undertake the execution of this deed, save the red-haired child. He went to the fountain where the camel was drinking, and with one kick he knocked her over, and with another kick he despatched her.

But the foal, seeing the fate of her mother, ran away, and the boy with the red hair and blue eyes ran after her.

Saleh, seeing what had taken place, cried, "The judgment of God is about to fall."

The people were frightened, and asked, "What shall we do?"

"The judgment of God will not fall as long as the colt remains among you."

Hearing this, the whole population went in pursuit of the young camel. Now it had fled to the mountain whence it had sprung, and the red-haired boy was close on its heels. And when the young camel heard the shouting of the inhabitants of the city, and saw the multitude in pursuit, it stood before the rock, turned round, uttered three piercing cries, and vanished.

The Thamudites arrived and beat the rock, but they could not open it. Then said Saleh, "The judgment of God will fall; prepare to receive it. The first day your faces will become livid, the second day they will become black, and the third day red."

Things happened as Saleh had predicted. And when the signs befel them which Saleh had foretold, they knew that their end was near. The first day they became ash pale, the second day coal black, and the third day red as fire, and then there came a sound from heaven, and all fell dead on the earth, save Saleh and those who believed in him; these heard the sound, but did not perish.

By the will of God, when the people were destroyed, one man was absent at Mecca; the name of this man was Abou-Ghalib. When he knew what had befallen his nation, he took up his residence in Mecca; but all the rest perished, as it is written in the Koran, "In the morning they were found dead in their houses, stretched upon the ground, as though they had never dwelt there."

From Saleh to Abraham there was no prophet. At the time of that patriarch there was no king over all the earth. The sovereignty had passed to Canaan, the son of Cush, the son of Ham, who was the son of Noah.[1]

The camel of the prophet Saleh was placed by Mohammed in the heavens, together with the ass of Balaam, and other favoured animals.

Now wonderful as is this story, it is surpassed by that related by certain Arabic historians of the mission of Saleh. This we proceed to give.

[1] Tabari, i. c. xlv.

Djundu Ibn Omar was king of the Thamudites, a people numbering seventy thousand fighting men. He had a palace cut out of the face of a rock, and his high priest, Kanuch Ibn Abid, had one likewise. The most magnificent building in the city was a temple which contained the idol worshipped by the people. This idol had the head of a man, the neck of a bull, the body of a lion, and the feet of a horse. It was fashioned out of pure gold, and was studded with jewels.

One day, as Kanuch, the high priest, was worshipping in the temple, he fell asleep, and heard a voice cry, "The truth will appear, and the madness will pass away." He started to his feet in alarm, and saw the idol prostrate on the floor, and its crown had fallen from its head.

Kanuch cried out for assistance, and fled to the king, who sent men to set up the image, and replace on its head the crown that had fallen from it.

But doubt took possession of the heart of Kanuch; he no longer addressed the image in prayer, and his enthusiasm was at an end. The king observed this, and sent two vizirs with orders to imprison and execute him. But Allah struck the vizirs with blindness, and he sent two angels to transport Kanuch to a well-shaded grotto, well supplied with all that could content the heart of man.

As Kanuch was nowhere to be found, the king appointed his kinsman Davud to be high priest. But on the third day he came to the king to announce to him that the idol was again prostrate.

The monarch set it up once more, and Eblis, entering the image, spoke through its mouth, exhorting all men to beware of novel doctrines which were about to be introduced.

Next feast-day Davud was about to sacrifice two oxen to the idol, when one of them opened its mouth, and thus addressed him :—

"Will you sacrifice creatures endued with life by the living

God to a mass of lifeless metal? O God, do Thou destroy this sinful nation!" And the oxen broke their halters, and ran away.

Horsemen were deputed to pursue and capture them, but they escaped, for Allah screened them.

But God in His mercy resolved to give the Thamudites another chance of repenting of their idolatry.

Raghwah, Kanuch's wife, had shed incessant tears since the disappearance of her husband. Allah dispatched a bird out of Paradise to guide her to the grotto of Kanuch.

This bird was a raven; its head was white as snow, its back was green as emerald. Its feet were purple; its beak of heaven's blue. Its eyes were gems; only its body was black, for this bird did not fall under the curse of Noah, as it was in Paradise.

It was midnight when the raven entered Raghwah's dark chamber, where she lay weeping on a carpet; but the glory of its eyes illumined the whole room, as though the sun had suddenly flashed into it. Raghwah rose from her place, and gazed in wonder on the lovely bird, which opened its beak and said, "Arise and follow me! God has seen thy tears, and will reunite thee to thy husband."

Raghwah followed the raven, which flew before her, and with the light of its eyes turned the night into day. The morning star had not risen, when they stood before Kanuch's grot. Then cried the raven, "Kanuch, open to thy wife!" and so vanished.

Nine months after that Raghwah had rejoined her husband, she bore him a son, who was the image of Seth, and had on his brow the prophetic light; and Kanuch, in the hope of drawing him to the knowledge of the true God and to a pious life, gave him the name of Saleh (The Blessed).

Not long after Saleh's birth, Kanuch died; and the raven of Paradise returned to the grotto to lead back Saleh to his own people.

Saleh grew in beauty and strength, to the admiration of his mother and all who saw him.

A war was being waged between the descendants of Ham and the Thamudites, and the latter had lost many battles and a large portion of their army, when Saleh suddenly appeared in the battle-field at the head of a few friends, and, by his personal heroism, turned the tide of victory, and routed the enemy.

This success drew upon him the gratitude and love of the people, but the envy of the king was kindled, and he sought the life of the young prophet. But as often as assassins were sent by the king to take his life, their arms shrivelled up, and were only restored at the intercession of Saleh. These circumstances tended to increase and confirm the number of his adherents, so that he was able to build a mosque, and occupy with worshippers of the true God one whole quarter of the city.

But one day the king surrounded the mosque with his troops, and threatened Saleh and his followers with death if they would not work a miracle to prove their worship to be the true one.

Saleh prayed, and instantly the leaves of the date-tree that stood before the mosque were transformed into serpents and scorpions, which fell over the king and his soldiers; whilst two doves, which dwelt on the terrace of the mosque, sang aloud, "Believe in Saleh, he is a prophet and messenger of God!"

But Saleh was moved with compassion when he saw the anguish of those who had been bitten by the scorpions and vipers, and he prayed to God, and the noxious reptiles were transformed back again into date-leaves, and those who had been stung were made whole. Nevertheless the king hardened his heart, and continued to worship false gods.

When Saleh saw the impenitence of the Thamudites, he besought God to destroy them; but an angel appeared to him in a cave, and sent him to sleep for twenty years.

When he woke he betook himself towards the mosque he had built, never doubting that he had slept but a single night

The mosque was gone, his friends and adherents were dead or dispersed, a few remained, but they were old, and he hardly recognized them. Falling into despair, the angel Gabriel came to him and said,—

" Thou wert hasty in desiring the destruction of this people, therefore God hath withdrawn from thy life twenty years, which He has taken from thee in sleep. Now He sends thee precious relics wherewith to establish thy mission, to wit, Adam's shirt, Abel's sandals, Seth's overcoat, Enoch's seal ring, Noah's sword, and Hud's staff."

Next day, as the king Djundu with his brother Schihab, and the priests and the princes of the people, formed a procession to an idol temple near the town, Saleh ran before the procession, entered the temple, and stood in the door.

"Who art thou?" asked the king in astonishment: for he did not recognize Saleh, so greatly had God changed him in his sleep of twenty years.

He answered: "I am Saleh, the messenger of the only God, who preached to you twenty years ago, and showed to you many signs and wonders, but you would not believe. And now once more I appear unto you to give you a proof of my mission. Ask what miracle I shall perform and it shall be done."

Then the king said, " Bring me here out of the rock a camel one hundred ells long, of every colour under the sun, whose eyes are like lightning, and whose feet are swifter than the wind."

Saleh consented. Then said Davud, " Let its fore feet be golden and its hinder feet silver, its head of emerald and its ears of ruby. Let it bear on its hump a tent of silver, woven with gold threads and adorned with pearls, resting on four pillars of diamonds!"

When Saleh agreed to this also, the king added, "And let it bring with it a foal like to its mother, just born, and running by her side; then will I believe in Allah, and in thee as His prophet."

"And wilt thou believe too?" asked Saleh of the high priest.

"Yes," answered Davud, "if she give milk without being milked, cold in summer and warm in winter."

"And one thing more," threw in the king's brother, Schihab; "the milk must heal the sick, enrich the poor, and the camel must of its own accord go into every house, and fill the pails with milk."

"Be it according to your will," said Saleh. "But I warn you,—no one must injure the camel, deprive it of its food or drink, attempt to ride it, or use it for any other kind of labour."

When they consented, Saleh prayed to God, and the earth opened under his feet, and a well of fragrant water gushed up, and poured over the rock, and the rock was rent, and the camel started forth in every particular such as the king and his high priest had desired. So they cried, "There is no God but God, and Saleh is His prophet."

Then the angel Gabriel came down from heaven, having in his hand a flaming sword, wherewith he touched the camel, and she bore instantly a foal like her parent.

Then the king fell on Saleh's neck, and kissed him and believed. But his brother Schihab and Davud attributed all that had been done to magic, and they laboured to convince the people that the camel was the work of necromancy.

But as daily the camel gave her milk, and, whenever she drank, said her grace with formality, the number of true believers increased daily, and the high priest and all the chiefs of the infidels resolved on her destruction. Schihab, the king's brother, hoping to overturn the king and take his place, by adhering to the established religion and ignoring all novelties, was resolute in his resistance to the true religion. Therefore he promised his daughter Rajan in marriage to whosoever should kill the wondrous camel.

Now there was a young man of humble origin, named Kaddar, who had long loved the maiden, but had never ventured to show his passion ; he armed himself with a great sword and attacked the camel as it was drinking, in the rear, and wounded it in the hock.

Instantly all nature uttered a piercing cry. Then the youth, filled with compunction, ran to the top of a mountain, and cried, " God's curse on you, ye sinful people ! "

Saleh betook himself with the king, who would not be separated from him, into the town, and demanded the punishment of Kaddar and his accomplices. But Schihab, who in the meantime had seized on the throne, threatened them with death, and Saleh, obliged to fly to save his life, had only time to speak this threat, " Three days are given you for repentance ; after that ye shall be slain."

Next day every man's face was yellow as the leaves in autumn, and wherever the wounded camel limped a spring of blood bubbled out of the soil.

On the second day the faces of all were blood-red, and on the third they were coal-black.

Towards evening the camel spread a pair of scarlet wings and flew away, and then mountains of fire were rained from heaven on the city, by the hands of angels; and the keepers of the fire beneath the earth opened vents, and blew fire from below in the form of flaming camels.

When the sun went down, all that remained of the Thamudites was a heap of ashes.

Saleh alone, and the king Djundu, were saved.[1]

[1] Weil, pp. 48-61 ; Abulfeda, p. 21.

## XXIII.

## THE TOWER OF BABEL.

FIRST we will take Jewish traditions, and then Mahommedan legends. The Rabbis relate as follows:—

After the times of the great Deluge, men feared a recurrence of that great overthrow, and they assembled on and inhabited the plain of Shinar. There, they no longer obeyed the gentle guidance of Shem, the son of Noah; but they cast the kingdom of God far from them, and chose as their sovereign, Nimrod, son of Cush, son of Ham.[1] Nimrod became very great in power. Having been born when his father was old, he was dearly beloved, and every whim had been gratified. Cush gave him the garment which God made for Adam when he was expelled from Paradise, and which Adam had given to Enoch, and Enoch to Methuselah, and Methuselah had left to Noah, and which Noah had taken with him into the ark. Ham stole it from his father in the ark, concealed it, and gave it to his son Cush. Nimrod, vested in this garment, was unconquerable and irresistible.[2] All beasts and birds fell down before him, and his enemies were overcome almost without a struggle.

It was thus that he triumphed over the king of Babylon. His kingdom rapidly extended, and he became daily more powerful, till at last he was sole monarch over the whole world.[3]

Nimrod rejected God as his ruler; he trusted in his own

[1] Pirke of Rabbi Eliezer, c. xi.   [2] Ibid. c. xxiv.   [3] Ibid. c. xi.

might, therefore it is said of him, "He was mighty in hunting, and in sin before the Lord; for he was a hunter of the sons of men in their languages. And he said to them, Leave the judgments of Shem, and adhere to the judgments of Nimrod."[1]

But Nimrod was uneasy in his mind, and he feared lest some one should arise who would be empowered by God to overthrow him; therefore he said to his subjects, "Come, let us build a great city, and let us settle therein, that we may not be scattered over the face of the earth, and be destroyed once more by a flood. And in the midst of our city let us build a high tower, so lofty as to overtop any flood, and so strong as to resist any fire. Yea, let us do further, let us prop up the heaven on all sides from the top of the tower, that it may not again fall and inundate us. Then let us climb up into heaven, and break it up with axes, and drain its water away where it can do no injury. Thus shall we avenge the death of our ancestors. And at the summit of our tower we will place an image of our god with a sword in his hand, and he shall fight for us. Thus shall we obtain a great name, and reign over the universe."

Even if all were not inspired with the same presumption, yet all saw in the tower a means of refuge from a future deluge; and therefore they readily fell in with the proposal of the king. Six hundred thousand men were set to work under a thousand captains, and raised the tower to the height of seventy miles (*i.e.* fifty-six English miles). A great flight of stairs on the east side was used by those carrying up material, and a flight on the west side served those who descended, having deposited their burdens. If a workman fell down and was killed, no one heeded; but if any of the bricks gave way, there was an outcry. Some shot arrows into the sky, and they came down tinged with blood, then they shouted and cried, "See, we have killed every one who is in heaven."[2] Curiously

---

[1] Targums, ed. Etheridge, i. p. 187.
[2] Bechaji, Comm. in 1 Mos. xi.; Pirke of R. Eliezer, c. xi.; Talmud, Sanhedrim, 109a; Targums, i. pp. 189-90, &c.

enough a similar story is told by the Chinese of one of their earlier monarchs, who thought himself so great that he might war against heaven. He shot an arrow into the sky, and a drop of blood fell. "So," said he, "I have killed God!"

At this time Abraham was forty-eight. He was filled with grief and shame at the impiety of his fellow-men, and he prayed to God, "*O Lord! confound their tongues, for I have spied unrighteousness and strife in the city!*"

Then the Lord called the seventy angels who surround His throne, that they should confuse the language of the builders, so that none should understand the other.

The angels came down, and cast confusion among the subjects of Nimrod, and seventy distinct languages sprang up, and the men could not understand each other; so they separated from one another, and were spread over the surface of the earth. The tower itself was destroyed in part. It was in three portions: the upper story was destroyed by fire from heaven, the basement was overthrown by an earthquake, only the middle story was left intact,—how, we are not informed.[1]

We will now take the Mussulman tradition. Nimrod, who, according to the Arabs, was the son of Canaan, and brother of Cush, sons of Ham, having cast Abraham, who refused to acknowledge him as supreme monarch of the world, into a burning, fiery furnace, from which he issued unhurt, said to his courtiers, "I will go to heaven and see this God whom Abraham preaches, and who protects him."

His wise men having represented to him that heaven is very high, Nimrod ordered the erection of a tower, by which he might reach it. For three years an immense multitude of workmen toiled at the erection of this tower. Every day Nimrod ascended it and looked up, but the sky seemed to him as distant from the summit of his tower as it had from the level ground.

[1] Talmud, Sanhedrim; see also the history of Nimrod in Yaschar, pp. 1107-8.

One morning he found his tower cast down. But Nimrod was not to be defeated so easily. He ordered a firmer foundation to be laid, and a second tower was constructed; but however high it was built, the sky remained inaccessible. Then Nimrod resolved on reaching heaven in another fashion. He had a large box made, and to the four corners he attached gigantic birds of the species Roc. They bore Nimrod high into the air, and then fluttered here and fluttered there, and finally upset the box, and tumbled him on the top of a mountain, which he cracked by his fall, without however materially injuring himself.

But Nimrod was not penitent, nor ready to submit to the Most High, therefore God confounded the language of his subjects, and thus rent from him a large portion of his kingdom.[1]

God sent a wind, says Abulfaraj, which overthrew the Tower of Babel and buried Nimrod under its ruins.[2]

Of Babel we find fewer traditions preserved amongst the ancient nations, than we did of the Deluge.

The Zendavesta makes no mention of such an event; and it is equally unknown to the Chinese books, though curiously enough, in Chinese hieroglyphics, the *tower* is the symbol of *separation*.[3]

The Chaldeans, however, says Abydessus, probably quoting Berosus, the priest of Bel, related, "That the first inhabitants of the earth, glorying in their own strength and size, and despising the gods, undertook to raise a tower whose top should reach the sky in the place where Babylon now stands; but when it approached the heavens, the winds assisted the gods, and overthrew the work of the contrivers; and its ruins are said to be still in Babylon; and the gods introduced a diversity of tongues among men, who till that time had all spoken the same language; and a war arose between Kronos

---

[1] Herbelot, s. v. Nimroud.   [2] Hist. Dynast., p. 12.
[3] Mémoires conc. les Chinois, i. p. 213.

## THE TOWER OF BABEL.

and Titan. The place on which they built the tower is now called Babylon."[1]

Alexander Polyhistor relates the events as follows, and quotes the Sibyl. "The Sibyl says, when all men had one speech, they built a great tower in order to climb into heaven, but the gods blowing against it with the winds, threw it down, and confounded the language of the builders; therefore the city is called Babylon."[2] The writings of this Sibyl, commonly called the Chaldean Sibyl, formed part of the sacred scriptures of the Babylonians. Eupolemus, quoting apparently Syro-phœnician traditions, relates the matter somewhat differently. "The city Babylon," says he, "was built after the Deluge by those who were saved. But they were giants, and they built the famous tower then. But when this was overthrown by the will of the gods, the giants were scattered over the whole face of the earth."[3] The Armenian tradition recorded by Moses of Chorene, is to this effect: "From them (*i.e.* from the first dwellers on the earth) sprang the race of the giants, with strong bodies and of huge size. Full of pride and envy, they formed the godless resolve to build a high tower. But whilst they were engaged on the undertaking, a fearful wind overthrew it, which the wrath of God had sent against it, and unknown words were at the same time blown about among men, wherefore arose strife and contention."[4]

The Hindu story of the confusion of tongues and the separation of nations is not connected with the erection of a tower, but with the pride of the Tree of Knowledge, or the world tree. This tree grew in the centre of the earth, and its head was in heaven. It said in its heart, I shall hold my head in heaven, and spread my branches over all the earth, and gather all men together under my shadow and protect them, and prevent them from separating. But Brahm, to punish the pride of

---

[1] Euseb., Præp. Ev., ix. 14; Cory, Ancient Fragments, pp. 34–50.
[2] George Syncellus, Bibl. Græc., v. p. 178.
[3] Euseb., Præp. Ev., ix. 17.   [4] Mos. Chorene, i. 9.

the tree, cut off its branches and cast them down on the earth, where they sprang up as Wata trees, and made differences of belief and speech and customs to prevail in the earth, to disperse men over its surface.[1]

The Dutch traveller, Hamel van Gorcum, found a tradition of the Tower of Babel, in the seventeenth century, in the Korea, in the midst of a sect which had not adopted Buddhism, but which retained much of the old primitive Schamanism of the race. They said, " That formerly all men spake the same language, but, after building a great tower, wherewith they attempted to invade heaven, they fell into confusion of tongues."[2]

The Mexican story was, that after the Deluge the sole survivors Coxcox and Chichequetzl engendered many children who were born dumb, but one day received the gift of speech from a dove, which came and perched itself on a lofty tree; but the dove did not communicate to them the same language, so they separated in fifteen companies. And Gemelli Carreri and Clavigero describe an ancient Mexican painting representing the dove with thirty-three tongues, answering to the languages and dialects he taught.[3]

At Cholula they related that Xelhuaz began to build a tower on Mount Tlalok to commemorate his having been saved along with his brothers from the Flood. And the tower he built in the form of a pyramid. The clay was baked into bricks in the province of Tlamanalco, at the foot of the Sierra Cocotl, and to bring them to Cholula a row of men was placed, that the bricks might be passed from hand to hand. The gods saw this building, whose top reached the clouds, with anger and dismay, and sent fire from heaven, and destroyed the tower.[4]

[1] Müller, Glauben u. Wissen. d. Hindus; Mainz, 1822, i. p. 303.
[2] Allgem. Hist. d. Reisen, vi. p. 602.
[3] Luken, p. 287; Amerikanische Urreligionen, p. 517, &c.
[4] Humboldt, Ansichten d. Cordilleren, i. p. 42.

## XXIV.

## ABRAHAM.[1]

### 1. HIS YOUTH AND EARLY STRUGGLES.

ABRAHAM or Abram, as he was first called, was the son of Terah, general of Nimrod's army, and Amtelai, daughter of Carnebo. He was born at Ur of the Chaldees, in the year 1948 after the Creation.

On the night on which Abraham was born, Terah's friends, amongst whom were many councillors and soothsayers of Nimrod, were feasting in the house. On leaving, late at night, they observed an unusual star in the east; it seemed to run from one quarter of the heavens to another, and to devour four stars which were there. All gazed in astonishment on this wondrous sight. "Truly," said they, "this can signify nothing else but that Terah's new-born son will become great and powerful, will conquer the whole realm, and dethrone great princes, and seize on their possessions."

Next morning they hastened to the king, to announce to him what they had seen, and what was their interpretation of the vision, and to advise the slaughter of the young child, and that Terah should be compensated with a liberal sum of money.

[1] For the Rabbinic traditions relating to Abraham I am indebted to the exhaustive monograph of Dr. B. Beer, "Leben Abraham's nach Auffassung der jüdischen Sage," Leipzig, 1859, to which I must refer my readers for references to Jewish books, which are given with an exactitude which leaves nothing to be desired.

Nimrod accordingly sent gold and silver to Terah, and asked his son in exchange, but Terah refused. Then the king sent and threatened to burn down and utterly destroy the whole house of Terah, unless the child were surrendered. In the meantime one of the female slaves had born a son; this Terah gave to the royal officers, who, supposing it to be the son of the householder, brought it before Nimrod and slew it.

Then, to secure Abraham, Terah concealed him and his mother and nurse in a cave.

But there is another version of the story, and it is as follows:—

Nimrod had long read in the stars that a child would be born who would oppose his power and his religion, and would finally overcome both.

Acting on the advice of his wise men, he built a house, sixty ells high and eighty ells broad, into which all pregnant women were brought to be delivered, and the nurses were instructed to put to death all the boys that were born, but to make handsome presents to the mothers who were brought to bed of daughters.

After seventy thousand male children had thus perished, the angels of heaven turned to the All Mighty, and besought Him with tears to stay this cruel murder of innocents.

"I slumber not, I sleep not," God answered. "Ye shall see that this atrocity shall not pass unpunished."

Shortly after, Terah's wife was pregnant; she concealed her situation as long as was possible, pretending that she was ill; but when she could conceal it no more, the infant crept behind her breasts, so that she appeared to every eye as if nothing were about to take place.

When the time came for her delivery, she went in fear out of the city, and wandered in the desert till she lighted on a cave, into which she entered. Next morning she was delivered of a son, Abraham, whose face shone, so that the grotto was as light as though the sun were casting a golden beam into it. She wrapped the child in a mantle, and left it there to the custody of God and His angels, and returned home. God heard the cry of the weeping infant, and He sent His angel Gabriel to the cave, who let the child suck milk out of his fore-finger. But according to another account he opened two holes in the cave, from which dropped oil and flour to nourish Abraham. Others, however, say that Terah visited the cave every day, and nursed and fed the child.

According to the Arab tradition, which follows the Jewish in most particulars, the mother, on visiting the cave, found the infant sucking its two thumbs. Now out of one of its thumbs flowed milk, and out of the other, honey, and thus the babe nourished itself: or, say others, from one finger flowed water when he sucked it; from a second, milk; from a third, honey; from a fourth, the juice of dates; and from the little finger, butter.[1]

When Abraham had been in the cave, according to some, three years, according to others ten, and according to others thirteen, he left the cavern and stood on the face of the desert. And when he saw the sun shining in all its glory, he was filled with wonder, and he thought, "Surely the sun is God the Creator!" and he knelt down and worshipped the sun. But when evening came, the sun went down in the west, and Abraham said, "No! the Author of creation cannot set." Now the moon arose in the east, and the stars looked out of the firmament. Then said Abraham, "This moon must indeed be God, and all the stars are His host!" And kneeling down he adored the moon.

But after some hours of darkness the moon set, and from the east appeared once more the bright face of the sun. Then said Abraham, "Verily these heavenly bodies are no gods, for they obey law: I will worship Him who imposed the law upon them."

The Arab story is this. When Abraham came out of the

[1] Weil, p. 69.

cave, he saw a number of flocks and herds, and he said to his mother, "Who is lord of these?" She answered, "Your father Azar (Terah)." "And who is the lord of Azar?" he further asked. She replied, "Nimrod." "And who is the lord of Nimrod?" "Oh, hush, my son," said she, striking him on the mouth; "you must not push your questions so far." But it was by following this train of thought that Abraham arrived at the knowledge of the one true God.

Another Rabbinical story is, that Abraham was only ten days in the cave after his birth, and then he was able to walk, and he left it. But his mother, who visited the grotto, finding him gone, was a prey to anguish and fear.

Wandering along the bank of the river, searching for her child, she met Abraham, but did not recognize him, as he had grown tall; and she asked him if he had seen a little baby anywhere.

"I am he whom you seek," answered Abraham.

"Is this possible!" exclaimed the mother. "Could you grow to such a height, and be able to walk and talk, in ten days?"

"Yes, mother," answered the youthful prodigy; "all this has taken place that you might know that there is but one living and true God who made heaven and earth, who dwells in heaven and fills the earth with His goodness."

"What!" asked Amtelai, "is there another god besides Nimrod?"

"By all means," replied the infant son; "there is a God in heaven, who is also the God who made Nimrod. Now go to Nimrod and announce this to him."

Abraham's mother related all this to her husband, who bore the message to the king. Nimrod, greatly alarmed, consulted his council what was to be done with the boy.[1]

---

[1] The Mussulman history of the patriarch relates that Azar brought Abraham before Nimrod and said, "This is thy God who made all things." "Then why did he not make himself less ugly?" asked Abraham,—for Nimrod had bad features.

The council replied that he had nothing to fear from an infant of ten days,—he, the king and god of the world! But Nimrod was not satisfied. Then Satan, putting on a black robe, mingled with the advisers of the monarch and said, "Let the king open his arsenal, arm all his troops, and march against this precocious infant." This advice fell in completely with Nimrod's own personal fears, and his army was marched against the baby. But when Abraham saw the host drawn up in battle array, he cried to heaven with many tears, and Gabriel came to his succour, enveloped the infant in clouds, and snatched him from the sight of those who came against him; and they, frightened at the cloud and darkness, fled precipitately to Babylon.

Abraham followed them on the shoulders of Gabriel, and reaching the gates of the city in an instant of time, he cried, "The Eternal One is the true and only God, and none other is like Him! He is the God of heaven, God of gods and Lord of Nimrod! Be convinced of this, all ye men, women and children who dwell here, even as I am Abraham, his servant." Then he sought his parents, and bade Terah go and fulfil his command to Nimrod.

Terah went accordingly, and announced to the king that his son, whom the army had been unable to capture, had, in a brief space of time, traversed a country across which was forty days' journey.

Nimrod quaked, and consulted his princes, who advised him to institute a festival of seven days, during which every subject and dweller on the face of the earth was to make a pilgrimage to his palace, and there to worship and adore him.

In the meantime Nimrod, being very curious to see Abraham, ordered Terah to bring him into his royal presence. The child entered the throne-room boldly, and going to the foot of the steps which led to the throne, he exclaimed: "Woe to thee, accursed Nimrod, blasphemer of God! Acknowledge, O Nimrod, that the true God is without body, evelasting, never slumbering nor sleeping; acknowledge that He created the world, that all men may believe in Him likewise!"

At the same moment all the idols in the palace fell, and the king rolled from his throne in convulsions, and remained in a fit for two hours.

When he came to himself again, he said to Abraham, "Was that thy voice, or was it the voice of God?"

Abraham answered, "It was the voice of the meanest of His creatures."

"Then your God must be great and mighty, and a King of kings."

Nimrod now suffered Abraham to depart, and as his anger was abated, the child remained in his father's house, and no attempts were made against his life.

Here must be inserted a legend of the childhood of Abraham, which I have ventured to render into verse.

### THE GIFT OF THE KING.

Nimrod the Cushite sat upon a throne
Of gold, encrusted with the sapphire stone,
And round the monarch stood, in triple rank,
Three hundred ruddy pages, like a bank
  Of roses all a-blow.
Two gentle boys, with blue eyes clear as glass,
And locks as light as tufted cotton grass,
  And faces as the snow
That lies on Ararat, and flushes pink
On summer evenings, as the sun doth sink,
Were stationed by the royal golden chair
With fillets of carnation in their hair,
And clothed in silken vesture, candid, clean,
To flutter fans of burnished blue and green,
  Fashioned of peacock's plume.
A little lower, on a second stage
On either side, was placed a graceful page,
  To raise a fragrant fume—
With costly woods and gums on burning coals
That glowed on tripods, in bright silver bowls;
And at the basement of the marble stair,
Sweet singing choirs and harping minstrels were,
In amber kirtles purple gilt and sashed.
The throbbing strings in silver ripples flashed,

Where slaves the choral song
Accompanied with psaltery and lyre,
In red and saffron, like to men of fire,
　　　Whilst hoarsely boomed the gong :
Or silver cymbals clashed, or, waxing shrill,
Danced up the scale a flute's melodious thrill.

Now at the monarch's signal, pages twain,
With sunny hair as ripened autumn grain,
And robed in lustrous silver tissue, shot
With changing hues of blue forget-me-not,
　　　Start nimbly forth, and bend
Before the monarch, at his gilded stool,
And crystal goblets brimming, sweet and cool,
　　　Obsequiously extend ;
But Nimrod, slightly stirring, stately, calm,
Towards the right-hand beaker thrusts his arm,
And, languid, raises it towards his lips ;
Yet ere he of the ruby liquor sips,
He notices upon the surface lie—
Fallen in and fluttering—a feeble fly,
　　　With draggled wings outspread.
Then shot from Nimrod's eyes an angry flare,
And passionately down the marble stair
　　　The costly draught he shed.
He spoke no word, but with a finger wave,
Made signal to a scarlet-vested slave ;
And as the lad before him, quaking, kneels,
Above him swift the gleaming falchion wheels,
Then flashes down, and, with one leap, his head
Bounds from his shoulders, and bespirts with red
　　　The alabaster floor.
And, mingled with the outpoured Persian wine,
Descends the steps a sliding purple line
　　　Of smoking, dribbled gore ;
And floats the little midge upon a flood
Of fragrant grape-juice, and of roseate blood.

Then Nimrod said : " I would yon ugly stain
Were wiped away ; and thou, my chamberlain,
Obtain for me a stripling, to replace
This petty fool. Let him have comely face,
　　　And be of slender mould :
Be lithely built, of noble birth ; a youth,
The choicest thou can find. His cost, in sooth !
　　　I heed not. Stint no gold,
But buy a goodly slave : for I, a king,
Will have the best, the best of everything—
Of gems, of slaves, of fabrics, meats, or wine ;
The best, the very best on earth be mine."
Then, prostrate flung before his master's throne,
The servant said, " Sire ! Terah hath a son

Whose equal in the whole round world is none,
    Belovèd as himself.
But, Sire! I fear the father will not deign
To yield his son as slave through love of gain,
    For great is he in wealth."
"Go!" said the monarch, "I must have the child:
Be sure the father can be reconciled,
If you expend of gold a goodly store,
And, if he haggles at your price, bid-more;
    I will it, chamberlain!
I care not what the cost. I'll have the lad!"
And then, he leaned him idly back, and bade
    The slaves to fan again.

Now on the morrow, to the royal court,
Terah Ben-Nahor from old Ur was brought—
Protesting loud he would not yield his son
As slave, at any price, to any one.
    "My flesh and blood be sold!
Fie on you! Do you reckon that I prize
My first-begotten as mere merchandise,
    To barter him for gold!
A curse on him who would the old man's stay,
That bears him up, with money buy away!
Require me not to offer child of mine
To serve and brim a tyrant's cup with wine;
To waste a life from morning to its grave,
Branded in mind and soul and body 'Slave!'
    How could I be repaid?
His artless fondlings, all his childish ways:
The reminiscences of olden days,
    That sudden flash and fade,
Of her who bore him—her, my boyhood's choice—
Resemblances in feature, figure, voice,
In gesture, manner, ay! in very tone
Of pealing laugh, of that dear partner gone?
Thou, Nimrod, to an old man condescend
To hear his story; your attention lend,
    And judge if acted well.
Last year to me thou gav'st a goodly steed,
From thine own stud, of purest Yemen breed:
    And thus it me befel.
A stranger offered me a price so fair
That I accepted it, and sold the mare."
"My gift disposed of!" with an angry start,
King Nimrod thundered: "Thou, old man, shalt smart
For this thy avarice. A royal gift,
Thou knowest well, must never owners shift,
    As thing of little worth."
Then Terah raised his trembling hands, and said,
"From thine own mouth, O King, has judgment sped.
    The Lord of Heaven and Earth,

> The King of Kings to me my offspring gave,
> And shall I sell His gift to be a slave?
> Nimrod! that child, which is His royal gift,—
> Thy mouth hath said it,—may not owners shift."

At this time idolatry was commonly practised by all. Nimrod and his servants, Terah and his whole house, worshipped images of wood and stone. Terah had not only twelve idols of the twelve months which he adored, but he manufactured images and sold them.

One day, when Terah was absent, and Abraham was left to manage the shop, he thought the time had come when he must make his protest against idolatry. This he did as follows. Every purchaser who came, was asked by Abraham his age; if he answered fifty or sixty years old, Abraham exclaimed, "Woe to a man of such an age who adores the work of one day!" and the purchaser withdrew in shame.

Another version of the incident is more full.

A strong lusty fellow came one day to buy an idol, the strongest that there was. As he was going away with it, Abraham called after him, "How old are you?"

"Seventy years," he answered.

"Oh, you fool!" said Abraham, "to adore a god younger than yourself."

"What do you mean?" asked the purchaser.

"Why, you were born seventy years ago, and this god was made only yesterday."

Hearing this, the buyer threw the idol away.

Shortly after, an old woman brought a dish of meal to set before the idols. Abraham took it, and then with a stick smashed all the gods except the biggest, into whose hands he placed the stick.

Terah, who was returning home, heard the noise of blows, and quickened his pace. When he entered, his gods were in pieces.

He accused Abraham angrily; but Abraham said, "My father, a woman brought this dish of meal for the gods: they all wanted to have it, and the strongest knocked the heads off the rest, lest they should eat it all." And this, say the Mussulmans, was the *first* lie that Abraham told, but it was not a lie, but a justifiable falsehood.

Terah said this could not be true, for the images were of wood and stone.

"Let thine ear hear what thy mouth hath spoken," said Abraham, and then he exhorted his father against idolatry.

Terah complained to Nimrod, who sent for Abraham, and he said to him, "Wilt thou not worship these idols? Well then, adore fire."

"Why not water which quenches fire?" asked Abraham.

*Nimrod.*—"Very well; then worship water."

*Abraham.*—"Why not the clouds which swallow the water?"

*Nimrod.*—"So be it; adore the clouds."

*Abraham.*—"Rather let me adore wind which blows the clouds about."

*Nimrod.*—"So be it; pray to the wind."

*Abraham.*—"But man can stand up against the wind, and build it out of his house."

Then Nimrod in a fury exclaimed, "Fire is my god, and that shall consume you."

According to another version, a woman came to Abraham to buy a god, because thieves had stolen her former god; this gave the patriarch a text for his homily against idolatry. The woman was convinced.

"Believe in the true God," said he, "and you will recover the things the thieves stole from your house."

A few days after, the woman recovered all her lost goods, amongst them her image. Then she took a stone, and smashed its head, saying, "Oh, thou blockhead, not to be able to preserve my property and thyself from thieves!"

The report of what she had said and done reached the king, who ordered her to be executed. But Nimrod was uneasy, and he announced a grand ceremony to last for seven days, during which every one was to produce his gods and carry them about the streets, which were to be hung with gold and silks. His object was to dazzle Abraham's eyes by the splendour of idol worship. He sent for Terah and Abraham, but the latter refused to attend. The Mussulmans say that Abraham excused himself thus: "I see in the stars that I am going to be very sick to-day." This was the *second* lie Abraham told, but it was not a lie, it was a justifiable falsehood. Then the king sent his guard, who arrested him and cast him into a dungeon.

He lay in the dungeon ten days. The angel Gabriel brought him food, and a crystal fountain bubbled up through the soil of his cell.

Nimrod called his council together, and it was unanimously decided that Abraham should be burnt alive. The king therefore published a decree ordering every man to bring wood or other fuel for the heating of the kiln.[1] The wood was piled about the furnace to the height of five ells, for a circle of five ells diameter, and for three days and three nights the fire was kept up, and the flames licked the heavens, so that the oven was at a white heat. Then Nimrod ordered his jailer to produce Abraham. The prison-keeper humbly answered, that it was impossible that Abraham could be alive, for he had been given neither meat nor drink. But Nimrod answered, "Produce him alive or dead."

Then the jailer went to the prison door and cried, "Abraham, livest thou?"

"I live," answered the prisoner, "and am hearty."

"How is that possible?" asked the jailer, astonished.

"Because the Almighty has wrought a miracle on my behalf.

---

[1] The Mussulman story, which is precisely the same as the Jewish, adds that the camels refused to bear wood to form the pyre, but cast it on the ground; therefore Abraham blessed the camels. But the mules had no compunction, therefore he cursed them that they should be sterile. The birds who flew over the fire were killed, the city was enveloped in its smoke, and the crackling of its flames could be heard a day's journey off.

He is sole God, invisible, the Creator of the world, and the Lord of Nimrod."

The jailer believed.

The news was conveyed to Nimrod, who ordered the immediate execution of the jailer; but as the executioner was about to smite off his head, he cried, "The Eternal One is alone the true God of the world, and the God of Nimrod who denies him." And lo! the sword was blunted, and shivered into a thousand fragments.

Here we must add a few particulars from Mussulman sources.

"Who is your God?" asked Nimrod of Abraham, when brought before him.

"He who kills and makes alive again," said Abraham.

"I can do that," exclaimed Nimrod, and he ordered two prisoners before him; one he slew, the other he spared.

But Abraham said, "Behold the power of my God!" and he bade a dead man who had been four years in his grave, rise and bring him a white cock, a black raven, a green pigeon, and a gaily-coloured peacock. The dead man rose and obeyed. Then Abraham cut up the birds, but preserved their heads; and lo! from the heads new bodies sprouted.

"Now," said Abraham, "do the same."

But Nimrod could not.

"If thou art a God," said Abraham again, "command the sun to rise to-morrow in the west and set in the east."

But this he could not do.[1]

Nimrod was highly incensed, and ordered that Abraham should be at once precipitated into the fire. When he was brought before the king, say the Rabbis, the soothsayers recognized him as the boy at whose birth they had warned the king that one was come into the world who would be the father of a great nation which would subdue that of Nimrod, and would possess the whole earth and heaven.

"This is the man against whom we cautioned you," they

[1] Weil, p. 73.

said; "his father Terah must have deceived you, O king, and not have given you up the right child."

Terah, on being questioned, owned the truth.

"Who gave you this advice?" asked the king; "confess it, and your life shall be spared."

Out of fear Terah told a lie, and said that Haran, his other son, had suggested the deception.

"For having given this advice," said Nimrod, "Haran shall perish along with Abraham. Cast them both into the flames." Abraham and Haran were now to be stripped and their hands and feet bound by ropes, and then they were to be thrown into the fire. But the servants of Nimrod who approached the brothers were caught by the flames which, like the tongues of serpents, shot out, curled round them, drew them into the fire, and consumed them.

Then Satan appeared to Nimrod, and instructed him how to make a catapult which would throw stones to a distance, and by means of which Abraham and Haran could be projected into the midst of the fire.

Haran was undecided in his mind whether to worship God or idols; sometimes he sided with Abraham, and sometimes with Terah. Now, the moment Haran was shot into the flames, his heart failed him, and he cried out that he would worship idols if his life were spared. But it was too late, he was burnt to ashes. But Abraham was unharmed. The cords which bound him were consumed, but for three days and nights he walked about in the flames, and felt no inconvenience.[1]

Then the king cried aloud, "Abraham, servant of the God of Heaven, come forth from the furnace to me."

And Abraham came forth. Then the king said to him, "How is it that thou art not consumed?" And Abraham answered,

---

[1] Both the Rabbinic commentators and the Mussulman historians tell a long story about the discussion carried on between Gabriel and Abraham in the air, as he was being shot into the flames. It is hardly worth repeating.

"The Lord God of Heaven and Earth, whom I serve, hath delivered me."

Instantly the flames were extinguished, and the wood burst forth into flower and fruit; and the pile was like a grove of flowering shrubs to look upon, and Angels descended and took Abraham and seated him in the midst.

The Arabic version of this part of the story is something different.

Nimrod could not see into the fire, so he ascended a high tower in his palace, and from the top looked down into the furnace, and saw that in the midst was a garden with flowers and a fountain of sparkling water, and Abraham seated on the grass beside the spring, conversing with an angel.[1]

Nimrod now loaded Abraham with presents, amongst which were two slaves named Oni and Eliezer; according to some, the latter was a son of the tyrant. Many followed Abraham home, and brought their children to him and said, "Now we see that the God in whom thou trustest, is the only true God; teach our children the truth, that they may serve Him in righteousness." Thus three hundred persons accompanied Abraham home, most of whom were servants of the king, and of noble race.

Here follows in the Mussulman account the story of Nimrod's attempt to reach heaven in a box, to which were attached four vultures. His object was, says Tabari, to kill the God of Abraham. He went up along with his vizir. After a night and day in the air, the king said to his vizir, "Open the window of the box towards the earth and tell me what you see." He did so, and replied, "I see the earth." After another day and night, he again looked out and saw the earth still; on the third day, at the king's command he looked out and saw nothing. Then said Nimrod, "Open the window towards heaven and look out." He did so and saw nothing. Then Nimrod shot three arrows into the sky, and they fell back with blood on them. So

[1] Tabari, i. p. 147.

Nimrod said, "I have killed the God of Abraham." But whence the blood came is unsettled. Some say that the arrows hit a bird which flew higher than the vultures; but others, with more probability, say they struck a fish, which was being carried by the wind, that had caught it up with the rain out of the sea.[1]

Abraham now married the daughter of his brother Haran, named Sarai or Jisha, "the seeress," because she was endowed with the spirit of prophecy, say some, or, say others, because she was so beautiful that every one wanted to see her. At the time of his marriage, Abraham was aged fifty; others, however, suggest twenty-five.

Two years later, Nimrod was visited with a dream. He saw himself and all his army in a valley, near the furnace into which he had cast Abraham. A man resembling the latter stepped out of the furnace and approached the king, holding a naked sword. When Nimrod recoiled, the man cast an egg at his head; the egg broke and became a mighty river, which swept all his host away, saving only three men; and on looking at them, the king saw that they wore royal robes, and exactly resembled himself. Then the stream retreated into the egg, and when all the water was gathered into it, from the egg hopped out a chicken, which seated itself on Nimrod's head, and pecked out one of his eyes.

Next morning the king sent for his soothsayers to explain the dream, and this was their interpretation: "Hear, O king! this dream presages to thee great misfortune, which Abraham and his posterity shall bring upon thee. The time will come when he will war with his forces against thee and thy forces, and will overcome them and put them to the sword. Thou alone wilt escape with three of thy confederates; but a messenger of Abraham will cause thy death. Therefore, O king! remember that thy council of wise men foretold this fifty-two years ago, in the stars at Abraham's birth. As long as Abraham

[1] Weil, p. 78.

bodies; then Ormuzd collected
placed it as a boundary to the
ocean formed."¹

The ancient Indian tradition i
sun-born monarch Satyavrata, the
and the whole human race destr
pious prince himself, the seven Ris
This general *pralaya*, or destruc
first Purana, or sacred poem; and
in the eighth book of the Bhagava
is an abridged extract:—"The de
loined the Vedas from Brahma w
whole race of men became corrup
and Satyavrata. This prince was
the river Critamala, when Vishnu ap
of a small fish, and after several
different waters, was placed by Sa
he thus addressed his amazed votar
tures who have offended me shall b
thou shalt be secured in a capacious
Take, therefore, all kinds of medici
for food, and, together with the sev
wives, and pairs of all animals, ent
shalt thou know God face to face, a
answered.' Saying this, he disappear
ocean began to overflow the coasts.
by constant showers, when Satyavr
saw a large vessel moving on the w
in all respects conformed to the in
the form of a large fish, suffered the
sea-serpent, as with a cable, to hi
the deluge had ceased, Vishnu sle
the Vedas, and instructed Satyavr

¹ Bundehesch, 7.
² On the Chronology of the Hindus,
searches, ii. pp. 116-7.

rought thee out of the furnace
this land to inherit it." And he
ll I know that I shall inherit it?
ul and true, and serve Thee the
gainst God, against Thee, as did
d as did the men of Shinar who

an heifer of three years old, or a
d a ram, and a turtle-dove, and a
all these and divided them in the
ne against another; but the birds
aid to him, "When, in after days,
me a temple, in it shall these five
me."
hould the temple be destroyed,
ost Holy, "they shall offer to me
heir sins." The beasts and birds
r which his seed was to reign; the
betokened the Gentile races, from
away their idolatry; but *the birds*
signified the elect nation.
ultures down upon the carcases, but
y (ver. 11); a symbol of the protec-
cord to the people, for His promise
r father Abraham, when the powers of
menaced them.

was going down, a deep sleep fell
12), and he saw the four realms,—the
bylonian, Medo-Persian, Syro-Grecian,
And God said to Abraham (ver. 13),
*that thy seed shall be a stranger in a land*
*shall serve them; and they shall afflict them*
in the fourth generation thy seed
n. xv.

lives thou art in jeopardy. Wherefore should he be suffered to live any longer?"

Nimrod believing what was said, sent a servant to assassinate Abraham. But Eliezer, the slave, whom Nimrod had given to the patriarch, had been with the councillors when this advice was given, and he fled and told Abraham before the emissary of the tyrant arrived; and Abraham left his house and took refuge with Noah and Shem, and remained hidden with them for the space of one month.

Here Terah sought him in secret; and Abraham addressed him a long discourse on the vanity of idol-worship, and the evil of serving the godless tyrant Nimrod. And Noah and Shem supported him.

Then Terah, who grieved over the death of his son Haran, consented to all that Abraham had said, and he went forth with Abraham and his wife Sarah, and Lot his grandson, the son of Haran, and all his household, and they settled at Charan, where the land was fruitful and well watered. The dwellers in Charan associated themselves with Abraham, who instructed them in the knowledge and fear of the Lord.

2. THE CALL OF ABRAHAM, AND THE VISIT TO EGYPT.

For three years Abraham dwelt in Charan, till God called him to go further with his wife Sarah, and to take up his abode in Canaan; but Terah and Lot remained at Charan. Abraham reached Canaan and pitched his tent among the inhabitants of that land; and on the spot where God promised that He would give him all that pleasant country for his inheritance, he erected an altar to the Eternal One.

For fifteen years he had dwelt in Canaan, and Abraham was now aged 70, when, on the 15th day of the first month (Nisan), on the self-same day on which, in after years, the children of Israel went out of Egypt, the voice of God came to him saying, "I am the Lord that brought thee out of the furnace of Chaldæa; to thee will I give this land to inherit it." And he said, "Lord God, whereby shall I know that I shall inherit it? Shall my descendants be faithful and true, and serve Thee the living God, or will they rebel against God, against Thee, as did the men before the Flood, and as did the men of Shinar who builded the tower?"

Then God bade him take an heifer of three years old, or a she-goat of three years old, and a ram, and a turtle-dove, and a young pigeon. And he took all these and divided them in the midst, and laid each piece one against another; but the birds divided he not.[1] And God said to him, "When, in after days, thy descendants shall build me a temple, in it shall these five kinds of victims be offered to me."

"But," said Abraham, "should the temple be destroyed, what then shall they do?"

"Then," answered the Most Holy, "they shall offer to me in spirit, and I will pardon their sins." The beasts and birds also signified the races over which his seed was to reign; the beasts he divided, and they betokened the Gentile races, from which they were to purge away their idolatry: but *the birds divided he not;* for the birds signified the elect nation.

Then came ravens and vultures down upon the carcases, but Abraham drove them away (ver. 11); a symbol of the protection which God would accord to the people, for His promise sake, and the sake of their father Abraham, when the powers of evil, or mighty princes, menaced them.

And when the sun was going down, a deep sleep fell upon Abraham (ver. 12), and he saw the four realms,—the horror-awakening Babylonian, Medo-Persian, Syro-Grecian, and Roman empires. And God said to Abraham (ver. 13), "*Know of a surety that thy seed shall be a stranger in a land that is not theirs, and shall serve them; and they shall afflict them four hundred years.* But in the fourth generation thy seed

---

[1] Gen. xv.

shall come hither again, after I have plagued the nation that has held them in bondage with 250 plagues."

"Is this decree spoken to punish me for my crimes?" asked Abraham.

"No," answered the Almighty: "*Thou shalt go to thy fathers in peace; thou shalt be buried in a good old age* (ver. 15); and Terah, who now bewails his former idolatry, has a share in the eternal happiness; also Ishmael, thy son, who shall be born to thee, will, in thy lifetime, repent and return to good, and the profanity of thy grandson Esau shalt thou not see."

And when the sun was set, it was dark, and the various periods of futurity passed before the eyes of the seer. He beheld *a smoking furnace* (ver. 17); this was the flaming Gehinom, Hell, where sinners shall expiate their iniquities. Then he saw *a burning lamp:* that was the Law given on Sinai, and it *passed between those pieces;* that is, he saw Israel go through the Red Sea.

Then said the voice of God to the patriarch, "I have showed thee the Temple-worship, Law, Bondage, and Hell. I must tell thee that in the times to come, through the sins of thy children, the Temple will be destroyed, and the Law will be disregarded. Choose now, whether thou wilt have for their punishment, Bondage or Hell."

And Abraham after long hesitation answered, "I choose Hell;" for he thought, "It is better to fall into the hands of God, than into the hands of men."

But the Lord answered and said, "Not so; thou hast chosen wrongly, for from Bondage there will come deliverance, but from Gehinom, never."

After that, Abraham returned to the land of Charan, and dwelt there many years; and he instructed the men, and Sarah the women, in the true religion. And when his father Terah was dead, God called him again, and bade him go forth to the land which God had promised him; and he went obediently, and Lot his brother's son accompanied him. And he reached the land of Canaan, and pitched first his wife's tent, and then his own, on the plain between Gerizim and Ebal; and he erected three altars in thanks to God for His call, for His having brought him into the promised land, and for having cast down his enemies before him. Then he went south, and pitched on the spot where stands Jerusalem.

And now a famine came upon the land; this was the third famine since the world was formed, and it was sent to prove Abraham. He murmured not, but went down with Sarah his wife, and his servants.

When he reached the River of Egypt (Wadi el Arisch), Abraham rested some days. As Abraham and Sarah walked together by the water-side, Abraham saw for the first time, reflected in the water, the beauty of Sarah; for he was so modest that he had never lifted his eyes to her face, and knew not what she was like, till he saw her in the water. Then, when he saw how beautiful she was, he persuaded her to pass as his sister in Egypt, for he feared lest he should be slain for her sake; but as a further precaution he shut her up in a chest.

On the frontier, the Custom-house officers insisted on his paying the customs due for the box, and required that it should be opened. Abraham offered to pay for the box as if it contained gold dust or gems, if only they would not enforce their right of search.

"Does it contain silk?" asked the officers.

"I will pay the tenth, as of silk," he answered.

"Does it contain silver?" they further asked.

"I will pay for it as silver."

"Nay, then it must contain gold."

"I will pay for it as gold."

"Maybe it contains the most rare and costly gems."

"I will pay for it as for gems."

In the altercation the chest was violently broken open, and lo! in it was seated a beautiful woman, so beautiful that her countenance illumined all Egypt; and the news reached the ears of Pharaoh. All this occurred in the night of the 15th of the month Nisan.

Abraham and Sarah were sorely troubled, and prayed to God to protect them. Then the angel of the Lord was sent to watch over Sarah, and the angel comforted her with these words, "Fear not; God has heard thy petitions!"

Pharaoh asked Sarah who that man was who accompanied her, and when she answered "My brother," Pharaoh bade him to be brought before him, and he gave him rich gifts.

And Pharaoh asked Abraham, "Who is this woman?" He answered, "She is my sister." This, say the Mussulmans, is the *third* lie that Abraham told; but it was not a lie, but a justifiable falsehood.

Pharaoh was filled with love for Sarah, and he offered her as his present for her hand, all his possessions of gold and silver and slaves, and the land of Goshen. And when he pressed his suit upon her with great vehemence, she cried to God and told him she was already married; then he was smitten with paralysis, and great plagues afflicted all his servants. But Pharaoh sent for Abraham, and returned him Sarah, his wife, and dismissed him with costly presents, and he gave to Sarah also his daughter, Hagar, to be her servant.

"Truly, my daughter, it is better," said Pharaoh, "to be servant in a house which God has taken under His protection, than to command elsewhere."

After a three months' sojourn in Egypt, Abraham returned to Canaan.

According to Tabari, Hagar loved Sarah greatly. On their way back to Canaan, the provisions failed, and Abraham went out one day to get food, with a sack on his back; but the day was hot, so that he laid down and went to sleep. He did not awake till evening, and then he returned, but was ashamed to appear with the sack empty before his wife, so he filled it with sand. On reaching the tent he put the sack under his head and went to sleep again. Very early in the morning Sarah said to Hagar, "What has Abraham in his sack? open it and look." So Hagar untied it, put in her hand and drew out flour. She and Sarah baked cakes of the flour, and woke Abraham and bade him eat. Then, full of wonder, he asked where they had obtained meal. They told him, and he understood that God had wrought a miracle.[1]

Now Abraham's flocks and herds, and those of Lot, pastured together. Abraham's cattle were muzzled that they should not feed in the lands of the neighbouring people; but Lot's cattle were not muzzled. And when Abraham's shepherds complained of this to those of Lot, the latter answered, "Your master is old, and has no children; soon he will die, and then all will belong to our master Lot."

But Abraham spake to Lot and said, "Thy ways and my ways do not agree: we must part; do thou go to the left, and I will go to the right." So they separated; and Lot departed from Abraham, and from the way of righteousness, and from the living God; but Abraham camped in Mamre.

### 3. THE WAR WITH THE KINGS.

After the failure of the Tower of Babel, and the people had been scattered over the whole earth, Chedorlaomer, one of Nimrod's chief captains, had left his service, and had established a kingdom of his own in Elam. He speedily brought into subjection all the Canaanitish peoples that dwelt in the fertile valley of Jordan,—Sodom, Gomorrah, Admah, Zebojim, and Zoar, and made them tributary to himself. These cities bore his yoke for twelve years, and then they rebelled. Five years after did Nimrod, who is also called Amraphel in

[1] Tabari, i. p. 156.

the sacred text,[1] march against Chedorlaomer, but Nimrod was defeated, along with his allies, Arioch, king of Ellasar, and Tidal, king of many confederate nations; and obliged to enter into alliance with his former general, Chedorlaomer; and agree to assist him in bringing back the revolted cities—Sodom, Gomorrah, Admah, Zebojim, and Zoar—to their allegiance.

Consequently a huge army of confederates, under Chedorlaomer, Nimrod or Amraphel, Arioch, and Tidal, overran the plain and valley of Jordan, and slew all the giants that were there. The country before them was a garden, and behind them it was a desert.

They resolved also to defeat, and utterly to destroy, Abraham, the servant of the Most High; for Nimrod (Amraphel) remembered the perils to which his soothsayers had assured him he was exposed so long as Abraham lived.

The rulers of the five cities—Bera (Ruffian), king of Sodom; Birsha (Evil-doer), king of Gomorrah; Shirrab (Covetous one), king of Admah; Shemeber (the Strong one), king of Zebojim; and the king (a nameless one) of Bela (the engulfing city)—went forth in battle array, and met the host of Chedorlaomer in the great plain of Siddim, from whose canals and fountains the Salt Sea, or Dead Sea, was afterwards formed; and there they were utterly routed, and fled in precipitate haste to the mountains and to the desert.

The king of Sodom alone escaped unharmed of all the five kings, by a miracle which God wrought, to exhibit His power to the dwellers in the plain, who had begun to doubt the truth of Abraham's deliverance out of the burning, fiery furnace.

The conquerors took the spoils of Sodom, and carried away Lot, who was like Abraham in face, thinking that they had taken Abraham captive; and they placed him in chains.

Abraham was, in prophetic spirit, performing all the sacred rites, and preparing the unleavened cakes for the Paschal feast,

---

[1] Gen. xiv. 19. The book Jasher also says that Amraphel and Nimrod are the same.

for it was the Eve of the Passover, when the only giant who escaped the overthrow of the Rephaim by Chedorlaomer and his confederate kings,—Og, who was afterwards king of Basan, and who had been saved alive in the Flood of Noah,—came in haste to announce to the Patriarch the captivity of Lot.

Now Og had long cast his lustful eyes on Sarah, and he thought in his heart, "This Abraham is full of fire and zeal, like a sportsman; that I know well. He will rush into battle to deliver his kinsman Lot, and will perish; and then Sarah, his beautiful wife, will be mine."

But, according to another version, it was the angel Michael who brought the news to Abraham; and to another, it was Oni, one of the slaves Nimrod had given him, and who had been sent to observe the progress of the war.

No sooner had Abraham heard the tidings than, filled with anxiety on Lot's behalf, and with sympathy for the Sodomites, his neighbours, he called all his neighbours together, and all those who had followed him, and in earnest words exhorted them to prepare to fight and rescue Lot. But they, knowing the disparity of numbers, would make no promise; then he threatened them, but could not persuade them to join in what they regarded as an infatuated course certain to lead to destruction. Consequently Abraham was obliged to go against the enemy with only his own servants. But as they neared the plain, and saw the devastation wrought by the host of Chedorlaomer, they also slipped away in the night, and Abraham was left alone with Eliezer, his trusty slave, and his three friends Aner, Eshcol, and Mamre. And he followed after the foe, as they retired with their spoil, till he reached one of the fountains of Jordan, which is named Paneas, or Dan.

Here his three friends forsook him, along with their wives, who had accompanied them thus far.

It was the night of the 15th Nisan, the self-same night in which in after-years the firstborn of Egypt would be slain; and Abraham's heart fainted as he overtook the mighty host, and saw that they were countless as the sands of the sea-shore, and as grasshoppers for number.

But lo! God fought for Abraham. The grass-blades changed into swords, and the stubble into spears, and battled all that night; and in the morning, when he looked upon the host, they were all dead corpses. Thus he delivered Lot and all the captives, men, women, and children, and the spoil that had been carried away; and none stayed them, for all their foes lay dead upon the ground.

The King of Sodom came forth to meet Abraham, full of pride of heart because he had been miraculously delivered, and attributing all the glory of the victory to Divine interposition on his own behalf. But all the people knew that Abraham was the favoured of God, and their deliverer, and they built a throne of the trees that covered the plain, and which had been burnt in the war, and set Abraham as their prince and king thereon; therefore is that place called to this day, "The king's dale."[1]

But Abraham was little pleased with this exhibition of honour, and he thought upon what he had learnt of old from that aged man, Shem, consecrated by God to be His priest, when he fled to him in his cave from the tyranny of Nimrod.

Shem reigned now in the city of Salem, which was in later years called Jerusalem, and from his righteous government he was named Melchizedek (king of righteousness). And Abraham thought, "Will Shem ever forgive me for having drawn the sword against his grandsons, the sons of Elam?"

But Shem was of no less noble and considerate temper than Abraham; and he mused within himself, and said, "What sort of opinion can Abraham have formed of me, that such godless and violent hosts should have sprung from my loins, and have devastated the fair plain of Jordan, and carried away captive even his near kinsman!"

Then Shem, full of noble resolution to reconcile himself with

[1] Gen. xiv. 17.

Abraham, rose up and went forth, bearing bread and wine as tokens of friendship.

The words of God flowed from his mouth; he instructed Abraham in all that appertained to the high priest's office, which was in future times to belong to his family; and before he left, he blessed Abraham with these words, "*Blessed be Abraham of the most high God, possessor of heaven and earth; and blessed be the most high God, which hath delivered thine enemies into thy hand.*"[1]

But in so saying, Melchizedek erred grievously, for he blessed Abraham before he blessed God, and the Creator should be blessed first, and the creature blessed afterwards; therefore the high priesthood was taken from him, and was given to Aaron in after-times.

Of all the spoil which Abraham had taken, he separated a tenth part, and he gave it to Melchizedek, as the offering due to the priest, and this was the first tithe paid in the history of the world. All the booty of Sodom Abraham returned to the king thereof, and he took an oath, "*I will not take from a thread even to a shoe-latchet, and I will not take anything that is thine, lest thou should say, I have made Abraham rich, save only that which the young men have eaten, and the portion of the men which went with me, Aner, Eshcol, and Mamre; let them take their portion.*"[2]

On account of this unselfishness, the remembrance of which was to be continued through all generations, God gave the descendants of Abraham maxims to be written on their phylacteries and shoe-latchets; and the promise was made, "*Over Edom will I cast out my shoe;*"[3] that is, Edom, the most cruel oppressor of the chosen people, should fall under the condemnation of the Most High.

The end of Nimrod and his confederate kings is related with greater fulness by the Mussulman historians.

According to Tabari, God sent an army of flies against the

---

[1] Gen. xiv. 19, 20.     [2] Gen. xiv. 23, 24.     [3] Ps. ix. 8.

host of Chedorlaomer and Nimrod, and these flies attacked the soldiers in their faces; and the flies were so numerous that the soldiers could not see one another; and the horses stung by them went mad, and leaped, and fell; so that, what with the horses and the flies, the army was entirely dispersed. Nimrod escaped to Babylon, but he was pursued by the meanest of the gnats of that host; it was blind of one eye and lame of one leg. When Nimrod sat down on his throne, the gnat settled upon his knee. Then the tyrant smote at it; and it rose, flew up one of his nostrils and entered his brain, which it began to devour.

Nimrod beat his face and his head, and when he did so the fly ceased gnawing at his brain, but he had no repose from his agonies, save when struck upon the head. Consequently there was, after that, always some one stationed by him to strike his head. The king had a large blacksmith's hammer brought into his throne-room, and with that his princes and nobles smote him on the head; and the more violent the blow, the greater was the relief afforded. Nimrod reigned a thousand years before he felt the torment of the gnat; up to that moment he had suffered no pains. He lived for five hundred years with the fly eating at his brain; and all that while, night and day, there were relays of men to strike his head with the hammer.[1]

Precisely the same story is told by the Jewish Rabbis of Titus.[2]

There is, however, another version of the tradition; which is, that the gnat fattening on the brain grew in size till it swelled to the dimensions of a pigeon, and then the skull of Nimrod burst, and the gnat flew away; and this was fifteen days after it had entered by his nose.[3]

More shall be told of Melchizedek in a separate article.

---

[1] Tabari, i. c. xlviii.
[2] Gittin, fol. 56 b; Pirke of R. Eliezer, fol. 49.
[3] Weil, p. 80.

### 4. THE BIRTH OF ISHMAEL.

Ten years passed, and yet Sarah was barren. Abraham, in sore distress, prayed to God, and reminded Him of His promises. Sarah then said to Abraham, "God has refused me children, therefore take Hagar to wife, the daughter of Pharaoh, who was given to be my servant; I give her thee in all goodwill, that my reproach may be taken away, and to her I give her freedom."

Abraham consented; but Hagar, who had been virtuously brought up by Sarah, objected modestly, till Sarah pointed out to her how great an honour it would be to be the concubine of such a holy man.

But no sooner was Hagar installed as second wife, and felt in herself that she was about to become a mother, than her character changed; she assumed the pre-eminence, and cast bitter words in the teeth of her mistress. "What," said she, "can Sarah be so holy and beloved of God, and He has never given her her heart's desire?"

Sarah was stung to the quick by these words of her former slave. She turned to her husband and said, "I demand of thee my rights. For thee I forsook my father's house, and followed thee into a strange land; for thee I passed myself off in Egypt as thy sister. And now what hast thou done? Thou hast suffered my slave to assume the chief place in the house, and to take upon herself airs, and thou holdest thy peace. Depend upon it, if she bear thee a son there will be no peace in the house, for she is a daughter of Pharaoh, who is of the race of Nimrod, who cast thee into the furnace of fire."

"Hagar is in thy power," answered Abraham; "but do her no harm. After thou gavest her her freedom, she may not again be brought into bondage."

But Sarah paid no attention to these words of gentleness, and treated Hagar with such cruelty, beat her, and cast an evil eye on her, so that she was delivered before her time of a dead child, and she fled for her life from the house.

The All-Righteous, for this offence, shortened Sarah's life, and made her die thirty-eight years before her husband.

Angels appeared to Hagar in the desert by the well of water whither she had fled, and bade her return to Abraham. So she went back, and was again pregnant, and bore a son, and called his name Ishmael.

### 5. THE DESTRUCTION OF SODOM AND GOMORRAH.

At noon on the 15th Nisan, the third day after the circumcision of Abraham, as recorded in the Book of Genesis, the heat of the sun was so great that Gehinom (Hell) was penetrated by it. And Abraham had not recovered the administration of the rite, which had been performed by the hands of Shem, king of Salem, priest of the Most High God.

Abraham was wont every day to go forth and invite any travellers he might see to feast with him. But this day, owing to the heat and to his being in pain, he sent Eliezer, his servant, forth, who looked and returned and said that there was no one to be seen.

But Abraham thought, "Can I trust the words of this slave, and neglect for one day the performance of my accustomed hospitality?"

Then, notwithstanding the heat and his suffering, he went and sat in the shade of the door, and he beheld in the plain of Mamre the glory of the Lord that appeared. Abraham would have risen, but the voice of God called to him, saying, "Remain where thou art, and let thy pious, sitting posture teach future generations in their prayer and instruction to be seated; and let judges, in delivering judgment, occupy the same position."

Then Abraham lifted his eyes, and beheld three men, who seemed to approach and then to withdraw. These were the angels Michael, Raphael, and Gabriel, sent to him with messages, whereof each bore one. They now stood before Abraham's tent, and they came to satisfy his desire to show hospitality: but when they observed the predicament in which he was, they attempted to withdraw, but Abraham supposed them to be travellers of the three neighbouring races of Saracens, Nabathæans, and Arabians; and as two of the angels were smaller of stature than the third, who stood in the middle—this was Michael—Abraham supposed him to be their chief; and he rose and bowed himself before him, and said to the Majesty of God which still shone, "If I have found favour in Thy sight, O Lord, may Thy majesty not depart from me whilst I receive hospitably these wanderers." And the Lord granted his request.

Then said Abraham to the men, "*Let a little water, I pray you, be fetched, and wash your feet, and rest yourselves under the tree; and I will fetch a morsel of bread, and comfort ye your hearts; after that ye shall pass on: for therefore are ye come to your servant.*"

Now the reason why he said "Let a little water be fetched and wash your feet," was, that he supposed the men were idolaters, and he would not have the dust from the feet of idolaters to pollute the floor of his tent.

And they said, "Do so."

Then Abraham hastened into the tent to Sarah, and said, "*Make ready quickly three measures of fine meal, knead it, and make cakes upon the hearth.*" And Abraham ran unto the herd, and fetched a calf which he had dressed, and set it before them; and he stood by them under the tree, and they did eat.

Abraham placed butter and milk on the table first, then calves' tongues, then the other dishes, and lastly Sarah's cakes; but some commentators doubt whether the men ate the cakes. It is asserted by some that the angels only appeared to eat, but by others we are assured that to reward Abraham's

# OLD TESTAMENT LEGENDS

... all kinds of beasts ...
... days; at last Tschi... 
... the beaver to look ...
... Then he sent out ...
... ing, but it had ...
... to see the earth, an...
... it become an island on ...
...¹

... of New Geor...
... were saved ...
... when the earth w...
... it to the surface
... Sakechah was a ...
... Master of Life, "...

... , Sakechah."

... of men supplic...
... for what I s...
... earth; I must
..."
... I done. M...
... destructi...
... thou hast
... the general do...
... , an...
... to the bott...
... of the ...
... of wild rice.
... and str...
... be gather...
... themselves
... the trunk.

...: Berlin...

201

, his legs were
.ith horror what
:e had recourse
e bed, because
1other never to
:ly after, having
.arment, Eliezer
1 over the head
l. Both being
·ate's decision :
bber for having
on took up a
1 he cut open,
:" and then he

.icked the city

spare the cities
is mighty with
hat if in Zoar,
be found, and
ild spare them.
morning early,
.he place where
for the cities of
a furnace, for
out of heaven,
ir inhabitants.
Lot, and Lot
.nembered how
.l not betrayed
.oh.

by God as a
.es of the plain

hospitality they really did eat, and this was the only occasion on which angels tasted the food of earth.

The angels, knowing that Sarah was within the tent, asked after her. And this betokens her great modesty, that she did not thrust herself forward to be seen of strange visitors. Abraham replied that she was within, engaged in women's household work. Then said Michael, the chief of the angels, "Truly shall such pious and seemly habits not pass unrewarded; but Sarah shall bloom again as fair as in her youth, and shall bear a son in her old age."

Sarah heard these words at the entrance of the tent; so did Ishmael, who stood near. Sarah stepped behind the angel, but the beauty of her countenance shone before her, and the angel turned to look at her, and then he saw she was laughing to herself, and saying, "I am good-looking, and smart dresses become me; I could perfectly well produce a son, but then my husband is old."

Then the word of God came to Abraham, and said, "*Wherefore did Sarah laugh?* Am I, the all-powerful God, too old to create miracles? *At the appointed time Sarah shall have a son.*" To Sarah, who, out of fear, denied having laughed, the word came, "Fear not, *but thou didst laugh.*"

Then Michael withdrew, for his mission was accomplished; and left the other two, Gabriel and Raphael, with Abraham. Then God revealed to Abraham, by Gabriel, that He was about to destroy the cities of the plain; and by Raphael, that He would deliver Lot and his family in the overthrow.

These cities were very guilty before God. Eliezer, having been sent by Sarah to her brother Lot with a message, some years before, arrived in Sodom. An acquaintance invited him to a meal. But hospitality was a virtue abhorred in Sodom, and the news of the invitation having got wind, Eliezer's friend was driven out of the city. Now it was a custom in Sodom to make every stranger arriving within the walls rest in a certain bed; and if the bed proved too long for him, his legs were pulled out to fit it; and if it proved too short, his legs were pared down to its dimensions. Eliezer saw with horror what it was that they purposed to do with him, and he had recourse to a lie of necessity; he declined to sleep in the bed, because he had taken an oath upon the death of his mother never to lie on a bed again; and thus he escaped. Shortly after, having seen a Sodomite rob a poor stranger of his garment, Eliezer attempted to interfere, but the robber struck him over the head and made a gash, from which he lost much blood. Both being brought before the judge, this was the magistrate's decision: —That Eliezer was indebted to the Sodomite robber for having bled him. The servant of Abraham thereupon took up a large stone, flung it at the judge's head, which he cut open, and said, "Now, pay me for having bled thee!" and then he fled out of the city.

From these incidents it may be seen how wicked the city was.

Now Abraham had interceded with God to spare the cities of the plain, for the intercession of His saints is mighty with God. And Abraham had obtained of God that if in Zoar, the smallest of the cities, five righteous could be found, and forty-five in all the rest of the country, God would spare them. Then God ceased talking with Abraham. Next morning early, Abraham arose and took his staff, and went to the place where God had met him, to make further intercession for the cities of the plain, but the smoke of them rose as from a furnace, for brimstone and fire had been rained upon them out of heaven, and they had been consumed along with their inhabitants. Only Zoar was spared, as a place of refuge for Lot, and Lot was kept alive and his daughters; for God remembered how he had been true to Abraham in Egypt, and had not betrayed the truth about Sarah when questioned by Pharaoh.

The Mussulman tradition is as follows :—

Lot, whom the Arabs call Loth, was sent by God as a prophet to convince the inhabitants of the cities of the plain of their ungodly deeds. But, though he preached for twenty years, he could not convince them. And whenever he visited Abraham he complained to him of the iniquity of the people. But Abraham urged him to patience.

At length the long-suffering of God was exhausted, and He sent the angels Michael, Gabriel, and Azrael, armed with the sword of destruction, against these cities.

They came to Abraham, who received them, and slaughtered a calf, and prepared meat and set it before them. But they would not eat. And he pressed them, and ate himself; but they would not eat, being angels. Then Abraham's colour went, and he was afraid, for to refuse to eat with a man is a token that you seek his life.

Seeing him discouraged, the angels announced their mission. But Sarah, observing her husband's loss of colour, laughed and said in her heart, "Why is he fearful, being surrounded with many servants and faithful friends?"

Now the angels promised to Abraham a son in his old age, and that they would rescue Lot in the overthrow of Sodom. Then they rose up and went on their way, and entered into Sodom; and they met a young maiden in the street, and asked her the way to Lot's house.

She answered, "He is my father, and I dwell with him; but know you not, O strangers, that it is against the laws of this city to show hospitality?"

But they answered her, "Fear not; lead us to thy father."

So she led them, and ran before and told Lot, "Behold three men come seeking thee and asking shelter, and they are beautiful as the angels of God."

Then Lot went out to them, and told them that the city was full of wickedness, and that hospitality was not permitted.

But they answered, "We must tarry this night in thy house." Then he admitted them, and he hid them. But Lot's wife was an infidel, a native of Sodom; and finding that he lodged these strangers, she hastened to the chief men of the city and said, "My husband has violated your laws, and the customs of this people; he has housed travellers, and will feed them and show them all courtesy."

Therefore the men of the city came tumultuously to the door of Lot's house, to bring forth the men that were come to him, and to cast them out of the city, having shamefully entreated them. They would not listen to the remonstrances of Lot, but went near to break in his door.

Then the three angels stepped forth and passed their hands over the faces of all who drew near, and they were struck blind, and fled from their presence.

Now, long before the day began to break, the angels rose up and called Lot, his wife and daughters, and bade them take their clothes and all that they had that was most precious, and escape out of the city. Therefore Lot and his family went forth.

And when they were escaped, the angel Gabriel went through the cities, and passed his wing over the soil on which they were built, and the cities were carried up into heaven; and they came so near thereto that those on the confines of heaven could hear the crowing of the cocks in Sodom, and the barking of the dogs in Gomorrah. And then they were overthrown, so that their foundations were towards the sky and their roofs towards the earth. And God rained on them stones heated in the fire of Hell; and on each stone was written the name of him whom it was destined to slay. Now there were many natives of these accursed cities in other parts of the land, and where they were, there they were sought out by the red-hot stones, and were struck down. But some were within the sacred enclosure of the temple at Mecca, and the stones waited for them in the air; and at the expiration of forty days they came forth, and as they came forth the stones whistled through the air, and smote them, and they were slain.

Now Lot's wife turned, as she went forth, to look back upon the city, and a stone fell on her, and she died.[1]

[1] Tabari, i. c. lii. ; Abulfeda, p. 25.

It is related further of Lot that, after he had escaped, he committed in ignorance a very great sin; and Abraham sent him to expiate his crime to the sources of the Nile, to fetch thence three sorts of wood, which he named to him. Abraham thought, "He will be slain by ravenous beasts, and so will he atone for the sin that he has committed."

But Lot after a while returned, bringing with him the woods which Abraham had demanded—a cypress plant, a young cedar, and a young pine.

Abraham planted the three trees in the shape of a triangle, on a mountain, and charged Lot with watering them every day from Jordan. Now the mountain was twenty-four thousand paces from Jordan, and this penance was laid on Lot to expiate his sin.

At the end of three months the trees blossomed; Lot announced this to Abraham, who visited the spot, and saw to his surprise that the three trees had grown together to form one trunk, but with three distinct roots of different natures.

At the sight of this miracle he bowed his face to the ground and said, " This tree will abolish sin."

And by that he knew that God had pardoned Lot.

The tree grew and subsisted till the reign of Solomon, when it was cut down, and this was the tree which the Jews employed to form the Cross of Christ.[1]

This tradition is, of course, Christian; though Jewish in origin, it has been adapted to the Gospel story.

### 6. THE BIRTH OF ISAAC.

The country was wasted; travellers were few; those who passed by, and accepted Abraham's hospitality, spoke with scorn of the sin of Lot, his nephew; and the neighbourhood became intolerable to the patriarch, who resolved to change his place of residence for a while.

---

[1] Apocrypha de Loto, apud Fabricium, t. i. pp. 428-431.

He therefore went south, between Kadesh and Sur, and dwelt in Gerar.

Now Sarah had bloomed again as fair as in her youth, as the angel Michael had foretold; and Abraham persuaded her to pretend again to be his sister, though Sarah, remembering the ill-success of this deceit before, hesitated to comply.

Abimelech, king of Gerar, hearing of Sarah's beauty, sent for her to his palace. He asked Abraham, "Who is this woman?" and he answered, "She is my sister." Then Abimelech inquired of the camels and of the asses, and they answered the same, "She is his sister." But that same evening, as it grew towards dusk, as he sat on his throne, he fell asleep; and in dream saw an angel of God approach him with a drawn sword in his hand to slay him. The king in his dream cried out to know why he was doomed to death; and the angel answered, "Because thou hast received into thy house the wife of another man, the mistress of a house."

Abimelech excused himself, saying that Abraham had concealed the truth from him, and had said Sarah was his sister.

"The All-Holy knows that thou hast sinned in ignorance," said the angel; "but is it seemly, when strangers enter thy land, to be questioning closely into their connexions? Know that Abraham is a prophet, and foreseeing that thy people would entreat his wife ill, he resolved to call her his sister, and he knew, being a prophet, that thou couldst not harm her."

That night—it was the Paschal eve,—the angel with the drawn sword traversed all the streets of the city, and closed the wombs of those about to bear.

Next morning early, while it was yet dark, Abimelech sent for Abraham and Sarah, and gave Sarah back to her husband, and paid him a thousand ounces of silver, and to Sarah he gave a costly robe, which might conceal her from her eyes to her feet, that none might henceforth be bewitched by her beauty. "But," said Abimelech to Abraham, "because thou

---

[1] Solomon Jarschi, Comm. on Moses, xx. 5.

didst deceive me, and blind my eyes with a lie, therefore thou shalt bear a son, whose eyes shall be dim so that he shall be deceived." And Abraham prayed to the Lord, and all the women that were with child in Gerar were delivered of men-children, without the pangs of maternity, and those who were barren felt themselves with child. The angel hosts besought the Lord to look upon Sarah, and to remember His covenant. "O Lord of the whole world! Thou didst hear the cry of Abraham, and grant his petitions when he prayed for the barren women of Gerar; and his own wife, from whom Thou didst promise him a son, is unfruitful and despised. Does it beseem a Lord, when he prepares a fleet, to free his subjects from pirates, but to leave the vessel of his best friend in bondage?"

Now it was the first day of the seventh month, Tischri, the day on which, at the close of the world's history, the Lord will come to judge the quick and the dead, that the Lord God remembered Sarah, and the promise He had made, and looked upon her, and she conceived a son in her old age, one year and four months after her sojourn in Gerar; and nine months after, say some, but, say others, six months and two days after; at mid-day say some, others say in the evening of the fifteenth of Nisan; or, as others affirm, on the first of Nisan she was delivered of a son, without suffering any pains in the bringing forth. And the same time that Sarah's womb was blessed, God looked upon many other barren women and blessed them also; and on the day that the child was born they were delivered likewise; and the blind saw, the dumb spake, the deaf heard, and the lame walked, and the crazed recovered their senses. Also, the sun shone forty-eight times brighter than he shines at Midsummer, even with the splendour that he had on the day of his creation.

And when eight days were accomplished, Abraham circumcised his son, and called him Isaac.

But many thought it was an incredible thing that Abraham

and Sarah should have a son in their old age, and they said, "This is a foundling, or it is the child of one of the slaves, which they pass off as their own." Now Abraham held a great feast on the day that Isaac was weaned, and he invited thereto all the princes and great men of the country. And there came Abimelech, king of Gerar, and Og, king of Basan, and all the princes of Canaan, sixty-two princes in all. Such an assembly was not seen before, yet all these princes fell in after-years by the hands of Joshua.[1]

Of this feast it is related that Og's companions said to him, "Do you believe that that old mule, Abraham, can be the father of this child?"

Og replied with scorn, "I could crack this imp with the nail of my little finger."

Then came there a voice from heaven, saying, "Thou despisest this little child, but know thou that tens of thousands shall spring from his loins, and that before them thy pride shall be humbled."

Also, Abraham's ancestors, Shem and Eber, and his father, Terah—though some say he was dead—and Nahor, Abraham's brother, attended the feast, and the Shekinah, the glory of the Lord, appeared to grace it.

But Satan also appeared in the form of a poor beggar-man, and he stood at the door and asked an alms. Now Abraham and Sarah were busy attending to their guests, so they perceived him not, but the servants thrust him away, and Satan received nothing; therefore he presented himself before the Most High, and laid an accusation of inhospitality and churlishness against the Friend of God.

In the meantime Sarah had assembled, and was entertaining all the wives of the guests of Abraham. And it happened that the women found that they had no milk in their bosoms to give their infants, and the babes screamed that no one could hear the voice of another. The mothers were in despair, for

---

[1] Josh. xii. 24.

the children were hungry, and they were all dry. Then Sarah uncovered her breasts, and there spirted from them jets of milk, and all the babes were nourished at her bosom, and yet there was more.

Now when they saw this, the women, who had doubted that the child was really the offspring of Sarah, doubted no more, and cried, "We are not worthy that our little ones should be nourished at thy bosom!" And the story goes that all those who afterwards joined themselves to the people of Israel, and all those in every nation who in after-times became proselytes, were descended from those who sucked the breasts of Sarah. In allusion to this incident it is said in the Book of Psalms: "*Thou makest the barren woman to keep house, and to be the joyful mother of* (i.e. giving suck to) *children.*"[1]

The child Isaac was shown to every visitor, and all were astonished at his resemblance to Abraham. Both the babe and his father were so much alike that it was impossible to distinguish one from the other, and all doubt as to whose it was vanished before such evidence of likeness to the father, and before the fulness of Sarah's breasts. But as confusion was likely to arise through the striking similarity between father and son, Abraham besought God to give him wrinkles and white hair, that he might not be mistaken for the babe Isaac, or the babe Isaac be mistaken for him.[2]

### 7. THE EXPULSION OF HAGAR AND ISHMAEL.

Ishmael grew up, and became skilful with his bow; he was rough and undisciplined, and he occasionally lapsed into idolatry, but without his father knowing it. But Sarah was aware of his sin, and was grieved thereat.

Ishmael often boasted, "I am the eldest son, and I shall have a double portion of my father's inheritance." These

---
[1] Psalm cxiii. 9.
[2] This climax of absurdity is found also in the Mussulman histories of the Patriarch.

words were reported to Sarah, and she hated Ishmael for them in her heart.

One day when Isaac was five years old, but others say fifteen, Ishmael said to him, "Come forth into the field and let us shoot." Isaac was well pleased. And when they were in the field, Ishmael turned his bow against his brother, but he did it in jest. Sarah saw him from the tent door, and she ran out, and caught away her son Isaac, and she went to Abraham and told him all the evil she knew of Ishmael; how he had gone after idols and had learnt the ways of the Canaanites that were in the land, how he had boasted of his majority, and how he had sought Isaac's life. And she said, "Give the maid-servant a writing of divorcement, and send her away. *Cast out this bond-woman and her son; for the son of this bond-woman shall not be heir with my son, even with Isaac.* Then she will no more vex Isaac. Do thou leave to Isaac all thy possessions. Never shall Ishmael inherit anything from thee, for he is not my son."

Abraham was grieved at heart, for he loved Ishmael his son, but nothing that he said could alter Sarah's determination. She insisted on the expulsion of Hagar and her son, and she stirred up the wrath of Abraham against Ishmael, because he had fallen into idolatry.

Sarah, say the Mussulmans, was so fierce in her jealousy, that she would not be satisfied till she had washed her hands in the blood of Hagar. Then Abraham quickly pierced Hagar's ears, and drew a ring through them, so that Sarah could fulfil her oath, without endangering the life of Hagar.[1]

It was long before Abraham could be brought to consent to Sarah's desire, but God appeared to him in a dream and said, "Fear not to obey the voice of Sarah, for she is the wife of thy youth, and was chosen for thee from her mother's womb. But Hagar is not thy wife; she is but a bond-woman. Sarah also is a prophetess, and sees into things that shall be in the

[1] Weil, p. 83.

latter days, further than thou. Unto Isaac and those of his seed who believe in the Two Worlds are the promises made; and they alone shall be accounted as thy seed."[1]

Abraham now did what he was commanded. Next morning he gave Hagar a writing of dismissal, and took twelve loaves of bread and a pitcher of water, and laid them upon Hagar, for Sarah had cast an evil eye upon Ishmael, so that he was ill, and unable to carry any burden. And Abraham attached the pitcher by a cord to the hips of Hagar, that all might know she was a slave, and the pitcher hung down and trailed on the sand. Ishmael was sent away without garments; he went forth naked as he came into the world: thus it may be seen how implacable was the anger of Sarah, because he had boasted of his birthright, and the wrath of Abraham, because he had fallen into idolatry.

But when they went along their way, Abraham looked after them for long, standing in the door of his tent, for his bowels yearned after his son, and he saw the trail in the sand of the water pitcher which Hagar had dragged sadly along, and thereby Abraham knew the direction which they had taken.

Now God forsook not the outcast in her affliction, but filled the pitcher with water as fast as she and her son drank out of it, and the water was always sweet and cold. Thus they penetrated the wilderness, and there they lost their way, and Hagar forgot the God of Abraham, and in her distress turned to the false gods of her father Pharaoh, and besought their protection, for she said, "Where are the promises of the God of Abraham, that of Ishmael would He make a great nation?"

Now Ishmael was sick of a burning fever, and the water in the pitcher failed when Hagar forsook the God of Abraham. So she cast him under a thorn bush, and went from him the space of two thousand ells, that she might not hear his cries. But Ishmael prayed to the Lord God of Heaven and Earth,

---

[1] It seems probable that S. Paul alludes to this traditional speech more than once, as for instance Gal. iii. 9.

and said, "O Lord God of my father Abraham! thou canst send death in so many forms; take my life speedily or give me a drop of water, that I suffer this agony no longer."

And the Lord in His compassion heard the prayer of the weeping child, and He sent His angel and showed Hagar that fountain which He had created on the sixth day at dusk, and of which the children of Israel were destined to drink when they came forth out of Egypt.

But the accusing angel murmured against this judgment of God, and said, "O Lord of the whole earth! shall this one, of whom a nation of robbers shall arise, who will war upon thine elect people, and be a scourge upon the face of the earth, shall he be delivered now, and given to drink of a fountain destined for thine elect?"

The Lord answered, "Is the youth guilty, or is he not guilty?"

The angel answered, "He is not himself guilty, but his posterity will sin."

Then God said, "I punish men for what they have done, and not for what their children will do. Ishmael hath not merited a death of suffering, therefore shall he not die." And God opened the eyes of Hagar, and she saw the spring of water, and filled her pitcher, and took it to Ishmael to drink. She filled the pitcher before she gave her son a draught of water, for she had little faith, and thought that the fountain would be withdrawn before she could return to it again.

Then Ishmael was strengthened and could go, and he and his mother went further, and were fed by the shepherds; and they reached Paran, and there they found springs of water, and they settled there. Ishmael took a wife, a daughter of Moab, named Aischa, or Aifa, or Asiah; but others say she was an Egyptian woman, and was named Meriba (the quarrelsome), and by her he had four sons and one daughter.

Ishmael lived a wandering life in tents with his wife and cattle; and the Lord blessed his flocks, and he had great possessions. But his heart remained the same; and he was a master of archery, and instructed his neighbours in making bows.

After three years, Abraham, whose heart longed after his son, said to Sarah, "I must see how my son Ishmael fares." And she answered, "Thou shalt go if thou wilt swear to me not to alight from off thy camel," for she hated Hagar, and feared to suffer her husband to meet her once more. So Abraham swore. Then he went to Paran, over the desert, seeking Ishmael's tent; and he reached it at noon, but neither Hagar nor her son were at home. Only Ishmael's wife was within, and she was scolding and beating the children.

So Abraham halted on his camel before the tent door, and the sun was hot in the blue sky above, and the sand was white and glaring beneath. And he called to her, "Is thy husband within?"

She answered, without rising from her seat, "He is hunting." Or, say others, she said without looking at him or rising, "He is gathering dates."

Then Abraham said, "I am faint and hungry; bring me a little bread and a drop of water."

But the woman answered, "I have none for such as thee."

So Abraham said to her, "Say to thy husband, even to Ishmael, these words: 'An old man hath come to see thee out of the land of the Philistines, and he says, The nail that fastens thy tent is bad; cast it away or thy tent will fall, and get thee a better nail.'" Then he departed, and went home.

Now when Ishmael returned, his wife told him all these words, and he knew that his father had been there, and he understood the tenor of his words, so he sent away his wife, and he took another, with his mother's advice, out of Egypt, and her name was Fatima.

And after three years, Abraham's bowels yearned once more after his son, and he said to Sarah, "I must see how Ishmael fares." And she answered, "Thou shalt go, if thou wilt swear to me not to alight from off thy camel." So Abraham swore.

Then he went to Paran, over the desert, seeking Ishmael's tent, and he reached it at noon; but neither Hagar nor her son was at home. Only Ishmael's wife, Fatima, was within, and she was singing to the children.

So Abraham halted on his camel before the tent door, and the sun was hot in the blue sky above, and the sand was white and glaring beneath. And when Fatima saw a stranger at the door, she rose from her seat, and veiled her face, and came out and greeted him.

Then said Abraham, "Is thy husband within?"

She answered, "My lord, he is pasturing the camels in the desert;" and she added, "Enter, my lord, into the cool of the tent and rest, and suffer me to bring thee a little meat."

But Abraham said, "I may not alight from off my camel, for my journey is hasty; but bring me, I pray thee, a morsel of bread and a drop of water, for I am hungry and faint."

Then she ran and brought him of the best of all that she had in the tent, and he ate and drank, and was glad.

So he said to her, "Say to thy husband, even to Ishmael, that an old man out of the land of the Philistines hath been here, and he says, The nail that fastens thy tent is very good; let it not be stirred out of its place, and thy tent will stand."

And he returned. And when Ishmael came home, Fatima related to him all the words that the old man had spoken, and he understood the tenor of the words.

Ishmael was glad that his father had visited him, for he knew thereby that his love to him was not extinguished.[1]

Shortly after, he left his wife and children, and went across the desert to see his father in the land of the Philistines. And Abraham related to him all that had taken place with the first wife, and why he had exhorted him to put her away.

[1] The same story is told by the Mohammedans: Weil, p. 90.

### 8. THE STRIFE BETWEEN THE SHEPHERDS.

Abraham lived twenty-six years in the land of the Philistines; then he went to Hebron, and there his servants dug wells, and there they encamped.

When Abimelech's servants heard of these wells that they had dug, they came with their flocks, and desired to use them also, and the largest of the wells they claimed as their own. But Abraham's shepherds said, "Let the well belong to those to whom it gives water. The Lord shall decide between us!"

To this the servants of Abimelech agreed. And when the flocks of Abraham came to drink, the well sprang up and overflowed; but when the flocks of Abimelech drew near, the water sank and disappeared.

Now when Abimelech heard of the strife, he came with Phicol, his chief captain, to seek Abraham, and to be reconciled with him. "God is with all that thou doest," said Abimelech; "He protected thee when Sodom was destroyed. He has given thee a son in thine old age. He rescued thy first-born when perishing in the desert. Swear to me, as I have offered thee my whole land, my own palace not excepted, in which to dwell, that thou wilt show equal love and liberality to my descendants to the third generation."

Abraham swore to him, and they made a covenant together.[1]

And Abraham set apart seven lambs as a witness and token, that just as the well had sprung up when his flocks had come to water at it, so, in after days should it spring up to water the descendants of Abraham; as it is said, "*From thence they went to Beer, that is, the well whereof the Lord spake unto Moses, Gather the people together, and I will give them water. Then Israel sang this song, Spring up, O well; sing ye unto it.*"[2]

But such condescension and courtesy ill became Abraham in his dealings with a rude and savage people, and therefore there

---
[1] Gen. xxi. 24–27.  [2] Numbers xxi. 16, 17.

came to him a voice from heaven which said: "Because thou hast given these seven innocent lambs into the hands of a barbarous nation, therefore seven of thy descendants shall be slain by their hands (Samson, Hophni and Phinehas, Saul and his three sons); also seven dwellings that thy people shall raise to my Name shall they destroy (the Tabernacle, Gilgal, Nob, Gibeon, Shiloh, and twice the Temple at Jerusalem), and seven months shall the ark of my covenant remain in the land of the Philistines."

### 9. THE GROVE IN BEER-SHEBA.

"*And Abraham planted a grove in Beer-sheba, and called there on the name of the Lord.*"[1] The reason was as follows:—

Once Abraham asked Shem the son of Noah, otherwise called Melchizedek, king of Salem, what service he and his father and brethren rendered to the Lord in the ark, which was so acceptable to God that He preserved them alive and brought them in safety to Ararat; and Shem answered, "The service we rendered to God, all the time of our sojourn in the ark, was charity."

And when Abraham wondered and asked how that could possibly be, as there were none in the ark save themselves and the beasts, Shem answered,—

"Even so; we showed charity and forethought and hospitality to the animals. We fed them regularly, and we slept not at night; so busy were we with them in making them comfortable. Once, when we had delayed somewhat, the lion was hungry and bit Noah, my father."

Then said Abraham to himself, "In very truth, if it was reckoned to Noah and his sons as so great righteousness, that they fed and tended the dumb and senseless beasts, how much more pleasing must it be to the Most High, to be kind and

[1] Gen. xxi. 33.

generous to men who are made in His image, after His likeness!"

Filled with this thought, Abraham settled at Beer-sheba, where was an abundant spring of fresh water, and there he resolved to do service acceptable to the living God, and to honour His name, as Noah and his sons had done Him service and honoured Him in the ark.

So Abraham planted a grove in Beer-sheba, one hundred ells long and one hundred ells broad, and he planted it with vines and figs, pomegranates and other fruit trees; and he built a guest-house adjoining this garden, and he made in it four doors, one towards each quarter of the heavens; and when a hungry man came by, Abraham gave him food; if there came a man who was thirsty, he gave him drink; if one who was naked, he clothed him; if one who was sick, he took him in and nursed him; and he gave to every man who passed by what he most needed for his journey.

He would receive neither thanks nor payment; and when any one thanked him, he said hastily, "Give thanks, not to me the servant, but to the Master of this house, *who openeth His hand, and filleth all things living with plenteousness.*"

Then when the traveller asked, "Who, and where is this Master?"

Abraham answered, "He is the God who rules over heaven and earth; He is Lord of all; He kills and makes alive; He wounds and heals; He forms the fruit in the mother's womb, and gives it life; He makes the plants and trees to grow; He brings man to destruction, and raises him from his grave again."

Thus Abraham instructed those whom he relieved. And if a traveller asked further, how he was to worship the great God, Abraham answered, "Say only these words, Praised be the Eternal One who reigns over heaven and earth! Praised be the Lord of the whole world, who filleth all things living with plenteousness." And no traveller went on his way without thanking God.

Thus that guest-house was a great school, in which men were taught the true religion, and gratitude to the Almighty God.

### 10. THE OFFERING OF ISAAC.[1]

Abraham loved the son of his old age, and Isaac grew up in the fear of God, and his good conduct heightened the love Abraham bore him; but the Patriarch thought in his heart, " I prepare gifts to give of my abundance to every man that asks of me, and to every passer-by; but to my Lord and God, the Giver of all good things, have I given nothing!"

There was a day when the sons of God (the angels) stood before the Eternal One, and amongst them was the accusing angel, Satan or Sammael. The Lord asked him, "Whence comest thou?"

"From walking to and fro upon the face of the earth," he replied.

"And what hast thou beheld there of the doings of the sons of men?"

The Accuser answered, " I saw that the sons of earth no longer praise Thee, and adore Thee; when they have obtained their petition, then they forget to give Thee thanks. I saw that Abraham, the son of Terah, as long as he was childless, built altars and proclaimed Thy name to all the world: now he has been given a son at the age of a hundred, and he forgets Thee. I went to his door as a beggar, on the day that Isaac was weaned, and I was turned away without an alms. I have seen him strike alliance with the King of the Philistines, a nation that knows Thee not, and to him has he given seven lambs. He has built a large house and he gives to strangers, but to Thee he gives no sacrifice of value. Ask of him any sacrifice that is costly, and he will refuse it."

"What shall I ask?" inquired the Almighty.

[1] The Mussulmans tell the story of Ishmael almost in every particular the same as that given below.

"Ask of him now his son, and he will refuse him to Thy face."

"I will do so, and thou shalt be confounded," answered the Holy One.

The self-same night God appeared to Abraham, and addressed him gently so as not to alarm him, and He said to him, "Abraham!"

The patriarch in deep humility answered, "Here am I, Lord; what willest Thou of Thy servant?"

The Lord answered, "I have come to ask of thee something. I have saved thee in all dangers; I delivered thee out of the furnace of Babylon; I rescued thee from the army of Nimrod; I brought thee into this land, and gave thee men-servants and maid-servants and cattle and sheep and horses, and I have given thee a son in thine old age, and victory over all thine enemies, and new temptations await thee, for I must prove thee, and see if thou art grateful in thy heart, and that thy righteousness may be manifest unto all, and that thy obedience may be perfected. Take therefore thy son——"

Abraham answered trembling, "Which son? I have two."

*The voice of God.*—"That son which alone counteth with thee."

*Abraham.*—"Each is the only son of his mother."

*The voice of God.*—"The one you love."

*Abraham.*—"I love both."

*The voice of God.*—"The one you love best."

*Abraham.*—"I love both alike."

*The voice of God.*—"Then I demand Isaac."

*Abraham.*—"And what shall I do with him, O Lord?"

*The voice of God.*—"Go to the place that I shall tell thee, where, unexpectedly, hills shall arise in sight out of the valley bottom. Go to that place whence once My Light, My Teaching issued, which My eye watches over untiringly, and where the smoke of incense shall arise to Me, to the place where prayer is heard and sacrifice shall be offered, where at the end of time I shall judge the nations, and cast the ungodly into the pit of

Gehinom;—to the land of Moriah that I shall show thee, there shalt thou take thy son Isaac as a whole burnt offering."

*Abraham.*—" Shall I bring Thee such an offering as this, O Lord? Where is the priest to prepare the sacrifice?"

*The voice of God.*—" I have taken from Shem his priesthood, and thou art clothed therewith."

*Abraham.*—" But in that country there are many hills; which shall I ascend?"

*The voice of God.*—"A mountain on which shall rest my Glory; there shalt it be told thee further what thou must do."

Abraham prepared to fulfil the command of God, but he dreaded the separation between Sarah and her son. If he took Isaac away secretly, then he feared that, in the excess of her distress, she would do herself harm. At last he decided on this course; he went to Sarah's tent, and he said to her, " My dearest, prepare this day a little banquet, that in our old days we may rejoice our hearts."

Sarah answered, "Wherefore this day, my husband? Are you about to lose anything this day?"

Abraham said, " Think, my wife, Sarah! how good God has been to us; therefore it behoves us to thank Him all the days of our life."

Sarah did as Abraham had commanded.

As they sat and ate, Abraham said, " Thou knowest well, dear wife, that I knew the One true God from the time that I was three years old. Isaac is older, and it behoves him to know more of the law of God. Therefore I design to take him with me to Shem and Eber, our ancestors, who live not far from here, that they may instruct him. Hast thou anything to object to this, Sarah?"

She answered, " No; do that which is pleasing in thine eyes; only let not Isaac be away too long, for thou knowest how precious the sight of him is to me."

Then Sarah put her arms round her son, and kissed him, and they parted with many tears; and she exhorted Abraham to have great care of the youth, that the journey might not be too great for him."

Next morning, very early, Abraham rose, and he saddled the ass himself, though he had many slaves, for he was eager to be gone, and to go where the Lord called him. This was the ass, born of the she-ass created by God on the eve of the sixth day, upon which Moses afterwards rode when he went to Egypt;[1] it is the ass which spake to Balaam, and it is the ass of which the prophet Zechariah has spoken, that on it Messiah shall ride.[2]

This ass was of a hundred colours.[3]

Sarah clothed Isaac in the garment that Abimelech had given her, and placed a jewel-studded fillet about his head. She provided the travellers with food for their journey, and accompanied them with her maids, till Abraham bade them return. Then she clasped Isaac once more to her breast, and said with tears, "God be gracious to thee, my son; how know I that I shall see thee again?"

Abraham had two to accompany him, Eliezer and Ishmael; he had cut fig and palm wood and made a faggot. On the way this discourse took place between Eliezer and Ishmael.

Ishmael said, "I perceive clearly that my father is about to offer Isaac as a whole burnt offering; therefore I, his eldest son, will inherit his possessions."

But Eliezer said, "That is false: I am his trusty servant! Did not thy father drive thee away from home? He will leave all to me."

Whilst they thus spake, there came a voice from heaven, "O ye fools! neither of you knows the truth."

Abraham in the meantime walked forward. Then came

---

[1] Exod. iv. 20.       [2] Zech. ix. 9.
[3] When King Sapor heard the R. Samuel explain that Messiah would come riding on an ass, the king said, "I will give him a horse; it is not seemly that he should ride an ass." "What," answered the Rabbi, "hast thou a horse with a hundred colours?" (Talmud, Tract. Sanhedrim, fol. 98, col. 1.)

Satan to him in the form of an old man bowed upon a staff, and said to him, "Whither goest thou?"

He answered, "I go to offer up my prayers."

"Wherefore this knife, and fuel, and fire?" asked Satan.

"I take them in case we have to spend much time on the mountain, that we may bake bread and slay beasts."

"Old man, thou deceivest me," said Satan. "Was I not by when a voice bade thee slay thy son, thine only son; and now, what art thou about to do? Thinkest thou that thou shalt have another son, now that thou art a hundred years old? Art thou then about to cut down with thine own hands the main pillar of thy tent, the staff on which thou mayest lean in thine old age? Knowest thou not the proverb, 'He who destroys his own goods, how shall he get more?' That was not the voice of God, it was the voice of the Tempter, and thou didst listen to it. Dost thou think that God, who promised to make of thee a great nation, and to bless all generations through Isaac, would thus persuade thee to make void His own promises?"

Abraham answered, "No, it was not the Tempter who spake, it was the voice of God; therefore I will not hearken to thy words, but walk on still in mine uprightness."

"But if God were to ask of thee some further sacrifice, wouldst thou grant it?"

"Of a truth would I," answered Abraham.

"Thy piety is folly," said Satan impatiently. "To-morrow God will punish thee for this murder thou art about to commit, since thou wilt shed the blood of thine own son."

But when Satan saw that Abraham was not to be moved from his purpose, then he took the form of a blooming youth, and joined himself to Isaac, and asked him the object of his journey.

Isaac replied that he was going to receive instruction in the law of the Most High.

"Art thou going to receive this instruction living or dead?" asked Satan, scornfully.

*Isaac.*—" Can a man receive instruction after he is dead?"

*Satan.*—"O thou son of a mother much to be pitied, knowest thou not that thy father is leading thee to death?"

*Isaac.*—" Nevertheless I shall follow him."

*Satan.*—"Then all the tears and prayers of thy mother, beseeching Heaven to grant her a son, end in this! All the pains and grief in childbearing! All the afflictions she laid on Hagar and Ishmael! All the care she has taken of thy youth! All the love she has expended upon thee! All these things for nothing!"

*Isaac.*—"As my father wills."

*Satan.*—"Then the inheritance passes to Ishmael. How he will glory in being the first-born, and his mother Hagar will despise Sarah, and maybe will drive her out!"

*Isaac.*—"I obey the command of my father and the will of God, be they what they may."

But these words were not without some effect on Isaac. With piteous voice he urged his father to suspend or delay what he had undertaken. But Abraham exhorted his son not to listen or give credence to the words he had heard, for they were the temptations of Satan, to draw him from the path of obedience and the fear of God.

They went a little further and came to a broad stream. Abraham, Isaac, and their followers sought to wade it; the water at first reached their knees, but when they were in the middle, it rose to their necks.

Abraham, who knew well the spot, and that there was neither brook nor river there by nature, recognized this as a deception of Satan, to divert them from the right way. He told Isaac that this was his opinion, and raising his eyes to heaven he prayed: "Thou, O Lord, didst declare to me Thy will, that I should take Isaac my son and offer him to Thee in pledge of my obedience. I did not hesitate, I did not refuse, and now the water overwhelms us and we sink; how then can I perform that which Thou badest me do?"

The Lord answered, "Fear not, through thee shall My Name be known."

Then the stream vanished away, and they stood upon dry land.

But now Satan made another attempt to turn Abraham from his purpose. He drew him aside and said, "The object of thy journey has failed. I caught a whisper in heaven, and it was this—God will prepare a lamb for the sacrifice, and not thy son."

Abraham answered, "Even if thy words be true, it matters not; for this is the penalty of liars, that when they speak the truth they are not believed."

Abraham journeyed on the rest of that day, without seeing his appointed place. Next day he retraced his steps, but could find no signs of the place. The Almighty had so ordered it, that men might not say Abraham was hasty and acted precipitately, but might see that he had leisure and time for reflection on what he was about to do.

On the morning of the third day,[1] they reached the height of Zophim, and thence Abraham saw a beautiful mountain-land, and on the top of one of the mountains was a fiery pillar, which reached from earth to heaven,—it was the Glory of the Lord appearing in the cloud.

When Abraham asked Isaac if he beheld this sight, he answered that he did so; but when he asked his other companions, they replied that they saw nothing save the brown hills and purple valleys. Some say they answered that one hill was to them like every other hill.

From this, Abraham concluded that God was well pleased with Isaac as a victim. Then he said to Eliezer and Ishmael:

"Tarry ye here with the ass, for you are not worthy to

---

[1] The day is uncertain. Some say it was the 3rd Nisan; others, it was the first of the seventh month, Tischri, New Year's day; others, that it was the Day of Atonement. Some say Isaac's age was 37; others say 36; others 26; others 25; others 16; others 13; others, again, say 5; and others say only 2 years.

behold the Shekinah nearer. But I and the youth will go on, *so many* only shall go."

Now, as he said these words, it suddenly came to his mind that God had promised him a great people descended from Isaac, *so many* as the stars for multitude, and with prophetic voice he said, "If the Lord will, *so many* as go on, *so many* shall return."

Then Abraham laid the wood of the sacrifice on his son Isaac, and took the fire and the knife in his hand; and they went on both together, Abraham joyous, and Isaac without fear or thought.

But after they had gone some way, Isaac turned to his father and said, "Father, whither are we going alone?"

*Abraham.*—" My son, we go to offer a sacrifice."

*Isaac.*—" But art thou a priest to execute this undertaking?"

*Abraham.*—" Shem, the High Priest, will prepare the victim."

A great fear fell upon Isaac when he saw that they had no animal with them to offer, and he said, "Here are the fire and the wood, but where is a lamb for the whole offering?"

*Abraham.*—" The lamb which is to be offered is foreknown to the Almighty. He will provide the lamb; and if none other is here, then must thou be the offering, my son."

Isaac was silent, for the fear of death came over him. But presently he recovered himself and said, "If God chooses me, I place my soul in His hands."

*Abraham.*—" My son! Is there any blemish in thee within? For the offering must be without blemish of any sort."

*Isaac.*—" My father! There is none. I swear by God and by thy life, that in my heart there is not the least resistance to the Divine will. My limbs do not tremble, and there is no quaking at my heart. With gladness do I say, The Lord be praised, who has chosen me for a whole sacrifice." [1]

[1] In the Rabbinic tradition, the type of Christ comes out more distinctly than in Genesis, for here we see Isaac not merely offered by his father, but also giving himself as a free-will offering, immaculate without in his body, and within in his soul.

*Abraham.*—"O my son, with many a wish wast thou brought into this world. Since thou hast been in it, every care has been lavished on thee. I hoped to have had thee to follow me and make a great nation. But now I must, myself, offer thee. Wondrous was thy coming into this world, and wondrous will be thy going out of it!¹ Not by sickness, not by war, but as a sacrifice. I had designed thee to be my comfort and stay in old age; now God himself must take thy place."²

*Isaac.*—"It were unworthy of thee were I to think to withstand the decree of God, and of thee. Had the decision been thine alone, I would have obeyed."

When they reached the top of Moriah, God said to Abraham,—

"This is the place where once Adam, when driven out of Paradise, built an altar to My name. Here also Cain and Abel offered their sacrifice. Then came the Flood, and when it was passed away, Noah offered victims to Me here. When the people were scattered from the tower at Babel, then this altar was overthrown. Now it is for thee, friend of God, to set it up again!"

Abraham built the altar, and Isaac brought him the stones. But, according to some authors, this was not so. Abraham hid his son in a cave, lest Satan should take advantage of the opportunity, with a stone or clod of earth, to blemish him.

And when all was ready and the wood laid in order, then Isaac said to his father, "Bind me hand and foot, lest in the fear of death I start and thou wound me, and so I be blemished. Fold thy garments together, and gird thy loins, and bare thine arm, and strike me with the knife and then burn me to ashes, and lay up my ashes in a coffer, and let this coffer be preserved as a memorial of me in thy house, before my mother; and when thou passest by it, bid her remember me. But remind her not

---

[1] Might not these words be spoken mystically of Christ?
[2] And these prophetic. Abraham means that God must take care of him in his old age. But they may also be taken by us thus, God must take thy place as the victim.

of it near a well, or on the edge of a precipice, lest she cast herself down in her grief." [1]

And he continued, "When thou returnest home, how wilt thou console my mother?"

Abraham answered, "Well I know that He who comforted us before thou camest, will comfort us after thou art gone from us." [2]

Abraham now stood over his son, who was bound with his hands to his feet, upon the wood laid in order; and the eyes of Abraham rested on the eyes of his son. But Isaac looked up into heaven, and saw the angel hosts crowded about God's throne. Abraham saw not this, and he lifted the knife; but he trembled and the knife fell from his hand, and he cried aloud, "O my son! Would that another offering were found instead of thee! But my help cometh only from the Lord who hath made heaven and earth!"

Then he gathered up his resolution, and took the knife and held it once more to strike; and Isaac's spirit left him, and he swooned away.

But the angels of God, who stood round about His throne, announced to the Most High all that took place, and they cried and wept, and even the fiery seraphim exclaimed, "Woe! He slays his son." And the tears of the angels fell upon the face of Isaac, and made him ever after sad of countenance.

Then God said, "Behold, and see how great is the faith of My servant Abraham, how on earth a man can hallow My great name, and devote his best and dearest to My service; see that, ye, who at the creation exclaimed, *What is man, that thou art mindful of him, and the son of man, that thou so regardest him?*"

---

[1] Here again—it may be fanciful—but I cannot help thinking we have the type continued of Christ's presence perpetuated in the Church, in the Tabernacle in which the Host is reserved, that all passing by may look thereupon and worship, and "Remember Me" in the adorable Sacrament. With a vast amount of utterly unfounded fable, the Rabbinic traditions may, and probably do, contain much truth.

[2] "If I go not away, the Comforter will not come unto you; but if I depart, I will send Him unto you." (John xvi. 7.)

Then He ordered Michael to fly swiftly, and stay the hand of Abraham.

And the archangel, when he came near, cried aloud, "Abraham! Abraham! what doest thou?"

Abraham looked in the direction of the voice, in doubt, and said, "*Here am I.*"

Then said the angel, "*Lay not thine hand upon the lad, neither do thou anything unto him.*"

And Abraham said, "Who art thou?"

Michael told him who he was. Then said Abraham, "The Most High appeared to me in a vision, and bade me take my son as a whole offering to the place which He should say, and I may take no command from a servant of God, against that which God Himself hath laid upon me."

Then heaven opened, and he saw the glory of God, and God said to him, "*Touch not the lad to do him harm, for now I know that thou fearest God, seeing thou hast not withheld thy son, thine only son, from Me.*"

And Abraham said, "How is this, O Lord! that Thou changest Thy purpose, and sayest one day, Do this, and the next, Do it not?"

And the Lord answered, and said, "I said not unto thee, Slay the lad as a burnt offering, but I said, Take thy son to the place that I shall tell thee, as a whole burnt offering. This hast thou done; thou hast fulfilled My command, I exact no more of thee. I change not My purpose, but I did suffer thee to misunderstand the purport of My command, and to think that I exacted more of thee; and this I did to prove thee. And now, *by Myself have I sworn; for because thou hast done this thing, and hast not withheld thy son, thine only son; that in blessing I will bless thee, and in multiplying I will multiply thy seed as the stars of the heavens, and as the sand which is upon the sea-shore; and thy seed shall possess the gate of his enemies.*"

Then Isaac revived, and Abraham cut his cords, and he

stood up and said, "Praised be the Eternal One, who quickeneth those that be dead."

And Abraham turned to the Shekinah and said, "Lord! how shall I depart hence without having offered to Thee a sacrifice?" The Lord answered, "Lift thine eyes, and thou shalt see a beast for sacrifice behind thee."

In the thicket of the wood was that ram which God created at dusk on the sixth day, that it might serve this purpose. An angel had brought it out of Paradise, where it had lived since its creation, and had fed under the shadow of the Tree of Life, and had drunk of the River that there flows. And when the ram was brought into this earth, all the earth was filled with the fragrance from its fleece, on which hung the odours of the flowers on which it had lain in Paradise.

But by Satan's fraud, the animal was frightened and strayed away, and Abraham tracked it by its foot-prints. Then Satan decoyed the beast behind some bushes and entangled its horns in the thicket; and Abraham would have passed by, and not seen it, but the ram caught him by his cloak. So Abraham slew it, and offered it in sacrifice, and sprinkled with its blood the altar he had made.

Now the Last Trumpets that shall sound, the one to call the just, the other the unjust, are made of the horns of this wondrous ram.

### 11. THE DEATH OF SARAH.

Sarah,—who, as we have seen, accompanied Abraham and Isaac part of the way to Moriah,—on her return to the tent, found an old man awaiting her. It was Satan.

He greeted her with profound respect, and asked after her husband and son.

She answered that they had gone forth on a journey.

"Whither have they gone?" asked Satan.

"My lord has gone to visit the school of Shem and Eber,

our grandsires, there to leave my son Isaac to be instructed in the law of God."

"Alas! alas!" exclaimed the Apostate Angel; "thou art greatly deceived."

Sarah was alarmed; and she asked wherefore he spake thus.

"Know then," said Satan, "that Abraham has gone forth with Isaac to sacrifice him, upon a mountain, to the Most High."

When she heard this, Sarah laid her head on the bosom of a slave, and fainted. When she came to herself she hurried with her maidens to the school of Shem and Eber, and inquired after her husband and son, but they had neither seen nor heard anything of them. So Sarah was convinced that what had been told her was true, and there was no spirit left in her.

Now when Satan knew that Abraham was bringing back his son, and that God had accepted the will for the deed, he was moved with envy and spite, and he could not rest to think of the joy that this would cause; so he went hastily to Sarah, and she was weeping in her tent, and sorely cast down and broken in spirit. Then he said suddenly to her, "Thy son liveth and is returning. God hath spared him!"

And she rose up and uttered a cry, and fell, and was dead; for the joy had killed her.

Abraham and Isaac in the meantime had returned from Moriah, and they sought Sarah at Beer-sheba, but she was not there; therefore they went to Hebron, and there they found her corpse. Isaac fell weeping upon the face of his mother, and he cried, "Mother, mother! why hast thou forsaken me? why hast thou gone away?"

Abraham wept aloud, and all the dwellers in Hebron wept and lamented over Sarah, and ceased from their labours, that they might mourn with Abraham and Isaac. Sarah's age was one hundred and seven-and-twenty years, and she was as fair to look upon when she died as in the bloom of her youth.

And as Abraham was bowed over the body of his wife, he

heard the laugh of the Angel of Death, and his words, "Wherefore weepest thou? Thou bearest the blame of her death. Hadst thou not taken her son from her, she would have been alive now."

Abraham sought a place where to bury her; and he went to the Hittites and asked them to suffer him to buy for his possession a parcel of land, where he might bury one dead body. But they said, "Nay, we will give thee land;" but he would not. So they said, "Choose now a place where thou wouldst have thy sepulchre, and we will entreat the owner for thee."

Then Abraham said, "I desire the double cave of Ephron the son of Zohar. *If it be your mind that I should bury my dead out of my sight, hear me, and entreat for me to Ephron the son of Zohar, that he may give me the cave of Machpelah, which he hath; for as much money as is worth he shall give it me, for a possession of a burying-place amongst you.*"

And this was the reason why Abraham desired that cave. When he had gone after the calf, to slay it for the three angels that came to him before the destruction of Sodom, the calf had fled from him, and he had pursued it into this cave; and on entering it, he found that it was roomy, and in the inner recesses he saw the bodies of Adam and Eve laid out with burning tapers around them, and the air was fragrant with incense.

The Hittites elected Emor their chief that he might deal with Abraham, for it did not become a chief and prince, like Abraham, to deal with an inferior; and Emor said in the audience of the people of the land, "*My Lord, hear me; the field give I thee, and the cave that is therein, I give it thee; in the presence of the sons of my people give I it thee; bury thy dead.*"

But this he said with craft, for he sought to take an advantage of Abraham.[1]

---

[1] This is one instance out of several in which the honourable and generous conduct of a Gentile is distorted by Rabbinical tradition; the later Rabbis being unwilling to give any but their own nation credit for liberal and just

Then Ephron said, "Put thine own price upon the land;" but this Abraham would not do.

Then Ephron said to Abraham, "*My lord, hearken unto me; the land is worth four hundred shekels of silver; what is that betwixt me and thee? bury therefore thy dead.*"

Now the land was not worth half that sum, but Emor said in his heart, "Abraham can afford to pay it, and he is in haste to bury his dead out of his sight."

Nevertheless, Abraham paid him in the sight of all his people. And the transfer of the land and cave was signed by Amigal, son of Abischna the Hittite Elichoran, son of Essunass, the Hivite; Abdon, son of Ahirah, the Gomorrhite; and Akdil, son of Abdis, the Sidonian.

Machpelah (double cave) was so called, because, say some, it contained two chambers; or, say others, because Abraham paid double its value; or, say others, because it became doubly holy; but others again observe with the highest probability, because Adam's body had to be doubled up to get it into the cave.

Because the Hittites dealt honourably, and sought to procure a place for Abraham, where he might lay Sarah, their name is written ten times in the Holy Scriptures.

They took also an oath of Abraham, that he and his seed should never attack their city Jebus with violence; and they wrote his promise on brazen pillars, and set them up in the market-place of Jebus. Therefore, when the Israelites conquered Canaan, they left the Jebusites unmolested.[1] But when David sought to take the stronghold of Jebus,[2] its inhabitants said to him, "Thou canst not storm our city, because of the covenant of Abraham, which is engraven on these pillars of brass."

David removed these brazen pillars, for they were in time honoured as idols; therefore the inhabitants of Jebus were

dealing. It may have been observed in the account of Abimelech, how the frank exchange of promises between Abraham and the Philistine prince was regarded by them as sinful.

[1] Joshua i. 21.   [2] 2 Sam. v. 6; 1 Chron. xi. 4.

*hated of David's soul;*[1] but he did not break the covenant of Abraham, for he obtained the city of Jebus, not by force of arms, but by purchase.[2]

Sarah was buried with the utmost honour; Shem (Melchizedek), his grandson Eber, Abimelech, Aner, Eshcol and Mamre, together with all the great men of the land, followed the bier. Abraham caused a great mourning throughout the country to be made for seven days. After that, Abraham returned to Beer-sheba, and Isaac went to be instructed in the law by Melchizedek. A year after, died Abimelech, king of Gerar, and Abraham attended his funeral. Soon after, also, died Nahor, Abraham's brother.

### 12. THE MARRIAGE OF ISAAC.

After the death of Sarah, say some, Abraham had a daughter named Bakila, by Hagar, who returned to him now that her enemy was dead; but, according to others, the great blessing of Abraham consisted in this, that he had no daughters. Ishmael abandoned his disorderly ways, and loved and respected his brother.

Isaac mourned his mother three years. When this time was elapsed, Abraham called to him his faithful servant Eliezer, and said to him, "I am old, and I know not the day of my death; therefore must I no longer delay the marriage of my son Isaac. Lay thine hand upon my thigh, and swear to me by God Almighty to fulfil my commission. Do not take for my son a wife of the daughters of the Canaanites, but go to Haran, to the place whence I came, and bring thence a wife for my son Isaac." And he added the proverb, "When you have wheat of your own, do not sow your field with your neighbour's corn."

---

[1] 2 Sam. v. 8.
[2] 2 Sam. xxiv. 24; 1 Chron. xxi. 24. This is, however, in direct contravention of the account in the fifth chapter of the 2nd Samuel.

Eliezer asked, "But how, if a woman of that place will not accompany me hither?"

But Abraham said, "Fear not; go, and the Lord be with thee."

So the servant of Abraham went with ten camels, and he reached Haran in three hours, for the earth fled under the feet of his camels, and Michael, the angel, protected him on his way.

When he reached Haran, he besought the Lord to give him a sign, by which he might know the maiden who was to be the wife of Isaac. "*Let it come to pass, that the damsel to whom I shall say, Let down thy pitcher, I pray thee, that I may drink; and she shall say, Drink, and I will give thy camels drink also; let the same be she that Thou hast appointed for Thy servant Isaac.*"

And there were many damsels by the fountain. And the servant said to them, "Let down the pitcher that I may drink." But they all said, "We may not tarry, for we must take the water home."

Then came Rebekah the daughter of Bethuel, son of Milcah, the wife of Nahor, Abraham's brother, out to the well, and she chid the maidens for their churlishness; and lo! the water in the well leaped to the margin, and she let down her pitcher and offered it to the man, and said, "*Drink; and I will give thy camels drink also.*" Then Eliezer leaped from his camel, and he brought forth his gifts, and he gave her a nose ring with a jewel of half a shekel weight, and bracelets of ten shekels weight. And he asked if he might lodge in her house one night.

She answered, "Not one night only, but many."

Now Rebekah's brother, Laban, so called from the paleness of his face,—or, say some, from the cowardice of his breast, which made him pale,—coveted the man's gold, and resolved to kill him. Therefore he put poison in the bowl of meat which was offered him. But the bowl was changed by accident, and it fell to the portion of Bethuel, and he ate, and died that same night.

And Laban would have fallen upon Eliezer with his own hand, but that he saw him lead the two camels at once over the brook, and he knew thereby that he was stronger than he.

After the engagement had been drawn up, as is written in the first book of Moses,[1] Eliezer urged for a speedy departure. Mother and brother consented, but on the following day they asked that, besides the seven days of mourning for Bethuel, they should tarry a year, or at least ten months, according to the usual custom. But Rebekah opposed them, and said that she would go at once.

It was noon when Eliezer and his retinue, together with Rebekah and her nurse Deborah, left Haran, and in three hours they were at Hebron.

At the self-same time Isaac was abroad in the fields, returning from the school of Seth, lamenting over his mother, and saying his evening prayer. Rebekah saw him with his hands outspread, and his angel walking behind him, and she said, "Who is that with a shining countenance, with another walking behind him?"

At the same moment she knew who it was, and with prophetic vision she saw that she would become the mother of Esau, and she trembled and fell from the camel.

Isaac took Rebekah to wife and led her into the tent of Sarah, and the door was once more open, and the perpetual lamp was again kindled, and it seemed to Isaac as if all the happiness that had gone with Sarah, had returned with Rebekah, so he was comforted for his mother.

Eliezer was rewarded for his faithful service, for Abraham gave him his freedom, and he was taken into Paradise without having tasted of death.

[1] Gen. xxiv. 34-49.

### 13. THE DEATH OF ABRAHAM.

Abraham, after the death of Sarah, had brought back Hagar, and she was called Keturah, which signifies " the Bond-woman," and this she was called because she had ever regarded herself as bound to Abraham, though he had cast her away. But others say that Keturah was not Hagar, but was a daughter of one of Abraham's slaves. She bare him six sons,[1] all strong, and men of clear understandings.

According to Mussulman traditions, she was the daughter of Jokdan, and was a Canaanitish woman.

Abraham said to the Most High, in gratitude of heart, " Thou didst promise me one son, Isaac, and thou hast given me many ! "

All his substance he gave to Isaac; but some say he gave him a double portion only, and the rest he made over to his other sons. And to Isaac only he gave the right to be buried in the cave of Machpelah, and along with that, his blessing. But others say that he did not give his blessing to Isaac, lest it should cause jealousy to spring up between him and his brothers. He said, " I am a mortal man ; to-day here, and to-morrow in the grave ; I have done all I can do for my children, and now I will depart when it pleases my heavenly Father."

He sent the sons of Keturah away, that they might not dwell near Isaac, lest his greatness should swallow them up; and he built them a city of iron, with walls of iron. But the walls were so high that the light of the sun could not penetrate the streets, therefore he set in them diamonds and pearls to illumine the iron city.

Epher, a grandson of Abraham and Keturah,[2] went with an army into Libya and conquered it, and founded there a kingdom, and the land he called after his own name, Africa.

Abraham was alive when Rebekah, after twenty years of

---

[1] Gen. xxv. 2.   [2] Gen. xxv. 4.

barrenness, bare to Isaac his sons, Esau and Jacob; and he saw them grow up before him till their fifteenth year, and he died on the day that Esau sold his birthright.

The days of his life had been 175 years; he reached not the age of 180, to which Isaac attained, because God shortened his life by five years, lest he should know the evil deeds of Esau.

The Angel of Death did not smite him, but God kissed him, and he died by that kiss; and because the sword of the angel touched him not, but his soul parted to the kiss of God, his body saw no corruption.

This is the Mussulman story of his death. The Angel of Death, when bidden to take the soul of the prophet, hesitated about doing so without his consent. So he took upon him the form of a very old man, and came to Abraham's door. The patriarch invited him in and gave him to eat, but he noted with surprise the great infirmity of the old man, how his limbs tottered, how dull was his sight, and how incapable he was of feeding himself, for his hands shook, and how little he could eat, for his teeth were gone. And he asked him how old he was. Then the angel answered, "I am aged 202." Now Abraham was then 200 years old. So he said, "What! in two years shall I be as feeble and helpless as this? O Lord, suffer me to depart; now send the Angel of Death to me, to remove my soul." Then the angel took him,[1] having first watched till he was on his knees in prayer.[2]

Isaac and Ishmael buried him in the double cave by the side of Sarah; and he was followed to his grave by all the inhabitants of Canaan, and Shem and Eber went before the bier. And all the people wailed and said, " Woe to the vessel when the pilot is gone! woe to the pilgrims when their guide is lost!"

A whole year was Abraham lamented by the inhabitants of the land; men, and women, and young children joined in bewailing him.

[1] Tabari, i. c. lvii.     [2] Weil, p. 98.

Never was there a man like Abraham in perfect righteousness, serving God, and walking in His way from the earliest youth to the day of his death.

Abraham was the first, say the Mussulmans, whose beard became white. He asked God when it became so, "What is this?" The Lord replied, "It is a token of gentleness, my son."

END OF VOL. I.

LONDON:
R. CLAY, SONS, AND TAYLOR, PRINTERS,
BREAD STREET HILL.

BY THE SAME AUTHOR.

In 2 Vols., crown 8vo., price 21s.

# IN EXITU ISRAEL,

AN

HISTORICAL NOVEL.

*OPINIONS OF THE PRESS.*

"The book is a remarkably able one, full of vigorous and often extremely beautiful writing and description. Some of its most powerful passages—and prodigiously powerful they are—are descriptions of familiar events in the earlier days of the Revolution. It would be easy to quote passages of great beauty, as well as of great power, while the fidelity of the local colouring, and the author's evident personal familiarity with the scenes he describes, give it a great freshness and vividness."—
  , *Literary Churchman.*

"The story is one of great power and vividness."—
  *British Quarterly Review.*

"Full of the most exciting incidents and ably portrayed characters, abounding in beautifully attractive legends, and relieved by descriptions, fresh, vivid, and truthlike."—*Westminster Review.*

"One of the most remarkable stories, if not *the* most remarkable story of the season."—*Illustrated Times.*

MACMILLAN AND CO., LONDON.

In crown 8vo. cloth extra, Illustrated, price 4s. 6d. each Volume; also kept in morocco and calf bindings at moderate prices; and in ornamental boxes containing Four Vols., price 21s.

## MACMILLAN'S
# SUNDAY LIBRARY.

A SERIES OF

*ORIGINAL WORKS BY EMINENT AUTHORS.*

The *Guardian:* "All Christian households owe a debt of gratitude to Mr. Macmillan for that useful 'Sunday Library.' It is a series which has been sustained with singular power throughout, combining in a rare degree attractive reading with real information."

*The following Volumes are now ready :—*

THE PUPILS OF ST. JOHN THE DIVINE. By the Author of "The Heir of Redclyffe."

THE HERMITS. By CANON KINGSLEY.

SEEKERS AFTER GOD. By the REV. F. W. FARRAR.

ENGLAND'S ANTIPHON. By GEORGE MACDONALD.

GREAT CHRISTIANS OF FRANCE—ST. LOUIS AND CALVIN. By M. GUIZOT.

CHRISTIAN SINGERS OF GERMANY. By CATHERINE WINKWORTH.

APOSTLES OF MEDIÆVAL EUROPE. By the REV. G. F. MACLEAR.

ALFRED THE GREAT. By THOMAS HUGHES, M.P., Author of "Tom Brown's School Days."

NATIONS AROUND. By MISS A. KEARY.

ST. ANSELM. By the REV. R. W. CHURCH, M.A.

THE LIFE OF FRANCIS OF ASSISI. By MRS. OLIPHANT.

PIONEERS AND FOUNDERS: or, Recent Workers in the Mission Field. By C. M. YONGE, Author of "The Heir of Redclyffe."

MACMILLAN AND CO., LONDON.

www.ingramcontent.com/pod-product-compliance
Lightning Source LLC
Chambersburg PA
CBHW032108220426
43664CB00008B/1174